THE WILDERNESS JOURNAL

365 Days with the Philokalia

ANGELA DOLL CARLSON

ANCIENT FAITH PUBLISHING
CHESTERTON, INDIANA

The Wilderness Journal: 365 Days with the Philokalia

Published by:
Ancient Faith Publishing
A Division of Ancient Faith Ministries
P.O. Box 748
Chesterton, IN 46304

ISBN: 978-1-944967-51-2

Printed in the United States of America

This book is dedicated to all my guides
and fellow travelers on this journey.
To each of you: I thank God for thee.

CONTENTS

Explorer's Notes

THE *PHILOKALIA* IS A COLLECTION of texts written between the fourth and the fifteenth centuries by spiritual masters of the Orthodox Christian tradition." This is the first line of the book in my hands. The book is the *Philokalia,* and I know of it from other books I've read on the road to becoming an Orthodox Christian. I see references to the *Philokalia* dropped into missives, emails, quotations from Church Fathers sprawled over pleasant backgrounds on social media outlets. These references are like fingerprints left behind on glass or bits of pottery from an archaeological dig. After two or three hints at the book, I recognize the synchronicity of that moment and decide that I should look to the source.

The word *philokalia* is best translated as "the love of the beautiful." How could I resist that? I pick up the heavy first volume and open to read the first line, and then I turn to the middle of the book. It's a habit I began years ago. I like first lines, and I like to see what's in the middle. In this case, the middle of the book hints at the structure of the whole of it—lines numbered with instructions, admonitions, micro-stories in which a whole world resides. This line from St. Hesychios leaps from the page: "With your breathing, combine watchfulness and the name of Jesus, or humility and the unremitting study of death. Both may confer great blessing."

I stop reading, let the words sink into my gray matter. I taste them on my tongue, breathing as instructed, and choking on the bitter truth that comes to my mind. I say that I am seeking beauty. I often talk about my monklike desires—humility, quiet, solitude, prayer. And I am failing day after day.

I decide to give up on this book. There is too much to see and do, and I am too busy, occupied, or maybe just afraid. What's the point for someone who is not living in solitude or seclusion? What's the benefit for someone not living a life befitting a monastic?

A few months later I find the volume on the floor under my nightstand. It is dusty. I have underlined the quotation from the middle of the book, and so I find it easily again. I am no further along the road than before. I am a little older; the sky is a bit more grey because it is winter. Can I live these words? I think. Can I find myself in them? Can I lose myself in them?

I decide to take a year and read a few lines, or maybe a page, each day. I read the words and then write something short, reflective of what's been given to me that day. The words I read are bread and water, bountiful and sumptuous, mildly sweet, often savory. I leave each sitting with a full stomach, or an aching head, sometimes satiated, often left wanting. Even so, I find the words of the Fathers linger, coming back to me as I wait for the bus or train, as I sweep the kitchen floor or fold laundry or binge-watch another television show.

Can I live these words, even though I am not a hermit in the desert? The answer is probably yes, but even now, after I reflect on the reading I've done so far in this first of four long volumes written centuries ago, it's not truly clear. All I can say is that I can try, and I should try. The effort was worthwhile; when the writing was done, I was startled to see that the ideas sparked were a kind of call and response. A voice calls out in the wilderness—make straight paths. So, with broom and rake, fuel in my tank, and hand scribbling on the page, I do what I can by keeping this sort of Wilderness Journal.

The advice I was given when I began reading the *Philokalia* was to have a guide. In fact, I ended up with several guides—friends, clergy, scholars, poets. I am honored to have had a good number of learned fellow travelers to walk alongside. So, *The Wilderness Journal,* then, is divided according to the writers in this volume, and each section has its own "guide" to give us some insight into the author of the text.

The readings essentially follow the Palmer, Sherrard, and Ware translation of the first volume of the *Philokalia* compiled by St. Nikodimos of the Holy Mountain and St. Markarios. We follow this translation page for page so that, in effect, we are reading this work together. (In fact, the adventurous reader may want to read the *Philokalia* day by day as well to get the full context of the quotations I've chosen.)

My reflections are sometimes bolstered by the church year or the season, sometimes bounded by my life as a middle-aged American woman living in the twenty-first century. Some reflections may seem out of place, or just barely brushing the surface of the text for the day. In any case, I mean to build support for the premise that the *Philokalia,* this love of the beautiful, offers something to find for anyone who is willing to seek. And it's important for me to say, as well, that what I've written here is less a book *about* the *Philokalia* and more a book about my *reading* the *Philokalia.* This is a view of my own wilderness, words from words, in dialogue with the text itself. Your dialogue might differ from mine. I encourage you to consider keeping a wilderness journal of your own along the way for this very reason.

The wilderness is here, whether the landscape resembles desert, mountains, or rain forest, small town, subdivision, or sprawling city. The Fathers speak to us all these centuries later in these many numbered lines and in the beauty of the instructions, admonitions, micro-stories in which a whole world resides. My world resides there, all concrete and cramped streets, and so does yours, no matter how or where you live. Can we live these well-aged words? I think so, yes. I think we can all live these words if we're willing to look for the beauty—no matter our lifestyle, circumstances, or landscape—with our breathing, combining watchfulness and the name of Jesus, or humility and the unremitting study of death.

May they confer great blessing.

Isaiah the Solitary

DAY 1

Introduction by Molly Maddex Sabourin

St. Isaiah the Solitary was a desert Father who lived around the year 370 and was a contemporary of Makarios the Great of Egypt. Though there is much uncertainty surrounding the details of his life, most historians believe he lived in Scetis, moved to Palestine around 431, and then later died near Gaza as a recluse on August 11, 491 (others say 489).

St. Nikodemos the Hagiorite wrote in the *Philokalia* that St. Isaiah the Solitary, also known as Father Isaiah the Anchorite, studied the divine Scriptures constantly, and "he drew from the founts of salvation abundant streams of spiritual wisdom and became the author of many and most beautiful words on various subjects of profit to the soul, so as to fill an entire book." Unfortunately, many of his writings were destroyed, but those that remain are beloved and profound. Specifically, these writings focus on the intellect and on protecting one's mind and soul from wicked thoughts.

St. Isaiah was a big proponent of ceaseless, prayerful vigilance. For those who wished to be free from the spiritual enslavement of oppressive, hateful, and demonic musings, he prescribed attentiveness and absolute dependence on Christ for aid in driving away each harmful thought as it comes. He preached alertness as essential for ongoing resistance to evil spirits:

> *If you find yourself hating your fellow men and resist this hatred, and you see that it grows weak and withdraws, do not rejoice in your heart; for this withdrawal is a trick of the evil spirits. They are preparing a second attack worse than the first; they have left their troops behind the city and ordered them to remain there. If you go out to attack them, they will flee before you in weakness. But if your heart is then elated because you have driven them away, and you leave the city, some of them will attack you from the rear while the rest*

> *will stand their ground in front of you; and your wretched soul will be caught between them with no means of escape. The city is prayer. Resistance is rebuttal through Christ Jesus. The foundation is incensive power.*

The writings and wisdom of St. Isaiah the Solitary are particularly applicable to those of us living in this age of obsessive self-expression. His holy texts draw us away from the noise and distractions of worldly tensions, back to the silent inner struggle for the mortification of our earthly passions and the salvation of our souls.

DAY 2

Let us stand firm in the fear of God, rigorously practicing the virtues and not giving our conscience cause to stumble.

St. Isaiah the Solitary, "On Guarding the Intellect," p. 22

Practice

AT THE BEGINNING OF THE year, I feel invincible. I make plans. I make resolutions. I make deep, heartfelt commitments to be better, do better, think better. I can see three miles down the road. I have pit stops planned and snacks in the passenger seat. The sun is shining on this start of the new year. There is no stumbling in sight.

But then clouds roll in, and the rain falls, soaking the plans, the resolutions, the map. I forget in all the mess what it was I meant to do; how I meant to be better, do better, think better. Here, I pull to the side of the road to remember. The windshield wiper sounds blend with the rain and thunder, a symphony made of man and nature.

The practicing of virtues, as St. Isaiah indicates, is the groundwork of contemplation. We may plan, we may resolve, but it is the practice, the dailiness of things, that makes up the road we follow. We won't get far without it. The fear of God is awe, wonder, the beginning of wisdom, as Proverbs 9:10 tells us.

Be there. Stand firm.

No matter what lies in the road ahead, I hope to stand firm in this awe. This is the start of a long trip ahead, and there will be some stumbling. I'll pull over, if needed, to remember what is important. Anything worthwhile takes practice.

DAY 3

The conscience is called an adversary because it opposes us when we wish to carry out the desires of our flesh; and if we do not listen to our conscience, it delivers us into the hands of our enemies.

St. Isaiah the Solitary, "On Guarding the Intellect," p. 23

Adversary

I DO NOT WANT TO BE at war with myself, and yet I know that I am already there. The voice in my head tells me the right way, but the voice in my head tells me the wrong way, too. In the grocery store or the coffee shop, the PTA meeting, the traffic jam—I am faced with choices in what I might say or do or think. There are consequences to each choice. I do not always know the full effects in the moment; often I do not see the ripples of the word, the action, or the thought until much later.

I sometimes hate that wise voice who shows me the way. I tell her, "I don't need you!" and run away fast, like a child angry with her parents. I sometimes hate that other voice, too, because she is convincing and carefree. She tells me what I want to hear, and then she runs away fast. I am left with sweeping up the remains of whatever I have broken. Shards of glass will hide in the grooves of the floorboards, cutting my feet when I least expect it.

I'll listen for the voice of this sort of adversary today—the parent voice, the wise friend voice, the teacher voice.

DAY 4

Unless a man hates all the activity of this world, he cannot worship God. What then is meant by the worship of God? It means that we have nothing extraneous in our intellect when we are praying to Him.

St. Isaiah the Solitary, "On Guarding the Intellect," p. 24

Distractions

THERE ARE NO BIRDS SINGING or dogs barking this morning. No trucks in the alleyway, no ringing telephones, only the whispering sound of the space heater blowing. It is frigid outside. Winter is shaking her fist at us today, but the sky is blue and the room is almost silent.

I am not calm or patient with the quiet. I am on the edge of my seat as I listen. I am waiting for the silence to break, because it will break. I am too used to disappointment, greedy with those silent moments because of the breaking. I wish for it to be more like tasting the fruit St. Isaac promises when he says, "Love silence above everything else, for it brings you near to fruit which the tongue is too feeble to expound." I imagine this silence is sweet and refreshing, though temporary and fleeting. I am hungry for it, even though it may have only a short time on my tongue.

I'll sit today in this silence and let this wash over me, the sweetness of it relaxing my fight-or-flight tendencies. The silence will break, of course it will, but I will delight in it in small doses. We take it as it comes, bring the fruit to our lips to taste it again and again. We never grow tired of that taste.

DAY 5

Once you have begun to seek God with true devotion and with all your heart, then you cannot possibly imagine that you already conform to His will.

St. Isaiah the Solitary, "On Guarding the Intellect," p. 25

Devotion

AT THIS MOMENT, I FIND I cannot remember what *devotion* means. I know the word on the page, I know the idea of it, but I cannot remember precisely what it means. A short trip to the dictionary reminds me that the root, from the Latin, means "to consecrate," and to consecrate means "to make sacred." To be devoted is to see the sacred, and that devotion is a kind of vow.

What are vows to me here and now? I vow to be true and faithful in my relationships. I vow to follow the practice of my faith. I vow to care well for people. I am devoted to all of this. My devotions are sacred, and they are also tested daily with the stress and strain of this ordinary life. The things to which I am devoted are woven like strings—my heart to his, hers, theirs—a warm blanket to keep us warm, a fine netting to hold us tight.

It is in the testing of these sacred things, these vows, these devotions that I see my lacking. The stressors press against that fine weave, pulling at it until I can see between the threads, until it threatens to break. What strength of devotion connects me to God like this? A warm blanket to keep us warm, a fine netting to hold us tight?

DAY 6

Examine yourself daily in the sight of God, and discover which of the passions is in your heart. Cast it out, and so escape His judgement.

St. Isaiah the Solitary, "On Guarding the Intellect," p. 26

Examination

IN THE SPRING, SUMMER, AND fall, I take my morning coffee to the deck. I check the plants there—pinch off dead buds, scoop up fallen leaves or dropped blooms, add water, pull up weeds. In the winter, I leave this task to the elements. Snow blankets the plants as the furniture is stored for the season. No one visits this place in the winter.

When the weather breaks in the spring again, the work will start up. I will have to clean up the remains of the dead plants, retill the soil, replace the perennials, trim back the dead branches. This clean-up time makes the garden ready to bloom again. It sets it up for success in the season of flowers and fruits. When I let the daily work of the garden lapse in the growing season, or the flowering season, it accumulates. The evidence of it shows in every part of the garden.

The struggle comes in the dailiness of the seasons, not in the accumulation, the buildup of the winter. We need to be looking daily for the work of our spiritual lives, or else every day becomes like the last day of winter.

DAY 7

Like a pilot steering a boat through the waves, he should hold to his course, guided by grace. Keeping his attention fixed within himself, he should commune with God in stillness, guarding his thoughts from distraction and his intellect from curiosity.

St. Isaiah the Solitary, "On Guarding the Intellect," p. 27

Piloting

WHEN THE WATER IS CALM, piloting is simple—not necessarily easy, but simple. The water is always a little bit unpredictable. Nature is like that. Life is like that. We do what we can to learn how to navigate the waves. Only one person could calm the waves with a word. I couldn't do it if I tried.

I sit with purpose in a stiff-backed chair for one minute, two, three, my back turned to everyday life to set the course for this daily prayer. I read, savor, read again, letting the words rush around in my brain just long enough to take them in, like medicine, like vitamins. Then I sit and silence the world, or so I think. The world won't bend at my word.

And so I decide instead to pilot the boat across the water one wave at a time. I cannot silence the world. I cannot calm the waves. I ride out the bumpy trip without cursing the weather or the water. The world is what it is—noisy and beautiful and enduring. I can only look ahead to the shore and hold to the course. Today it means letting the phone ring, ignoring the dog barking, taking a deep breath and returning to these words when the waves crash against the side of the boat, for one minute, two, three.

DAY 8

We have practiced virtue and done what is right, turning desire towards God and His will, and directing our incensive power, or wrath, against the devil and sin. What then do we still lack? Inward meditation.

St. Isaiah the Solitary, "On Guarding the Intellect," p. 28

Winter

FROM WHERE I SIT, I can see the snow falling. The snow is heavy, bordering on sleet. I hear the snowfall today as dull thuds on the roof, becoming softer as it accumulates. I won't go outside today. I'll lie here on the couch, wrap the blanket around myself, put on an extra pair of cotton socks to keep the cold from my feet.

I feel stationary in the winter, like an art installation here on this warm couch—*Woman Reclining*. I can live with this winter body, this woman reclining, but only for a little while before I slide into criticism. I hear the critic voice speaking: *Get up, do something*!

But in those moments as I move toward complaint, I think instead about my steady breath: into the lungs, out of the lungs, oxygen fueling the blood in my body and the thoughts in my head. It leads me to prayer. I make a path here. I breathe the Jesus Prayer to quiet the chiding—

Get up

Lord Jesus Christ

Do something

Have mercy on me

I breathe the Jesus Prayer to quiet me and to reverence Him, to seek Him and taste Him, to have joy in Him. The snow falls, building up, cushioning sound. I pull the blanket closer. The critic voice is persistent, even now. There's no joy in it. This, I know.

Evagrios the Solitary

DAY 9

Introduction by Dr. Nicole Roccas

EVAGRIOS THE SOLITARY, OFTEN REFERRED to as Evagrius of Ponticus, was a contemporary of St. Basil the Great (under whom he was ordained a reader) and St. Gregory of Nazianzus (under whom he was ordained a deacon). Prior to his retreat into the wilderness, Evagrius struggled with a multitude of severe passions, especially vainglory and lust. He eventually sought refuge in the Nitrian Desert of Egypt as a monk. The form of monasticism Evagrius adopted was cenobitic, or communal, meaning that instead of full-fledged solitude, he lived in close proximity to his brother monks. This allowed him to observe the nuances of spiritual struggle in both himself and those around him.

His most well-known writings outline the pathology of spiritual sickness and therapeutic antidotes to the passions. In fact, he is sometimes nicknamed the father of psychotherapy because he helped classify the dominant psychological or spiritual temptations. His template, known as the "eight evil thoughts," sought to help monastics diagnose the thought patterns (*logismoi*) from which virtually all sin and spiritual sickness were thought to originate. These archetypal logismoi included gluttony, greed, sorrow, acedia, lust, anger, vainglory, and pride. Over the centuries, this template would evolve into the so-called seven deadly sins.

Although Evagrius is not commemorated as a saint in most canonical Orthodox jurisdictions, his insights have guided many of the most beloved souls in our tradition, particularly St. John Cassian.

DAY 10

For the practice of stillness is full of joy and beauty; its yoke is easy and its burden light.

Evagrios the Solitary, "On Asceticism and Stillness," p. 31

Stillness and Beauty

THERE IS NO END TO housework. It is a daily task, like prayer, like waking up, like sleeping. Dust seems to find its way back to wherever it began immediately after I've wiped it from the top of the dresser. I avoid this cleaning, especially this dusting, because it means I have to shift everything from the top of the dresser to reach the dirt. I walk past this task three times, four times in a day. I see it and nod to it. I know it ought to be done, but it's the least loud of all the housework and so I let it go.

When, at last, I finally get too fed up with the sight of it, I make it like a ritual. The dust rag, the spray, the careful removal of trinkets and paperwork, various and sundry items that have no other lasting home. I place each thing on the floor until the surface is clear. Outlines of the items show me where each took up space, a clearing in the dust field. I take my dust rag, spray the dresser, wipe away the grime.

It will have to be done again before too long, I think as I replace each trinket, piece of paper, or item that has no other home. Until then, I'll take time to appreciate the beauty of this simple task.

DAY 11

Be careful, then and do not desire wealth for giving to the poor. For this is another trick of the evil one, who often arouses self-esteem and fills your intellect with worry and restlessness.

Evagrios the Solitary, "On Asceticism and Stillness," p. 32

Empty Wells

IT'S A WARM DAY FOR this time of year. I pull to the end of the off-ramp, ready to turn, and see him standing there. His sign is dirty. It's been written and rewritten. His clothes are torn, his shoes flop on his feet as he walks. They are too big. I can see it from the safety of my car while I wait for the light to go from red to green.

I dig in my purse and come up empty. I dig in the wells in the car doors and come up empty. I have nothing to give. It's warm today, I think to myself. He'll be all right. It's enough to keep the worry from nagging as I drive away. I'll offer a prayer. I'll assign him a backstory. I'll move on to something more pressing the moment I go into the store and fill my cart with groceries. I had nothing to give.

On the way home I am struck with an idea. I should pull to the side of the road and root through the groceries for something to offer. I should stop at the bank and pick up some cash. I should write a check to the charity of my choice. I should always keep change in the car door so that the well is never empty.

I don't stop. I don't fill. I'll move on to something more pressing the moment I pull into my driveway, step into my kitchen, my daily routine of life. If I had more, I'd give more, I think to myself. But I know that isn't true—the widow's mite and all that. Some find a way to give even from empty wells because they know this—even empty wells are not truly empty.

DAY 12

Do everything possible to attain stillness and freedom from distraction, and struggle to live according to God's will, battling against invisible enemies.

Evagrios the Solitary, "On Asceticism and Stillness," p. 33

Temporary

NEW-FALLEN SNOW MUFFLES THE GROUND, insulates the noises outside. In the country, the snow is a blanket thrown over a warm feather bed. It is already quiet out here. After the snow, I still hear tree branches swaying in the wind, clacking one against another. I still hear my footfalls as I make tracks on the trail. But the snow makes every sound crisp, present tense. There is an urgency in breaking the stillness with these sounds when all the other distractions are covered.

When snow falls in the city, it makes a hush sound in a crowded room. Sounds far in the distance travel as though underground now. They are a hum under the sidewalk. Snow seems to freeze us in place. I sit in my warm house and watch it fall in large flakes until everything is painted white. Even the grime of the city is made beautiful again wearing this winter apparel.

If I'm not careful, the clothing of winter can become the distraction instead of the cure. I remind myself today—remember that this is all temporary, but let this hush make you quiet long enough to breathe and pray.

DAY 13

Endure fearlessly, and you will see the great things of God, His help, His care, and all the other assurances of salvation.

Evagrios the Solitary, "On Asceticism and Stillness," p. 34

Fearless

I ARRIVE EARLY EVERYWHERE I HAVE to go. The traffic is one reason, and parking, yes, but also the preparation I take on before going into new situations, or meeting people, or running errands to locations I've never seen. I'll arrive early, and I'll wait. I practice the words I will need to say; I imagine what each scene will be. I want to be prepared because I am afraid.

What if I misspeak? What if I trip and fall? What if I have the wrong time written down, the wrong place, the wrong meeting?

I will sit in the car and wait quietly, praying and rehearsing, and hoping for the best. Once in a while, I chicken out and leave. I go home and kick myself for it later, but the sense of relief I get from leaving is palpable.

We cannot know what is ahead; the fears may be warranted, but the gifts in following through cannot be received if we run away. Being fearless means we walk through the things that scare us, leaving them along the side of the road and moving toward the goal. We do not pick them up, we do not store them away. We arrive at our destination without fear, arms open and ready to gather up the great things of God.

DAY 14

Provide yourself with such work for your hands as can be done, if possible, both during the day and at night, so that you are not a burden to anyone, and indeed can give to others.

Evagrios the Solitary, "On Asceticism and Stillness," p. 35

Work

WHEN THE PHYSICAL THERAPIST ASKS about my work, I say, "I'm a writer," and I mime my hands in front of me, as if at a keyboard, my shoulders shrugged forward and hunched. She nods understanding. She smiles and tells me she knows just what I need.

It's a closed posture, hunching over like this. The heart is protected, frozen in place by those shoulders. The muscles become tight in the front, mirroring that hunch no matter what position I take. The muscles of the back are overstretched, and the neck cranes my head forward. I lead with my head, my heart held captive, a postural burden carried on my back.

It's not the work that does this, not really. It's the hiding behind the work. It's my reluctance to stand up and walk around and meet people and stretch. The physical therapist pulls my shoulders back. My heart is exposed like that. The muscles are relieved. The pain subsides. She helps me work the weak muscles of the upper back, retract my head. I am an inch taller that way. I can see the whole world from here.

DAY 15

Sit in your cell, and concentrate your intellect; remember the day of death, visualize the dying of your body, reflect on this calamity, experience the pain, reject the vanity of this world, its compromises and crazes, so that you may continue in the way of stillness and not weaken.

Evagrios the Solitary, "On Asceticism and Stillness," p. 36

Death

FROM THIS CUSHY CHAIR OVERLOOKING the dirty alley behind my garage, I can see litter peeking out from under a soft layer of snow. The snow won't last. It's too warm to stick around for long. The weather is odd for this time of year, making big swings from one end of the thermometer to the other. It used to be that the season shifts helped me to know what was coming, but it seems less and less predictable every year.

I sit and consider the instruction today—to remember the day of death, to visualize the dying of my body. I used to be able to predict with some certainty how well I'd feel day to day, but like the weather, my body has become finicky. This body will die one day, of course it will. How can we help but want to cling to it? As if that's what lasts after all.

And now, as systems start to falter or fail, I'm struck by the small things I notice, the red truck on the corner, the bright neon signs downtown, the gray-white litter that withers under the melting snow. There's something beautiful in the temporary nature of it all, something enduring that undergirds the beauty, something eternal. This eternal underpinning, the hand of God at work in all things. Cling to this. Hold fast to this.

DAY 16

If you are disheartened, pray, as the Apostle says (Jas 5:13). Pray with fear, trembling, effort, with inner watchfulness and vigilance.

Evagrios the Solitary, "On Asceticism and Stillness," p. 37

Pray

THERE ARE THREE SHELVES ABOVE my prayer altar at home. The top shelf is lined with candles— tea lights tucked into a holder. Lit daily, they can burn at their own pace, safe on that shelf, away from anything that might catch fire, even if I forget about them. In the mid-morning, I sometimes catch sight of them as I go about my day, their wicks burning down as they throw just a little light against the wall.

Wisps of smoke sometimes rise from the tin container as they finally burn to their completion, and I stop what I'm doing to root myself here in this moment. It's not as thrilling as looking up on a moonless night to see a shooting star, but to see the smoke rising at just that moment is still something.

The timing is right. The conditions are clear. I pray whatever comes to mind first—about beginnings, about endings, about the endless cycle of birth and death. Tomorrow, the tea lights are replaced in their holder. The day begins in earnest with rising, with coffee or tea, with prayer, with flame.

DAY 17

Of the demons opposing us in the practice of the ascetic life, there are three groups who fight in the front line: those entrusted with the appetites of gluttony, those who suggest avaricious thoughts, and those who incite us to seek the esteem of men. All the other demons follow behind and in their turn attack those already wounded by the first three groups.

Evagrios the Solitary, "Texts on Discrimination," p. 38

Front Lines

IT'S NOT ENOUGH THAT THERE are distractions, but there are distinct categories of distractions. They lie in wait in the deep pile carpeting and grab my shoes as I sit and watch the light change. They cling to my legs when I brush them on my morning walk.

I should have. I ought to. I wish I had.

The pantry seems empty. The work list seems longer. The grass in the neighbor's yard is greener, well trimmed; flowers bloom in the middle of winter. How can it be?

I want more. I deserve better. How do I get mine?

Some days those thoughts circle through my brain without my even seeing them as destructive. We get used to the sounds outside, to the dirty streets, to the long grey days of winter. We get so used to it that when presented with quiet mornings, swept stoops, and ample sun, we are stunned and disoriented. Our "normal" is disrupted. Our "everyday" is challenged. And this is right, and this is good—take days as they come but pay attention. Take nothing for granted. We're on the front lines, always.

DAY 18

For through demonic agitation the intellect mentally commits adultery and becomes incensed. Thus, it cannot receive the vision of God, who sets us in order: for the divine splendor only appears to the intellect during prayer, when the intellect is free from conceptions of sensory objects.

Evagrios the Solitary, "Texts on Discrimination," p. 39

Dancing

SOME DAYS, THE ACTS OF daily living feel like dancing—hopping from one foot to the other, shifting weight, arms raised and joy overflowing, free from worry. But some days, those same acts feel like a boxing match—punches coming fast and hard. If I let down my guard, I expose my weakness. I am hit in the gut or the jaw. Though the floor under my feet is steady, my head reels. I will fall and I will fall hard, the ache of it keeping me down.

I did not intend to be this hungry or tired when I stood to pray this morning. I slept poorly. The winter days are cold, and the cupboard is bare. I warm my hands on the coffee mug, close my eyes long enough to find some focus, utter "Lord, have mercy" and make my cross. I touch the floor—deep *metania*—and the hard wood surprises me. I stay there, bent at the waist for a moment, maybe two. The floor under my feet is steady and solid.

This practice of prayer, making my cross, deep metania, roots me to this moment. It withers the distractions, dispels the punches, nudges my straying heart—*Get up, start again*. It offers the freedom I need and desire, with arms raised, joy overflowing. Today there may be dancing.

DAY 19

It is impossible to overcome these passions unless we can rise above attachment to food and possessions, to self-esteem and even to our very body, because it is through the body that the demons often attempt to attack us. It is essential, then, to imitate people who are in danger at sea and throw things overboard because of the violence of the winds and the threatening waves.

Evagrios the Solitary, "Texts on Discrimination," p. 39

At Sea

IN THE DREAM, I AM standing on the deck of a ship, old and wooden, sails whipping in the wind. I am watching the shore grow smaller on the horizon. I have just begun this journey. It will be a long time before I see land again. In the dream, I feel alone and afraid. In the dream, I am not eager about the crossing; there are storms, choppy waters.

What will I have to leave behind?

Who, at the start of a trip, thinks about what they'll have to give up? We pack heavy or we pack light, but we almost always bring it all back home from wherever we were. On this journey, while at sea, we're cautioned about what we may need to throw overboard. We are pondering our future discomfort here. Loss is on the itinerary.

What am I willing to give up? Why am I so uneasy about giving up these things?

DAY 20

Just as it is possible to think of water both while thirsty and while not thirsty, so it is possible to think of gold with greed and without greed.

Evagrios the Solitary, "Texts on Discrimination," p. 40

Thirsty

I FORGET THIRST—MY SKIN DRIES OUT and my mouth is parched, and still I'll keep moving through the day without stopping to fulfill this primary need for water. It's an easy need for me to meet; my water is clean and readily available. It is so available that I do not even have to think about it. So I don't think about it.

Water becomes a necessary thing that I ignore for as long as my body allows it. I fill the need in other ways—strong coffee, rich red wine. My heart pounds when the caffeine kicks in. My head spins with the alcohol in my blood. Neither of these will do the work of the water, and I am stuck in the static push and pull—swimming, floating, drowning.

Nothing fills us like water; nothing else nourishes as well. We gravitate toward the feel of our forgotten thirst. This, we remember—the forward motion of swimming into His open sea, His arms supporting us, floating there. The spirit soars, inebriated and spinning, drowning in His love.

DAY 21

The divine word can bear no fruit being choked by our cares.

Evagrios the Solitary, "Texts on Discrimination," p. 41

Cares

WHENEVER WE COME TO THE Cherubic Hymn in the liturgy, my children all take turns heading to the bathroom. The hymn is long and drawn out, "now lay aside all earthly cares" repeating over and over. They were already antsy, distracted by the thoughts of everything they'd rather be doing just then. So, one at a time, like clockwork, as I was trying to "lay aside all earthly cares" one would tap me on the shoulder, ask to be excused, and make a noisy departure. Just as I was resetting myself to the course of laying aside those cares, the first would return and the next would tap me on the shoulder. And on it went until all the children had made their porcelain pilgrimage.

My annoyance built over time. It crept up as pressure pushes to the top of the almost-sleeping volcano, but it always simmered there, never exploded. My agitation always faded before too long, stemmed by the angelic hymn, by the repeated prayers, by the supportive smiles of my fellow parishioners, the contrition of each child as he returned from the restroom.

It was a messy way to lay aside cares, unplanned and less effective than some forethought would have been. But, like water finding a way through rock, we find our way through. The pattern is ragged, the pressure is real, but we make it to the other side intact eventually and see, only in hindsight, the path we made.

DAY 22

Sometimes thoughts are cut off, and sometimes they do the cutting off. Evil thoughts cut off good thoughts, and in turn are cut off by good thoughts. The Holy Spirit therefore notes to which thought we give priority and condemns or approves us accordingly.

Evagrios the Solitary, "Texts on Discrimination," p. 42

Traffic

THERE IS A CONSTANT STREAM of traffic in my head. Thoughts never seem to stop at lights when they ought to; they do not wait patiently for other thoughts to pull through the intersection. Thoughts weave in and around and through other thoughts. They collide. They yell curses at each other out their windows.

The idea of stillness in this busy brain seems impossible. There is so much to consider, to worry about, to debate. Thinking is necessary, like having a car in a place with no good public transportation or well-paved pedestrian walkways.

But if we're to travel this way, in a head full of thoughts, I imagine the act of prayer, the act of stillness ought to function as a sort of traffic cop.

Slow down. Stop here. Wait for your turn.

And then, in allowing that stillness to direct the busy brain, perhaps we have time finally to take a look around. We see leaves on the trees beginning to bud. We see children crossing the road, walking home from school. We see the faces of the people in the cars around us. All of us busy. All of us worried. All of us ready for some break in the gridlock.

DAY 23

Angelic thought is concerned with the true nature of things and with searching out their spiritual essences. For example, why was gold created and scattered like sand in the lower regions of the earth, to be found only with much toil and effort? And how, when found, is it washed in water and committed to the fire, and then put into the hands of craftsmen who fashion it into the candlestick of the tabernacle and the censers and the vessels . . . ?

Evagrios the Solitary, "Texts on Discrimination," p. 42

Gold

IN A FIT OF DESPERATION, I poured myself into sweats and a T-shirt, dug out my running shoes, and enticed the dog to come outside with me. The sun made an appearance after many grayish days. The temperature would climb today into the 50s. I had been stuck inside the house for too long, and the walls were beginning to close in on me.

We picked our way through the melting snow, the gutters dripping from above my head until we reached the gate. My poor dog was already sporting muddy paws and shivering. The thermometer had not caught up with the forecast. I jumped up and down a little to warm up my muscles, to get my knees ready to move some distance.

For the length of three blocks we ambled along, not running. Then at the end of the last block I broke into a little sprint. My furry companion kept up easily, his Chihuahua head bobbing. I did not think of the bills on my desk, or the dishes in the sink, or the work deadline approaching. There was only blue sky dotted with clouds, mud splattering under the weight of my shoes, the soft click of small dog feet on the sidewalk. Even for only a block or two, I thought—how miraculous is this world.

DAY 24

There is a demon, known as the deluder, who visits the brethren especially at dawn, and leads the intellect about from city to city, from village to village, from house to house, pretending that no passions are aroused through such visits; but then the intellect goes on to meet and talk with old acquaintances at greater length, and so allows its own state to be corrupted by those it encounters.

Evagrios the Solitary, "Texts on Discrimination," p. 43

Delusions

THESE DAYS, WHEN DAWN COMES I'm already awake. The day begins with an alarm, dark mornings of stumbling to my slippers, shivering in the cold. It's a nice surprise when, in making coffee or waking the last late-sleeping child, I notice that it's already becoming light outside. There's some hope to it, some encouragement.

The hope and the encouragement are short-lived, though. Shouts for a missing shoe or pants too short, the news blaring in my ears despite my resolve to begin the day in the vacuum of this present moment. This bad news or good news or indifferent news creeps in. It sets the tense and the tone for the day.

"Did you hear . . ." I'll say when I talk to my friends. And then their day is set too. We are swimming in it. We are basking in it. We are feeling maybe a little less alone with it, regardless of the situation, and this is what I'm after—not being alone.

But instead, maybe barring "the deluder" means something besides making these agreements with myself to avoid the news or distractions. Maybe defeating this demon means we ought to try to remember when the light spreads across the living room in the morning that this is already true—we are not alone.

DAY 25

Hatred against the demons contributes greatly to our salvation and helps our growth in holiness. But we do not of ourselves have the power to nourish this hatred into a strong plant, because the pleasure-loving spirits restrict it and encourage the soul again to indulge in its old habitual loves.

Evagrios the Solitary, "Texts on Discrimination," p. 44

Hatred

I TOSS THE WORD AROUND AS though it's nothing at all. "I hate the cold weather" or "I hate the way this sweater fits." I could move somewhere warm, but I won't. I could give away the sweater, but it remains there in the back of my closet. I'll take it out from time to time to make sure I still hate it. Maybe something has changed in the meanwhile, but I doubt it.

These things I say I hate live on some invisible list I keep—black truffle oil, people who throw litter out their car window, packing materials that scatter all over the rug when I open the box, world hunger, poverty, cheating, injury and illness.

The list grows in the quiet dark of my daily comforts. Once again, distraction is the naked soil of doubt and fear. The cure means moving outside the comfort zone, and who wants to give up warmth for cold? Exchange satiation for an aching belly? We do not even know the depth of our comfort. Who among us would be willing to plumb those depths? And for what?

So how do I respond to the temptation to default to hate? When I am tempted to throw the word at food choices or weather, what would it look like to remind myself instead of my present comforts? My deep and abiding tendency toward sin? My reluctance to move away from indulgences in favor of moving toward God?

DAY 26

Now what am I to say about the demon who makes the soul obtuse?

This is one of those demons that seldom approach brethren living in community. The reason is clear: when people around us fall into misfortune, or are afflicted by illness, or are suffering in prison, or meet sudden death, this demon is driven out; for the soul has only to experience even a little compunction or compassion and the callousness caused by the demon is dissolved.

Evagrios the Solitary, "Texts on Discrimination," p. 45

Compassion

THERE IS A RISK IN compassion, in "suffering with" other people. I like to think I'd be the Good Samaritan, stopping to attend to the wounds of the stranger. I like to think so, but how often do I walk by in a rush because I have places to go and people to see? How often do I turn a blind eye?

It's impossible, I tell myself as I move quickly to my dentist appointment, or the grocery store, or the office. It's impossible to help everyone. There is too much, there are too many. The need is too great. And so I'll circle the wagons and attend to the deep wounds I see in my own feet and hands.

That stinging I feel in my chest as I walk past, though, that's real. I don't want to grow a hard exterior when I see pain. I don't want to rush by. I don't want to not care.

DAY 27

All the demons teach the soul to love pleasure: only the demon of dejection refrains from doing this, since he corrupts the thoughts of those he enters by cutting off every pleasure of the soul and drying it up through dejection, for 'the bones of the dejected are dried up' (Prov. 17:22. LXX).

Evagrios the Solitary, "Texts on Discrimination," p. 45

Inertia

NEWTON'S FIRST LAW OF MOTION stays with me. I forget the laundry in the dryer until the mildew settles into each fiber. I forget the reason I stopped at the grocery store and leave there without milk or bread. I forget so many things, but Newton's first law of motion, inertia, stays with me: An object at rest tends to stay at rest.

There are moments in my day in which I feel as though I'm sitting on a swing, waiting and unmoving. My legs are long enough now to reach the ground. I can put my feet down, edge my way back, stretch them out until they leave the ground, and let my body swing forward. I know how to pump my legs to keep myself flying, gliding, until I stop or, perhaps, I jump.

But there are moments, too, in which I recognize that I am afraid to try. I'm too tired or too stubborn. I will not push back. I will not move forward. The feel of the air on my face as I swing is not enough motivation. I give in to inertia; a body at rest tends to stay at rest unless or until an outside source gives a push. What hands will I feel on the chain above my own, pulling me like a slingshot setting up? What palms on my back to push me forward and gain height? The feel of wind on the face ought to be enough, whether we have someone to push us or not.

DAY 28

There is scarcely any other virtue which the demons fear as much as gentleness.

Evagrios the Solitary, "Texts on Discrimination," p. 46

Gentleness

WHEN I CONSIDER GENTLENESS, MY impulse might be to associate it with weakness. Even learning that the word *gentle* takes its root from *genere,* "to give birth, to beget," sets my teeth on edge. What has gentleness ever gotten me? Where does gentleness even show up in my day-to-day life?

When my children were young, a virus hit our house. One by one, night after night, the vomiting claimed another kid. I spent a week in the service of cleaning up their beds, their clothing, the floor, the toilet. Each night I'd pray that this was the last one to get it.

I cleaned every morning, trying to kill whatever germ was traveling so freely among us. I was exhausted and cranky. I wandered the halls of the house getting water for one person, bringing towels to another. I scowled all the way down the hallway, but when I entered the room of the afflicted child I felt my face relax. I softened my voice. I soothed with words that were confident and caring. "It's all right. Sip this. Just sleep now."

I would leave the room still exhausted, nearly defeated by the growing mound of laundry and the potential next patient on the list. But there was something shifted in me, in my manner or my mind. That small act of care, the gentleness with which it was delivered, changed me. That gentleness brought forth something new, something redeeming, some ability to persevere. There is an immense power to gentleness. It is dressed in the clothing of kindness.

DAY 29

Self-esteem gives rise in turn to pride, which cast down from heaven to earth the highest of the angels, the seal of God's likeness and the crown of all beauty. So, turn quickly away from pride and do not dally with it, in case you surrender your life to others and your substance to the merciless (cf. Prov. 5:9). This demon is driven away by intense prayer and by not doing or saying anything that contributes to the sense of your own importance.

Evagrios the Solitary, "Texts on Discrimination," p. 46

Pride

In the photo my long skinny legs show bruised knees. My mother made the halter top from a wild-patterned remnant. My hair is curly, courtesy of the home perm. The top is flat, though, making a sort of triangle of hair on my head as the curly edges spill out to the sides. I am drinking a large soda through a straw. I am twelve or maybe thirteen, standing next to a group of kids. I am making a face that shows my self-consciousness. I have never been comfortable in this body, in the company of people, in front of the camera. I might have said at one time that I had low self-esteem. I may have read that in a book somewhere.

There's nothing wrong or sinful about self-care or confidence in one's abilities, but the girl in the picture had no idea what it meant to see herself through the eyes of the Maker of all things. She could only see herself reflected in the mirror of the culture that surrounded her.

I wonder how it might have felt, growing up, to know and understand that I am made in His image, to know that I belong to Him. This sort of rootedness leads not to pride but to trust that I am beloved of God. Where pride is a fragile cloth I put on as if playing dress-up, trust that I am beloved is my very skin.

DAY 30

Let us sit still and keep our attention fixed within ourselves, so that we advance in holiness and resist vice more strongly. Awakened in this way to spiritual knowledge, we shall acquire contemplative insight into many things: and ascending still higher, we shall receive a clearer vision of the light of our Savior.

Evagrios the Solitary, "Texts on Discrimination," p. 47

The Voice

ONE VOICE THAT LIVES IN my head is purely administrative. It tells me that the dust is too thick on the bookcase. It tells me that the dishes are piled in the sink. It tells me I forgot to pay the bills, or pick up the dry cleaning, or file that report. This voice interrupts the movie I'm enjoying or the book I mean to finish.

This voice fills in the gaps, like crack filler into cement. Where there is space, this administrator voice seeps in. There is always something else I should be doing. This voice loves quiet, because quiet offers space to fill. That must be why this voice loves prayer time. It is ripe with opportunity for the voice to interrupt like a nosy assistant with a bad sense of timing.

I sit, I close my eyes, I listen and breathe and launch into prayer, and the voice chimes in: *Look here, pay attention to this instead.* A good friend offered this advice in those moments: Imagine that when that nosy assistant rushes into the room, we simply usher her out. Quietly, calmly, with a sense of authority. "You are in charge here," she told me. "Remind yourself of that when the assistant rushes in." In this way, we train our mind to listen and our spirit to be attentive.

DAY 31

Our incensive power is also a good defense against this demon. When it is directed against evil thoughts of this kind, such power fills the demon with fear and destroys his designs. And this is the meaning of the statement: 'Be angry, and do not sin' (Ps. 4:4). Such anger is a useful medicine for the soul at times of temptation.

Evagrios the Solitary, "Texts on Discrimination," p. 47

Anger

HOW MANY THINGS ARE A sort of medicine for the soul? Compassion, grace, mercy, kindness? I find that compassion cures envy, grace ministers to doubt, mercy gives relief from judgment, and kindness goes a long way to shake me from bitterness. But anger? When I think of anger, I think of destruction instead of medicine. Anger expels, tears down, moves out from deep places of quiet seething, yelling, crying, storming off in frustration. But what if my idea of anger is shortsighted? What if anger, at its core, can be an agent of change, an agent of healing?

When I step back from this, I can see the walls my sin builds, especially sins that have their roots in my thought life. I become a fortress of thinking, fantasy, cut off at once from both real life and God. And when I am alone and lonely, what may rise is anger, directed outward like a weapon unleashed against those who camp around the walls I've built. But what if I can turn that destructive anger against the temptation to tear down the walls instead?

In this way, destruction and anger are necessary—to take down walls built where there ought to be open fields, for attitudes developed without good information. Anger applied to that which separates us from God, from one another, even from ourselves, is necessary and good.

DAY 32

If a certain listlessness overtakes us as a result of our efforts, we should climb a little up the rock of spiritual knowledge and play on the harp, plucking the strings with the skills of such knowledge. Let us pasture our sheep below Mount Sinai, so that the God of our fathers may speak to us, too, out of the bush (cf. Exod. 3) and show us the inner essence of signs and wonders.

Evagrios the Solitary, "Texts on Discrimination," p. 48

Listless

THIS EARLY IN THE CALENDAR year I am still filled with high motivation to change. The effects of my New Year's resolution are still lingering. By March, it will feel more like a bad hangover, and I know I will openly rebel against whatever good habits I had hoped to begin.

By April, the resolution will be a footnote on the year. I'll settle into acceptance that once again, I have failed to do the thing I set out to do. I'll stop there, maybe having come a bit further than where I began. The effort was intense but short-lived. If listlessness sets in, it comes from fatigue, and from disappointment.

The invitation here from Evagrios is to climb just a little higher in those moments. It is as though he asks us to move from the dark corner of disappointment into a seat nearer the window, where the sun peeks out over the mountain, where we can see once again that there is still more to this journey. I cannot say that I readily accept the invitation to climb just a little higher every time, but perhaps it's enough to simply listen for the call, to look up and see that the higher places offer something worth striving toward.

DAY 33

Our spiritual nature, which had become dead through wickedness, is raised once more by Christ through the contemplation of all the ages of creation.

Evagrios the Solitary, "Texts on Discrimination," p. 49

History

THE PICTURE IS OLD, DOG-EARED at the corners, faded with thirty years' time hidden in a box in my mother's closet. We stand in rows by height and gender, boys on the left, girls on the right. I am in the back, my veil puffed up behind me, the blue sash of my First Communion dress peeking through between the girls in front of me. I hold my hands in front of me, like everyone else, in a posture of prayer, fingers pointing straight up to remind us to look to God in heaven.

My mother pulls another photo from her boxes. This one shows her in a similar dress, in a similar class of peers, hands held in prayer; she is smiling. I was born into this tradition, like my mother, like my grandmother. This is our history together.

Often, I am tempted to think that I am, somehow, at the center of all things. I recognize the anxiety of that belief creeping up on me. I feel alone, like a reluctant explorer. I did not want this assignment on Earth, whatever it is. Relief comes when I remember my history, when I look back on the ages that have come before me and that will live long after I am gone. I am not at the center of things. I am not the first to walk this path, not alone on this journey.

DAY 34

When the intellect has shed its fallen state, and acquired the state of grace, then during prayer it will see its own nature like a sapphire or the color of heaven.

Evagrios the Solitary, "Texts on Discrimination," p. 49

Elemental

ELEMENTAL FORCES MAKE SAPPHIRES BLUE. Titanium and iron plus pressure plus time make the color cast on my palm from the sun as I hold my mother's ring in my hand. Her birthstone, my sister's, and mine is the sapphire.

Her jewelry box was a treasure chest when I was a kid. The sapphire ring was my favorite. In the scheme of things, in genealogical terms, the presence of these elements, titanium and iron plus pressure plus time, are considered impurities in what might otherwise be a clear stone. Impurities bring color. You can keep your diamonds; I'll take this blue—Mother Mary blue, clear sky blue.

Clear, cloudless skies show blue because of the molecules in the air. Blue light from the sun is scattered more than red light. It's a trick of the light. We see what is there and what is not there, the essence and the energies, light from light, true God from true God. I take it as a good sign that all these things bring me back to the Creed, to the Mother of God, to those days looking through my mother's jewelry box, holding that blue-stone ring in my small hand, with the sun hitting it just so.

DAY 35

When one of the enemy approaches you and wounds you, and you wish to turn his sword back into his own heart (cf. Ps. 37:15), then do as follows: analyze in yourself the sinful thought that has wounded you, what it is, what it consists of, and what in it especially afflicts the intellect.

Evagrios the Solitary, "Texts on Discrimination," pp. 49–50

Persistent

IF I CONFESS MY VULNERABLE spot, it is the heart. For some, it may be the knees, or the arms, perhaps the wrists, the feet, the head. For me, it is the heart. I am tender-hearted even despite the constant wounding from the enemy. I soothe the scar tissue every day, massaging in the oils that come of prayer and forgiveness. I do not want to shut myself off, to withdraw and hide away.

This tender heart makes me vulnerable to attacks, and yet it makes me vulnerable to my fellow travelers, too. There is no shame in vulnerability, but there is risk.

So I take time to fortify the heart from inside, to make it beat more strongly, more efficiently, without hardening on the outside with callouses or the inside with calcification. To keep the heart strong enough to resist the wounding, to heal well time after time, takes some strategy, knowing where to risk, how much to give, how much to take, whom to trust in any given moment. It means knowing my limitations, becoming intimate with my struggle, while still edging ever closer to God, staggering but persistent.

DAY 36

Whenever unclean thoughts have been driven off quickly, we should try to find out why this has happened. Did the enemy fail to overpower us because there was no possibility of the thought becoming action?

Evagrios the Solitary, "Texts on Discrimination," p. 50

Debrief

THE MOST INSIGHTFUL CONVERSATIONS I have had in my life have been with children. Whether they were my children or someone else's, in these conversations I've learned deep and honest truths about the world.

It begins, with most children, with the long series of "why" questions they'll ask us. It can feel frustrating to keep answering their "why." They want you to go deeper. They want you to unpack it for them, not to be annoying, but to understand. We cannot understand fully without doing this deep diving debrief.

What is more satisfying, though, is at some point in the conversation to stop being the answerer and start being the questioner. I turn it around on them and ask them what they think the reasons might be. Each time I ask this of a child I've not spoken to before, they look surprised. It takes them a moment to wrap their mind around the idea that an adult, who ought to have the answers, wants to hear what they think on a given subject. But I do want to know, because perspective is everything, and I don't have all the answers.

What would this world look like if we all learned to ask questions instead of always trying to be the one answering?

DAY 37

All the impure thoughts that persist in us because of our passions bring the intellect down to ruin and perdition. Just as the idea of bread persists in a hungry man because of his hunger, and the idea of water persists in the thirsty man because of his thirst, so ideas of material things and of the shameful thoughts that follow a surfeit of food and drink persist in us because of the passions.

Evagrios the Solitary, "Texts on Discrimination," p. 52

Lingering

SOMETHING LINGERS THERE, IN THE pit of my stomach or the back of my head. A nagging hunger, a nagging thirst, a nagging thought that keeps me awake at night. After a full and delicious meal, when I say out loud, "I could not eat another bite!" I know it's a lie. I could, and I do. It's not because I'm still hungry.

My mother used to ask me when I rooted through the pantry after dinner, "Are you really hungry or are you bored?" and I never could answer it straight. Why question it? Doesn't my stomach give me good advice? Doesn't my head just want what is best for me while it puzzles away at the injustices, the imbalances, the slights from the day?

If I chip away at it, if I give it a minute and ask the right questions, I imagine that one day I won't always feel that persistent emptiness. There will be a crack in the wall of the fortress that protects my passions, big enough to grant access. Healing will enter and wrap itself around those lingering passions. This is how change happens.

DAY 38

If you long for pure prayer, keep guard over your incensive power; and if you desire self-restraint, control your belly, and do not take your fill even of bread and water. Be vigilant in prayer and avoid all rancor. Let the teachings of the Holy Spirit be always with you; and use the virtues as your hands to knock at the doors of Scripture. Then dispassion of heart will arise within you, and during prayer you will see your intellect shine like a star.

Evagrios the Solitary, "Texts on Discrimination," p. 52

Tow Rope

IN THE MORNING, THE MOMENT I put my feet on the cold floor, the list begins to run in my head—food, prayer, clothing, appointments, permission slips. Don't forget, I tell myself. I repeat things a few times so that I keep it straight, but I'd rather tuck my legs back under the comforter, gather myself up around the soft pillow, and let the world wash away while I sleep.

Just getting out of bed in the morning is a struggle. Though I have never been a morning person, some days are harder than others. The alarm is not enough. The list of things to do is not enough. I lie there under warm covers and listen to the rain falling, the trucks hitting potholes on the busy street outside my window.

When my kids would complain about getting up for school, I would say, "I know it's hard. Do it anyway." On the mornings when it is most difficult to get up, I remind myself of this blurry-eyed advice. Exercising control, leaning into prayer, knocking on the doors of Scripture become a tow rope to pull me from being left to my own devices. The evidence of our need is clear when the struggle pushes in on us before we're even out of bed.

DAY 39

A monk should always act as if he was going to die tomorrow; yet he should treat his body as if it was going to live for many years. The first cuts off the inclination to listlessness, and makes the monk more diligent; the second keeps his body sound and his self-control well balanced.

Evagrios the Solitary, "Texts on Watchfulness," p. 53

Balance

WE ARE CAUGHT IN A loop between that which is temporary and that which is eternal. We rehearse it at liturgy, standing at that intersection of the past, the present, the future. We rehearse it too in housework: the laundry that never seems to end, the bed that must be made, the dishes that do not clean themselves.

I wake each morning to the reality of that loop. Each day means a decision to follow through or risk the mounting of today's work into tomorrow's work. Each day offers the chance to care well for this house, this family, this body, this community.

And when we miss that chance? When we're too tired to clean, to cook, to take out the trash, to reach out, to offer hope? What then?

Here's where we make room for the mystery, the bowl that is filled by leaving it empty sometimes. When we're tired, we rest, not to give up or lie down in defeat—but because balance means we believe we're worthy of preservation. We take care because our time here is temporary, this body is temporary, this housework is temporary, but care of the temporary shores us up for that which is eternal.

DAY 40

He who has attained spiritual knowledge and has enjoyed the delight that comes from it will no longer succumb to the demon of self-esteem, even when he offers him all the delights of the world; for what could the demon promise him that is greater than spiritual contemplation?

Evagrios the Solitary, "Texts on Watchfulness," p. 53

Someday

"SOMEDAY," I SAY TO MY family, "this house will be spotless." I say that my workout routine will be consistent, or that I'll choose the foods I eat without any guilt or shame, or that I'll finally make it to liturgy without being tempted to just sleep in. "Someday" is powerful. It holds out hope. It means that all is not lost.

There's still time.

When I was young, "someday" was a long way off. I wanted to throw it aside in favor of the "right now." Impatient and untrusting, I lived in the skin of the pessimist. And then time and experience and some strong work crafted "someday" into that hopeful posture. "I am working on it" becomes my motto instead of "if only I had" or "I never will."

I hold out hope even in the face of my shortening time on earth. The older I get, the more that pressing "someday" feels elusive again. I am tempted to resort to the young thinking I wandered from years ago. But there is some taste in my mouth, still, that reminds me of the sweetness of "someday." It's not a full meal or even the richness of exquisite dessert I've already eaten. It is only that taste, that promise that there is more ahead if I am patient, if I am working on it.

DAY 41

Spiritual reading, vigils and prayer bring the straying intellect to stability. Hunger, exertion and withdrawal from the world wither burning lust. Reciting the psalms, long suffering and compassion curb our incensive power when it is unruly. Anything untimely or pushed to excess is short-lived and harmful rather than helpful.

Evagrios the Solitary, "Texts on Watchfulness," p. 54

Straying

I LOST THE THREAD OF THE explanation about halfway through. My son had waded into deep video-game water. He'd gone all out to tell me about not only the game itself, but also the company that produced it and the developers who worked on the project. I kept bringing my attention back to his words, or at least I kept trying to bring my attention back.

This is not important to me. The thought kept winging me away from his descriptions of the characters, the plot, the layout. This is not important to me.

As he talked, I drove. We were headed to his school. It was raining, pouring in one continuous deluge of water. The streets were flooded. I did not want to leave him standing at the bus stop in this. I did not want him to have to navigate the flooded streets to cross when he arrived at his destination, so I drove him there. But my thoughts kept straying as he talked. I nudged them back, one word at a time. At a stoplight, I looked at him. He was excited to tell me this. It occurred to me that it would not be long before he would be away from home at college, or just out on his own.

I rooted myself there, in that moment. Breathed one quick prayer of thanksgiving for the rain, this ride, this conversation. The world is filled with distractions. This boy is not one of them.

DAY 42

The way of prayer is also twofold: it comprises practice of the virtues and contemplation.

Evagrios the Solitary, "On Prayer," p. 55

Good Intentions

GOOD INTENTIONS DON'T WASH THE floor or buy the groceries or finish the reports that are due. They don't pick up the children at school. They don't weed the garden, pick up the mail, pay the bills, or put gas in the car. Action is necessary. I have to *do it*.

I told my friend yesterday at lunch that I know I should do the things but I don't want to do the things. I just want to crawl into bed and plead sick. I want to adopt the best teenager whine and say, "But I don't feel like it!" And some days, truth be told, the desire to quit, or at least to hide away and avoid everything and everyone, is overwhelming. Sometimes—not often, but sometimes—I give in.

And while I lie there and hear the noise below me of dishes rattling and television blaring, I find some source of light. I hear the noise below, but I also hear my breathing, I feel my heart beating in my chest. I find a rhythm there. "Lord, Jesus Christ . . ." I begin. It's work to focus, to calm my brain, to put aside the long list of all I'm avoiding. "Have mercy," I say aloud, because mercy is what is needed here.

That small moment, setting aside some time to just open the lines of communication, feels like everything. I may drag myself from the bed or stay there and sleep. Both options become prayer, as washing the floor is a prayer, paying the bills is a prayer, weeding the garden is a prayer.

DAY 43

You will recall how Christ did not reject the widow's mites (cf. Mark 12:44), but accepted them as greater than the rich gifts of many others.

Evagrios the Solitary, "On Prayer," p. 57

Enough

WHATEVER YOU HAVE, IT'S ENOUGH. I say this, but I don't believe it easily. I must remind myself all the time because so many messages I get from the world around me contradict this. I am tempted, when I am at my worst, to withdraw any support I could offer. I'll use the excuse, "well, it's not much" or "it's not enough." But something is better than nothing to someone who has so little.

Or I take the having-enough lie deep inside. I fold in on myself and translate the message to read, "I am not enough." No longer am I concerned with what I must give, what I must offer, but with who I am. I am not good enough, strong enough, wise enough, talented enough. And not being "enough" means that I am bad, I am weak, I am foolish, I am worthless. There is no middle ground—I am enough or I am nothing.

For as long as we see ourselves as profoundly lacking, we will not offer ourselves to another person. We won't give, we won't reach out. What is at risk today in knowing that in Christ, I am enough—not perfect, but enough?

DAY 44

When Moses tried to draw near to the burning bush he was forbidden to approach until he had loosed his sandals from his feet (cf. Exod. 3:5). If, then, you wish to behold and commune with Him who is beyond sense-perception and beyond concept, you must free yourself from every impassioned thought.

Evagrios the Solitary, "On Prayer," p. 57

Holy Ground

THE MUSIC REACHES OUT FROM the dance floor. I am sitting at a large round table at the wedding reception. I am young, maybe twelve, maybe thirteen. My cousin has gotten married. Her youngest sister and I are best friends. She is a junior bridesmaid. I watch them all dance together, arms pumping and legs moving. I am envious of them. My mother tells me to go and join them, but I don't because I am painfully aware of my awkward preteen body.

This memory lives on in me, and it stops me from dancing. I often feel that I got stuck there, at twelve or maybe thirteen. The awkwardness of that changing body, long lanky limbs that jutted out into space a little off-beat from the music playing. Now, I will wait and watch from the table while I see people run to the dance floor. I will sink into some envy and wishing I were as free and joyful as those I see before me.

It is these cagelike thoughts that keep us pent up and constrained. What does pure joy feel like now? What does it look like in action? I imagine myself choked by the passions I hold on to for dear life—envy in particular. They are heavy-weighted sandals on my feet. The envy keeps me from dancing. And it occurs to me that it's not the people I see before me that bar me from having joy. They do not cause my envy. I can take off those sandals. I am free to join the dancing.

DAY 45

Pray with tears and all you ask will be heard. For the Lord rejoices greatly when you pray with tears.

Evagrios the Solitary, "On Prayer," p. 58

Tears

IT BEGINS LIKE A VIBRATION in my chest, then moves into my throat. My words catch. The more I talk, the less able I am to form my lips around letters, and I am mute. I hate this part. I hate not being able to explain my emotion.

If I push past this part, I can talk my way out of this emotion. I am good at that. I can articulate the hurt, the anger, the disappointment. I will use sweet words. I will pull apart the problem and look at each piece. See how the light shines on this corner? See how the edges are rough here? This is where I was cut. This is why I bleed as I stand before you now.

But if I am in tears, I cannot talk. I cannot piece the problem in my head. I am living in my heart, in my body, in the flow of water from my eyes. It is a vulnerable position, far more vulnerable than any sweet words I can summon. And it terrifies me to be seen like that, vulnerable and unable to talk about it as we sit together in the park, or drink coffee in the place down the road, or even when I am alone. Even then, I turn from tears, afraid of what those tears have to tell me.

DAY 46

When the demons see you truly eager to pray, they suggest an imaginary need for various things, and then stir up your remembrance of these things, inciting the intellect to go after them: and when it fails to find them, it becomes very depressed and miserable. And when the intellect is at prayer, the demons keep filling it with the thought of these things, so that it tries to discover more about them and thus loses the fruitfulness of its prayer.

Evagrios the Solitary, "On Prayer," p. 58

Needs

THAT CRACK ON THE CEILING is not getting any smaller. The paint flakes around the crease; no bulging yet, as far as I can see, but the crack is there. Last time the room was painted was a year ago. It was a kind of treat to have our bedroom painted professionally. It was probably the first time we had not painted a room in our house ourselves. We have all the materials. I have painted a lot of rooms.

The speed with which the painters got the bedroom finished was remarkable. Nothing got in their way. The high ceilings were no match for their well-outfitted truck. One man saw the crack where the pitch of the roof met the dormer. He pointed to it, sent another man out to the truck, and they taped and patched and primed and painted. "It will come back," he said. He also said it was nothing to worry about. It's natural with the age of the house. It's all settling now.

I stare up at that crack as I sit today, trying to pray. I am preparing to write, to work, to parent. I ought to quiet my mind as Evagrios suggests, but this crack in the ceiling catches me. I want to leave this chair and climb up on a ladder, run my fingers over the paint peeling away from the jagged line. I want to fix it, but I know I can't. It's like this with prayer these days.

DAY 47

Those who store up grievances and rancor in themselves are like people who draw water and pour it into a cask full of holes.

Evagrios the Solitary, "On Prayer," p. 59

Two Steps Forward

WHAT I NEED IS TO make headway. Progress is better than perfection, I know, but I need some headway. I need to feel as though I'm making some strides, getting some results. It's always two steps forward and one step back. Some days it feels like two steps, even three steps back.

The trouble comes from the interior, but it's easy to look around me and point fingers at my circumstances. If I were stronger or better looking, I could handle things. If I had a newer house or car, I could finally get things done. If I had more, I could be more.

I collect disappointments. I store up grievances. I know this rancor well. It's a mistake for me to believe that one change of fate can wipe away my storehouse of collected things. When we're thirsty, that collection of disappointment and grief can't offer hydration. What does it look like for me to cast aside that storehouse and pick up a new cask?

What if that new cask doesn't reside outside of us but inside of us? We can store up water here, in the body. It's all about the interior.

DAY 48

Do not pray only with outward forms and gestures, but with reverence and awe try to make your intellect conscious of spiritual prayer.

Evagrios the Solitary, "On Prayer," p. 59

Connection

A FEW YEARS AGO, I BEGAN the practice of praying when I dropped my boys at school. I would drive away, cross myself, fall to prayer. I would repeat my morning prayers or the Jesus Prayer or the Lord's Prayer, whatever I could muster while navigating the traffic from the carpool line.

It's a habit now. I find that without even thinking about it, every time I get into the car I am praying. My lips are moving, and I barely even register it's happening. Is this praying without ceasing? I'm not sure. I think maybe it's groundwork for praying without ceasing.

I wonder today, having read about the "outward gestures," if this habitual prayer is adequate. I wonder if there is some spiritual connection I'm missing here. Is my habit monastic or simply a kind of conditioning?

This is not to say that my small act of prayer, in this circumstance, is not valuable, but it's important for me to remember that the pursuit of the *beautiful* is never-ending. Better questions today sound like asking, What is the next level? Where is the deeper layer?

DAY 49

Often when I have prayed I have asked for what I thought was good, and persisted in my petition, stupidly importuning the will of God, and not leaving it to Him to arrange things as He knows is best for me. But when I have obtained what I asked for, I have been very sorry that I did not ask for the will of God to be done; because the thing turned out not to be as I had thought. What is good, except God? Then let us leave to Him everything that concerns us and all will be well. For He who is good is naturally also a giver of good gifts.

Evagrios the Solitary, "On Prayer," p. 60

Good Gifts

EVERY NIGHT BEFORE BED MY oldest son rattles off a prayer he began saying when he was very young. He asks for God to protect us. He asks for everyone he knows to be healthy and happy. When he first started repeating this prayer, I tried to get him to aim a little wider, a little higher. I tried to steer him toward praying for God's will. He resisted. He questioned, "What is God's will? How can we know?" and I was at a loss. In that moment, I had no idea how to explain the concept of "God's will," and so he persisted in his prayer, night after night.

My resistance to his prayer was its specificity. And the knowledge I have as an adult that people do get sick, people do have accidents, people do die. The world is dangerous and uncertain. I have suggested that we pray for the strength to handle whatever comes our way, regardless, and this is still good advice, I think. But there is more, something instinctive that he knew as a child, something I'd forgotten—the goodness of God.

Bad things happen. Difficult times come. We do need strength, and we can ask for strength, but we shouldn't forget that God is naturally good and that He is the giver of good gifts. We can have this truth living in us. We can carry that into prayer too.

DAY 50

When you pray, keep close watch on your memory, so that it does not distract you with recollections of your past. But make yourself aware that you are standing before God. For by nature the intellect is apt to be carried away by memories during prayer.

Evagrios the Solitary, "On Prayer," p. 61

Inward

THE DOG IS BARKING. AGAIN. He hears everything that happens outside, even if he cannot see a thing. When we first got him, he was almost a year old and had been living on somebody's front porch. I assume he took on the role of the watchdog, though he's only six pounds and some change. His bark is loud and persistent. He is an alert dog by nature. I imagine his post on that porch trained him to hear things, to listen, and to make noise. This is his history. It is how he was raised.

So he barks to alert us because he thinks that is his job. Once confronted, he is not aggressive, though; he is fearful, cowering with tail tucked. It takes a long time to convince him that it's all right. I think it will be a long time before he trusts us when we tell him everything is as it should be.

Our memories may carry us away during prayer because the mind wants in everything to be the one in charge. I am a thinker; my brain is an alert barker—it wants to show me all the things around me, to listen to all the things outside of me, to remember all the things it has stored up. I think it will be a long time before I learn to let those things go, to turn off that alert for a little while, at least, and just allow the silence to stand.

DAY 51

What is it that the demons wish to excite in us? Gluttony, unchastity, avarice, anger, rancor, and the rest of the passions, so that the intellect grows coarse and cannot pray as it ought. For when the passions are aroused in the non-rational part of our nature, they do not allow the intellect to function properly.

Evagrios the Solitary, "On Prayer," p. 61

Cravings

I DROVE THREE MILES OUT OF my way for a cupcake.

I woke up with a headache. The dog got sick. Someone broke a glass in the kitchen. My car's "check engine" light went on. It began to rain. After dropping the kids at school, I stopped at my usual coffee place. Nothing appealed to me.

I sat in the car as the rain pounded on the roof. I wanted a cupcake. It was that specific—a vanilla cupcake with vanilla frosting. I wanted the sugary sweet of the buttercream. I wanted the spongy mass of the cake. Just one cupcake, nothing else.

The first bakery encountered did not have it. The second was closed. I drove three miles in the wrong direction to reach the third place, but it finally paid off. I drove home eyeing the cupcake in my passenger seat. I felt guilty in advance of eating it. It took too long to get. I'll wear this on my thighs and hips now. I'll feel sick after eating this. To stop the flow of guilt, I pulled over and ate it quickly, as though that were an act strong enough to ease my anxiety.

And maybe it was enough, at least for that moment. There's nothing wrong with wanting something, nothing wrong with having it, nothing wrong with craving it and finding it and taking it in. It was not until later that I asked myself, "What do you need, I mean, really *need* here?" and the answer was "comfort," because the trouble wasn't hunger, it was pain.

DAY 52

If you are a theologian, you will pray truly. And if you pray truly, you are a theologian.

Evagrios the Solitary, "On Prayer," p. 62

Theologian

GOD, WORD, DWELLER.

When I think of "theologian" a vision of stuffy old academics in tweed coats comes to mind, or perhaps robed bishops with long beards whitened with age. I say all the time, "Well, I'm no theologian but . . ." as though this caveat will lend some context or some passing credit to whatever I say next.

Evagrios tells me today that my prayer lends credit and context, but how? My living room houses a prayer corner, cards and books stacked haphazardly on the windowsill nearby. Candles go unlit for weeks at a time when I'm busy. I pass the prayer corner in the morning, the afternoon, the evening, and I nod to it. "Yes, soon," I think to myself. Drive-through prayers. Is this truly praying?

But I see today that I'm not absent prayer. Not completely. In the car, on the dog's walk, the grocery store, the after-school reading program where I sit next to a boy struggling with words, prayer comes here. It lives here. It dwells among us, in everything we do and say. God. Word. Dweller.

We reserve a room in the heart and the head when we dwell in prayer, and in word, and in deed. With each dwelling, we increase the space we devote to God. With each word, each deed, we furnish ourselves with care and faith and peace until at last, over time, we are filled. Theologians, praying truly.

DAY 53

When you are praying, do not shape within yourself any image of the Deity, and do not let your intellect be stamped with the impress of any form: but approach the Immaterial in an immaterial manner, and then you will understand.

Evagrios the Solitary, "On Prayer," p. 63

Image and Likeness

WHEN I WAS A CHILD, I pictured God as the kindly grandfather complete with long flowing robes and full white beard. His hands were soft and yet strong. He could lift any burden, scatter any fear, dispel any trouble. The picture faded with time and maturity. I wonder today what image I used to fill that space.

What image fills my head now when I pray? When I think of God? When I speak of Him?

Perhaps now I am most likely to pray with eyes open rather than closed. The visual reminders of God become buds on trees in early spring, or piles of laundry on the bed. The image of God is a mirror of the faces of people I meet at work, at home, at the shopping center. He is reflected in the water I see at the edge of the pond, round rocks that line the walking path, bright sun muted by heavy clouds.

We cannot help but desire an image, a likeness, a shape. We cannot help but hope for arms to comfort, long robes to touch for healing. But God is essence, a formless wonder, beyond us, in us, among us.

DAY 54

You cannot attain pure prayer while entangled in material things and agitated by constant cares. For prayer means the shedding of thoughts.

Evagrios the Solitary, "On Prayer," p. 64

Shedding

THE THERMOMETER IS CREEPING UP too far today for February. I left the house at 8 AM with layers on layers—T-shirt, pullover, scarf, winter coat, gloves. One at a time as the day wore on I peeled off layers—first the gloves, then the coat. With each shedding, I took a moment to let the air hit one more area of exposed skin. The cool breeze in bright sun offers a stark contrast. The air reminds me it's still winter. The sun blazes hot despite the season, thumbing its nose at the calendar. I adapt, picking my way through errands and side trips, adjusting the dial on my thermostat at home and in the car. I'm reminded of how heavy it feels to travel in the winter, bundled up and weighted down.

I notice the buds beginning on the weeping redbud tree in my yard. It's too soon for them. The tree stands in the corner of the front yard with its branch arms bared. We may yet have a cold snap. There is nothing we can do to protect those buds if a freeze comes. They will wither and die. The tree is waking up now, hopeful for spring. It will survive this early warm-up, I'm sure of that. I remind myself that the roots are well established and this is not its first bloom. Even if the cold comes back, those branch arms will find a way through. It adapts, picks it way through drought and flood and leaf-shedding and bud-blossoming.

I am like this tree, shifting with the seasons, the climate, the conditions. I long for the spring and the shedding of the weight of winter. It feels like freedom.

DAY 55

When the angel of God comes to us, with his presence alone he puts an end to all adverse energy within the intellect and makes its light energize without illusion.

Evagrios the Solitary, "On Prayer," p. 64

The Day's Weight

IN THE BEST MOMENTS, EVERYTHING feels possible. I wake up, have my coffee; the world is bright and ready and ripe with possibility. I can accomplish just about anything after my first cup of coffee. By mid-morning, the optimism is wearing thin. I can finish, perhaps, this one big thing, a few small things, and I'm thinking about lunch or laundry. The day presses on, and it begins to feel like a knapsack I carry on my back. I scoop up the things I have yet to do and toss them into the pack—for later, I think to myself. By day's end the pack is pushing me into a hunched position. My nose skims the floor because of the weight of the day.

I wonder what it might feel like today, rather than rushing into the caffeine-fueled possibility, to sit a moment and just gather myself in prayer, leave the agenda open a bit and take it as it comes, as it were. I wonder what it might feel like to let the day's tasks undone stay unpacked instead of carrying them on my back. Would the presence of God sustain me? Would the angel of God make his home here?

DAY 56

Spiritual knowledge has great beauty: it is the helpmate of prayer, awakening the noetic power of the intellect to contemplation of divine knowledge.

Evagrios the Solitary, "On Prayer," p. 65

Great Beauty

I KEEP THINKING THAT SOMEWHERE INSIDE there is a hidden button that I have only to tap and the world will open up. I make these ideas—prayer, noetic power, spiritual knowledge—a kind of treasure in a mystery box. It seems to be hidden from me, locked away. If there is a key, I do not have it. If it is a puzzle, I don't have the time or the patience or the aptitude to solve it. I've never been good at puzzles.

But what if it's not this at all? What if the elements that I feel are far from my reach have been entwined on my fingers all along? I have recognized great beauty. I have closed my eyes and tried to sear the image in my memory. We seek it out, having done that. We yearn for it, even in the most desolate of places. We remember real and true beauty as a kind of balm when we are burned. It is what keeps us going forward. I know this.

So, then, I put aside the puzzle and move forward, seeking out the beauty that spiritual knowledge promises, with prayer and thanksgiving. Every day a new song. There is so much more to discover.

DAY 57

You should wish for your affairs to turn out, not as you think best, but according to God's will. Then you will be undisturbed and thankful in your prayer.

Evagrios the Solitary, "On Prayer," p. 66

Undisturbed

THE WORDS DO NOT SAY what I want them to say, so I inject little asides in between the lines:

"Having arisen from sleep, we fall down before Thee, O Blessed One,"

What will this day bring? Traffic, car repairs, bills to pay.

"and sing to Thee, O Mighty One,"

We need more time to pay these bills.

"the angelic hymn: Holy! Holy! Holy! art Thou, O God;"

We need more money to pay these bills.

"through the Theotokos, have mercy on us."

Mercy, mercy, mercy, mercy.

I am left with mercy. The word stays on my tongue, and I say it over and over and over again. Mercy, we need mercy. I close my eyes tight before the icon of the Theotokos, afraid to even look into her eyes. Desperation does this to me—it makes me want to hide away, focus on the intricacies of my dilemma and dwell in it, even as God reaches out a hand to offer comfort.

I want to find that place of thankfulness, of gratitude and grace. I want to set aside my cares, especially now as I stand before these icons who are family to me, ready to help, willing to help, loving arms reaching to me, asking me to trust in God's will and leave my own by the wayside—at least for now.

DAY 58

If you cultivate prayer, be ready for the attacks of demons and endure them resolutely; for they will come at you like wild beasts and maltreat your whole body.

Evagrios the Solitary, "On Prayer," p. 66

Plate Spinners

THE CLOCK IS MOVING TOO fast. I have left too many things undone this week, and now they are stacked up on my desk and in my head, waiting for attention. Everything is screaming for my attention. My heart is racing, even now, in the early morning before anyone else is awake. I have too much to do. I don't have time for this.

What could happen? No, I don't even want to think about what could happen if I let all the spinning plates drop.

Here's what I know about spinning plates: First, we choose to spin them. Plates have no care about whether they spin or not. Second, professional plate spinners use heavy plastic plates that will not break if dropped. They do this because the process of learning to spin plates means that they do drop, and often. Third, plate spinning requires balance and attention. Last, it's all for show.

Stop. Take a breath. The plates can remain where they are for now. There is time enough to pray. Prayer builds balance, strength, perception, and patience. *You can pick up the plates when you're done,* I tell myself. For now, I'll leave them stacked, and I'll breathe.

DAY 59

Cultivate great humility and courage, and you will escape the power of demons.

Evagrios the Solitary, "On Prayer," p. 66

Someone Else

I HAVE ALWAYS THOUGHT I'D LIKE to keep a list. I'd write names on scraps of paper, tuck them into my pockets, leave them on my night stand or kitchen counter, to remind me to pray for all the people I love, the vision for the world to come, to overcome the fears that pile up day after day and nearly drown me in my own body. Writing it down feels like a solid act, gets all the words out of my crowded head, my congested heart, my unbalanced spirit.

To pray is the goal, to write it down, to follow through, to resist the desire to blind myself to any need but my own, because my own needs are so present and so strong. To think instead, pray instead, for someone else—this is an incredible act of love, of trust, and of courage.

DAY 60

Bread is food for the body and holiness is food for the soul; spiritual prayer is food for the intellect.

Evagrios the Solitary, "On Prayer," p. 67

Bread

COOKING IS ALCHEMY, BUT BAKING is chemistry, pure and simple. I can work around ingredients I'm missing for the dinner meal, substitute or leave out altogether. But if I'm making bread I must have the right mix of flour and water, rising agent, fats, add-ins. And they must be in the proper proportions, too; an excess of one thing will make the dough too tough or too sticky. The lack of something is also apt to wreak havoc. The bread can be thick, absent the air, absent the richness in taste or texture and everything that makes it breadlike. I bake a stone or a soupy mess, and it ends up going into the trash can in the end.

But more than the recipe of the bread, there is the mixing, the kneading, the shaping, the baking. This, too, contributes to the merit of the bread. Bread-baking mirrors the act of prayer and contemplation in this way. Choosing the ingredients of our practice—icons, words, time and space. Choosing to practice, knead and shape and bake, and then to consume. All taken in the right measure, the right timing, the right temperature, this feeds us.

DAY 61

Do not let your eyes be distracted during prayer, but detach yourself from concern with body and soul, and give all your attention to the intellect.

Evagrios the Solitary, "On Prayer," p. 68

Eyes to See

THE CHAIR IS HARD AND the birds are singing. The dog barks. The light changes. It's still cold outside, still winter despite the sun streaming in. My heater kicks on, and the air blows from the vent. I can hear it and I can feel it, even though my eyes are closed.

I move to the couch and lie down. I close my eyes, but I still hear every sound. Now the sounds are even more present. Pictures begin to fill in the darkness from behind my closed eyes: the car needs to be picked up at the shop, the credit card payment is overdue, the birds are singing outside, and spring is coming.

My heart is racing, my thoughts are racing, and all I wanted to do is spend five minutes in prayer. I set my timer. I find a comfortable position. I close my eyes. I try to focus, but I am reduced to head-shaking and plugging my ears. The world is too much.

Later, while doing the dishes, I notice the warm water on my hands. I thank God for the water. While at a stoplight, I notice the buds on the trees. I thank God for the blossoms to come. I kiss my son on the forehead because he had a rough day at school. I thank God for this kid.

If we cannot block out the world while praying, perhaps we have not yet come to understand the beauty of it well enough and have not yet given thanks often enough to its Creator to rest in prayer. In time, I trust I'll be able to shut my eyes and leave aside the distractions. Then I'll give thanks for that moment, too.

DAY 62

Blessed is the intellect that, undistracted in its prayer, acquires an ever-greater longing for God.

Evagrios the Solitary, "On Prayer," p. 68

Longing

FIRST, I MUST UNDERSTAND LONGING. I have to open up my hands and place them palm up on my lap so that I can feel the emptiness there. Palms waiting to be filled with—what? Gifts? Blessings? I have to conjure some memory of a longing. Was it for love or recognition or companionship?

I think, too, I have to consider the feeling of longing. It is a deep tug on the body. It doesn't begin in the hands or the head but in the heart, here at the center of myself. That place where I like to locate my intellect, my *nous*. I sit in that position a long time, thinking and feeling and waiting. I'm in touch with the empty hands, the tugging heart. Is it real and true, or just a fabrication of my imagination?

It is hard to imagine arriving here, at this place of longing for God, without a map, great effort, a nap, or a snack to keep my pacing right. Perhaps it is a tug, perhaps a taste on the tongue. And that taste, once acquired, ignites the longing. That tug, once felt, is a recognition of the heart toward the One to whom we have always belonged.

DAY 63

Let the virtues of the body lead you to those of the soul; and the virtues of the soul to those of the spirit; and these, in turn, to immaterial and principal knowledge.

Evagrios the Solitary, "On Prayer," p. 69

Walking

THIS IS THE TIME OF year when the weather begins to change and I am venturing out into the promise of spring after the long indoor hibernation of winter. The weather changes, and I walk three blocks to the trail that runs along the old elevated railroad track, now planted with trees and shrubs, paved with soft rubber running trails. I just feel better, in body, in spirit, after that short walk. It does not take much, especially after the cramped conditions of being snowbound or stuck in a car all day.

A quote from Thoreau comes to me as I walk: "An early-morning walk is a blessing for the whole day." I have no long errand to run, no timeline to meet, no goal in mind apart from breathing the outside air and moving my legs in long strides, feeling the freedom of the walk.

As I walk, I pray, simply and quietly—maybe the Jesus Prayer if I'm feeling unfocused, especially the Jesus Prayer if anxiety about not being "productive" creeps in, and it does. I let the rhythm of my feet drive the pace of the prayer. Each step adds to the heart beating, lungs expanding. My head clears, my spirit is buoyed. It is miraculous, this simple task.

DAY 64

If you do good to one person, you may be wronged by another and so feel injured, and say or do something stupid, thus dissipating by your bad action what you gained by your good action. This is just what the demons want; so always be attentive.

Evagrios the Solitary, "On Prayer," p. 70

No Good Deed

NOT FIVE MINUTES AFTER I handed a dollar to the homeless man who stands at the onramp, a well-dressed woman in a fancy car rear-ended me. In the minutes between, my son asked why I gave the haggard old man money whenever I saw him. I explained that I had a dollar on hand, and he seemed to need a dollar at the moment. He asked and I gave. It was as simple as that. Perhaps, I told my son, it's wise to think of how we'd want to be treated if our places were changed. I felt pretty good about my actions, especially the fact that my son was moved by my actions.

Boosted by the glow of my good deed, I turned left onto Cortland Avenue, and a hard bump came from behind. The crunch of bumper on bumper was immediately replaced with loud swear words coming from my mouth. I turned to check on my son, who was fine, though a bit surprised to hear the string of cursing on my part. "Sorry," I said, "you okay?" and he nodded.

The anger rose as I pulled over and got out of the car, ready to lay into whoever it was that had just made my day complicated and costly. The look on the face of the well-dressed woman was a mix of embarrassment and fear. We inspected the damage together as she apologized and asked if anyone was hurt. The cold anger about complication and cost melted fast. Perhaps, I thought to myself, it's wise to consider how I'd want to be treated if our places, also, were changed.

DAY 65

So long as you have not renounced the passions, and your intellect is still opposed to holiness and truth, you will not find the fragrance of incense in your breast.

Evagrios the Solitary, "On Prayer," p. 70

Passions

TALK OF "PASSIONS" COMES UP throughout the *Philokalia*. Just when I begin to feel comfortable that I understand what the Fathers mean, I stumble across another reference. I look it up in the back of the book to be sure I can put my fingers on their meaning again. In simplest terms, they are "appetites or impulses that violently dominate the soul."

The word *violently* leaps from the page. Do I carry this violence in me, latent and fed by old hurts and angers? Is it waiting in me, ready to rise when I am provoked? Or perhaps, the passions that thread themselves through my day are a different sort of violence—a quiet, destructive mechanism I allow to seed sarcastic one-liners in conversation, negative judgments I store up for later, or grudges I grip as though they were food in a land struck with famine.

The passions feel valuable, or else why would I keep them around? They serve me in some way, or at least they give this impression. To give them up, to let go and have my storehouses suddenly empty, seems an unfair thing to ask, but this emptying is necessary. Those storehouses are filled with food steeped in slow-acting poison. This is what I try to remember today—the passions pale when holiness and truth are tasted at last.

DAY 66

Just as persistent staring at the sun in its noonday brilliance will not cure a man suffering from ophthalmia, so the counterfeit practice of fearful and supernal prayer—which is properly to be performed in spirit and in truth—will in no way benefit an intellect that is passionate and impure; on the contrary, such practice will provoke the wrath of God against the intellect.

Evagrios the Solitary, "On Prayer," p. 70

Staring at the Sun

WE CAN ALWAYS FIND DARK. We can hide in dark places, close the shades; we can create dark by simply closing our eyes. Light comes from somewhere else, somewhere outside of us, sourced by the sun, by the lamp, by the glow of the moon at night.

The first step to seeing is recognizing that I am in the dark. I might believe I see the outline of my hand, I might feel it against my face or thigh, but seeing requires light. In some struggles, though, the light can blind me if I move too quickly toward it. I must inch forward, trusting that the way out will not be closed off from me before I arrive there. So, with the light ahead, I take my time, adjusting my sight with each step forward, anticipating it, savoring it.

My mouth waters with the promise of what will greet me when I finally step into the fullness of this light. What colors? What senses? What sounds? What sights? The impulse, halfway there, is to run, but no—keep walking, one foot in front of the other. Look down at the hands and watch as color begins to appear in the shadowy forms of fingers, where the ground turns from solid black to grainy gray brown sand. Keep the eyes open and motion going forward, prayerful and patient.

DAY 67

If you seek prayer attentively you will find it; for nothing is more essential to prayer than attentiveness. So, do all you can to acquire it.

Evagrios the Solitary, "On Prayer," p. 70

Rest Day

SOME DAYS, I'M TIRED OF paying attention. It's exhausting. I always hope to paint myself as the picture of a hummingbird darting from one flower to another, discovering beauty and nectar and everything good and life-giving. But I am not the hummingbird today. I am moving slowly, slothlike, as I'm surrounded by all the many things that demand my attention. On this day, I wonder what the fuss is about. I wonder why it's so very important at all. Some days I only want to close my eyes and stay asleep for as long as possible, block everything out and just retreat.

This is when context plays a vital role in the daily living out of our lives. Even with the words of Evagrios dished out each morning like spiritual vitamins, I lose sight of the bigger picture. My life is bigger than myself, my small corner of the universe, my stand of flowers from which to gather nectar.

This act of paying attention, for a while now, has felt like an active filling of my spirit, darting and filling and darting again. So I take a step back today, make a firm commitment to wander in some open spaces of my heart and brain, walking slowly and breathing and not "trying" at all. Imagine my surprise, then, when in the rest I am filled even so, carefully and sweetly—God pouring in where I have need.

DAY 68

If when praying no other joy can attract you, then truly you have found prayer.

Evagrios the Solitary, "On Prayer," p. 71

True Love

YOU'LL KNOW IT WHEN YOU find it, they would say. They were, of course, talking about true love. I grew up thinking that the "moment" would look a certain way, feel a certain way. That look and feel came from television or trashy novels. I waited a long time for that certain look and feel. In the end, I was impatient and maybe a little angry, too.

Joys in love don't come piled up when the door is opened. They are not stored somewhere waiting to be let loose. Joys come in small moments, smiles and good words and kind gestures. Joys come in fits and spurts, in negotiation and forgiveness and mercy. No one will tell you that part. We don't see that on television or read about it in trashy novels. Plot lines in real life are jagged and uncertain, complicated and painful more often than not.

If prayer is a relationship, does true love exist in it? Do I expect that the joy of prayer has been hiding behind a closed door waiting for me to pick the lock or give the secret knock that opens it? Yes, prayer is a relationship, with the One who made me, and yes, true love exists in prayer. The joys are not stacked and waiting but given out freely all the time, moment by moment. I do know it when I find it, so long as I recognize it, hold it close, pour it into my heart like blood, because that is what true love does for us.

John Cassian

DAY 69

Introduction by Katherine Bolger Hyde

PERHAPS THE GREATEST LEGACY OF St. John Cassian is the bridge he provided between Eastern and Western monastic spirituality. He lived and wrote in the time when monasticism was becoming firmly established in Christendom and its character and structure were being solidified. John himself contributed significantly to this development.

John was born around 360, most probably in Scythia Minor, in what is now Romania, although some sources say he was born in Gaul. He received a good education and was bilingual in Latin and Greek. As a young man, he spent about fifteen years in the monasteries of the East, notably those of Egypt, absorbing the wisdom of the elders there.

In about 399, Cassian moved to Constantinople, where he was ordained a deacon under Patriarch John Chrysostom. When Chrysostom was exiled in 404 due to conflicts with the emperor, Cassian was sent to Rome to plead his cause before Pope Innocent I. Thus began the period of Cassian's work and influence in the West.

Based on his experience in Egypt, Cassian founded a monastery near Marseilles that included a community for men and one for women. There he wrote his two major works, known briefly as the *Institutes* and the *Conferences*. The *Institutes* deal with the external organization of monastic communities and formed the foundation of St. Benedict's later Rule. The *Conferences of the Desert Fathers* contain all that Cassian absorbed about monastic spiritual life from his time in Egypt.

In the tradition of Evagrios, Cassian emphasized the eight vices and how to combat them. In opposition to Augustine, whose ideas were quite influential in the West at that time, Cassian taught that the human will was capable of the first stirrings of striving toward God, which would then be assisted and completed by divine grace.

Cassian's ideas influenced later theologians in both East and West, including Benedict of Nursia, Ignatius Loyola, John Climacus, and John of Damascus, as well as more recent thinkers such as John Henry Newman and Michel Foucault. His advice on struggling against the flesh resonates with those of all eras who seek to be united with Christ. John Cassian is honored as a saint in the Orthodox as well as the Roman Catholic Church.

DAY 70

To eat moderately and reasonably is to keep the body in health, not to deprive it of holiness. A clear rule for self-control handed down by the Fathers is this: stop eating while still hungry and do not continue until you are satisfied.

St. John Cassian, "On the Eight Vices," p. 76

Gluttony: Always Hungry

WHEN STANDING WITH THE REFRIGERATOR door open, staring into the cool air, I sometimes feel paralyzed. Am I hungry or bored? I was never quite sure when I was young. I was a skinny girl, "skin and bones" as my grandma would say before handing me another cookie or slice of rhubarb pie. Even now, all these years later, hunger is a slippery concept for me. Boredom is even more slippery.

How can anyone be bored in these times? Between media and errands and work and parenting, boredom feels like an insult to the good gifts around me, or a denial of responsibilities. Am I hungry?

Perhaps I am always just a little bit hungry, though I've learned to ignore the hunger or let it simmer too long. I let it simmer in favor of reading another chapter, running to the store, putting in a load of laundry, finishing this project or that. I let it simmer so long that when I do stand in the kitchen looking for food, I am too hungry to care what I eat or how much of it I eat. I know, in that desperate search for food, that I am hungry. Nothing else matters. Food, then, ceases to be about nourishment or gift or blessing. I am greedy for it.

This greed pours out in other areas of my life, in my time and my commitments, my possessions, my self-worth. I ask myself today, considering these words, why am I not always hungry for God?

DAY 71

No virtue makes flesh-bound man so like a spiritual angel as does self-restraint, for it enables those still living on earth to become, as the Apostle says, "citizens of heaven" (cf Phil. 3:20).

St. John Cassian, "On the Eight Vices," p. 77

Gluttony: Flesh-Bound

ONE DAY, I THINK, I may be at home in my body. It is not as though I feel like an alien or a foreigner in the flesh, but there is some disconnect there. I curl and uncurl my toes, my legs, my hands, my arms. I ask my body to move and it does, usually. And yet, I heap abuse on it time after time when I'm feeling stressed, bored, or angry, as though this flesh were a cage that keeps me from some higher truth, some higher peace, some higher or better love.

I wonder what it might feel like, instead, to partner with this body, this flesh given to me, entrusted to me, by the One who makes all things, the One who made the heavens and the earth, the angels and the air.

This body gives shelter to the spirit, a home for that which longs to be rejoined to the Creator. It's a mistake for me to discard it so easily, to feed it so poorly, to think that my citizenship in heaven has no connection to the shelter of these arms and legs and belly and breath.

DAY 72

And we will not be granted true spiritual knowledge so long as the passion of unchastity lies hidden in the depths of our souls.

St. John Cassian, "On the Eight Vices," p. 77

Unchastity: Hidden

THE PLANTER STAND ON MY patio is covered with snow this morning. It is the late Chicago winter's last gasp. I considered planting bulbs in it last fall, but I knew that I'd need to replace the soil first. And so I neglected to get the bulbs in. The old soil from three previous years still occupies that planter, now covered with four inches of snow.

When the snow melts, I'll see weeds start to appear as early as month's end. The root systems from last year's tomatoes still rot under the surface. Clumps of old, untilled soil still make up most of the dirt. I'll have to empty it all and dispose of the old earth, someplace. Green space is not abundant in my city yard. I'll most likely cart it to the front yard and mix it in along the base of the weeping redbud, kicking at the soil with my gardening clogs, breaking up the clay and last year's root systems.

What lies hidden is no mystery to me. I know where I've fallen and what I've buried and what I've ignored for too long. It's the snow piling up on top today that reminds me of all that's hidden. What we leave buried escapes the eye, moves to the bottom of the to-do list, allows us to operate unencumbered by the past. But before long, without some care, those weeds will sprout, thriving in the old, clay-clumped soil. Before long, we do begin to see the result, the culmination of seasons in which we denied the work we were meant to do to produce the flowers and fruits of spring.

DAY 73

The sickness of avarice, on the contrary, can with diligence and attention be cut off more readily, because it enters from outside.

St. John Cassian, "On the Eight Vices," p. 78

Avarice: Outside

YES, BUT WHO WOULDN'T WANT to be wealthy? I tell people all the time that I would be so great at being wealthy. Want to eat healthy? Personal chef. Want to work out more often? Personal trainer. Want to spend wisely? Personal financial consultant. I would hire an army of assistants to keep me on task. I'd never want for anything. It sounds like heaven.

And maybe it is. I don't know wealthy people to ask or even judge accurately.

The things I "want" are fine and good: health, fitness, philanthropy, fiscal responsibility. It isn't wrong, necessarily, to want these things. But the belief that they cannot be obtained except through some grand windfall of money, and money alone, is the trouble. Am I waiting even to try for good health or fiscal responsibility or philanthropy? Do I use my lack of funds to excuse or hide my bad behavior?

Do I yearn for the money? Do I sit in my house and wish for it, pine for it, worry over it? If I do, when I do, perhaps today I'll remember that the yearning knocks from the other side of the door. It does not begin in the heart. And I don't have to answer that knocking.

DAY 74

In all this we should remember how uncertain is the hour of our death, so that our Lord does not come unexpectedly and, finding our conscience soiled with avarice, say to us what God says to the rich man in the Gospel: "You fool, this night your soul will be required of you: who then will be the owner of what you have stored up?" (Luke 12:20).

St. John Cassian, "On the Eight Vices," p. 78

Avarice: Legacy

After my grandmother moved from her small house on Briarcliff to a nursing home a few months before she died, my uncles and aunts went through her house to get it ready to sell. In the basement, shelves lined all the walls, filled with her homemade canned vegetables, fruits, and jams. It was a storehouse of goods from her garden, and the collection was years in the making. They saved a few but, in the long run, ended up throwing out most of it.

The furniture was divided among the siblings if it was wanted. Old photos and heirlooms mostly found homes with my aunts, who pledged to scan and upload them onto a disk for us all. Even as a whole lifetime of things was cleared from the ranch-style house, the strongest pieces I remembered were the photos and the canned goods.

It's striking to me to realize that, in the end, what my grandmother left us was not money, furniture, or any other sort of worldly thing, but instead, a lasting legacy—the essence of her life here on earth, a story told in photographs, memory, and canned goods.

DAY 75

No matter what provokes it, anger blinds the soul's eyes, preventing it from seeing the Sun of righteousness. Leaves, whether of gold or lead, placed over the eyes, obstruct the sight equally, for the value of the gold does not affect the blindness it produces. Similarly, anger, whether reasonable or unreasonable, obstructs our spiritual vision.

St. John Cassian, "On the Eight Vices," p. 83

Anger: Temporary

Anger gives me cover. It hides deep hurt, fear, sadness, loneliness, abandonment. When I am angry I can feel forceful and in control, because sadness and loneliness are vulnerable positions. Anger gives me cover long enough to recover myself, to be able to stand on two feet again without worrying that I may hurt again in the meantime.

But if I stay too long under the cover of anger, I'm cut off from the world, from my fellow human, from the opportunity to build muscles strong enough to hold me upright. I am stuck, crouched under the weight of the cover, likely to be crushed by the very thing that was meant to keep me safe. Anger gives me cover, but it's temporary, a lean-to in a snowstorm. I cannot live there for long.

When the time is right, when the storm lets up perhaps, I stand and stretch my legs and look to the sky. I feel the smallness of my position, the inadequacy of my cover, and I set out again on the road. Under the shelter of anger, I am protected—but not for long, not forever.

DAY 76

The Gospel teaches us to cut off the roots of our sins and not merely their fruits. When we have dug the root of anger out of our heart, we will no longer act with hatred or envy.

St. John Cassian, "On the Eight Vices," p. 86

Anger: Roots

THE ROOTS OF THE DAYLILY are tuberous, and rather than one large bulb, as one might see with a tulip or daffodil, these come in groups. When we moved into our first house in Chicago, we had overgrown daylilies in clumps throughout the yard. The result of the crowding of the plants was a preponderance of long green spiky leaves and a shortfall of orange blooms. It was jungle-like in the front yard, and I hated what I saw when the spring came.

The first time I properly thinned the daylilies, I had to dig deep, all the way around each of the plants. It was difficult, having to dig up the entire bed of plants, separate the clump of tubers, and replant a portion. Once the task was completed, the landscape changed; I could see the earth again, clean and ready. In time the jungle dissolved into a stand of lovely orange blooms.

Anger is not without its bloom. We are angry sometimes for good reason. Anger, like pain, tells us something. But if left unchecked, it grows out of control and chokes the possibilities of beauty in the spring until all we can see is the spiky green leaves. The deep work of anger is regular maintenance for the soul. What lies buried beneath that emotional earth?

DAY 77

Our fifth struggle is against the demon of dejection, who obscures the soul's capacity for spiritual contemplation and keeps it from all good works. When this malicious demon seizes our soul, and darkens it completely, he prevents us from praying gladly, from reading Holy Scripture with profit and perseverance, and from being gentle and compassionate towards our brethren.

St. John Cassian, "On the Eight Vices," p. 87

Dejection: Cast Down

THE WORD, LITERALLY, MEANS "to cast down." Imagine that you can take your spirit in your hands, hold it there, look at it, and in remembering your situation or your history, you cast your spirit down from you. When we are dejected we throw down, away from us, that which brings us life.

Contrast, for a moment, the word *depressed,* which means closer to "a pressing down." The weight of depression presses down on me, like a great hand from the sky pushing on my upper back, bending it into a kind of question mark until my heart feels as though it is scraping the road as I walk.

But when I am tempted to dejection, it takes my own hand to reach inside and pull out that which brings joy. The voice in my head tells me that I do not deserve this joy, or that only pain will come of it. The voice is lying, and yet I may choose to believe it. I cast my spirit down. I let it lie there in the road, this empty place in my heart still throbbing from the loss of it.

It's never too late to gather my spirit back up, tenderly and sweetly, and tuck it safely into my heart again. It's never too late to cast down the lies instead, and just keep walking.

DAY 78

If our purpose is to fight the spiritual fight and to defeat, with God's help, the demons of malice, we should take every care to guard our heart from the demon of dejection, just as a moth devours clothing and a worm devours wood, so dejection devours a man's soul.

St. John Cassian, "On the Eight Vices," p. 87

Dejection: Weighted

THINGS ARE TIGHT FINANCIALLY," I say. My son has asked for something, a toy, a game, a visit to a restaurant we like. When he asks I say no and move on. He asks again, though, because he's a kid and this is part of their operating system. They ask and then they ask again. Persistence will pay off. It's a good strategy. Except that now, I say no and I have to keep saying no because, as I tell him, "things are tight financially." I leave it at that. He'll ask again tomorrow, not understanding how the flow of income to expense works for grown-ups.

When I am alone, then, I stare holes into the bills on the counter, as though it might cause them to burst into flame and disappear from the ledgers of the creditors. Wishful thinking then takes a left turn and crashes into a wall of worry. I begin to perseverate on the worst-case scenarios: we'll never dig out of the debt, we'll never get ahead, we'll never feel ease around these issues. My soul sinks to the hardwood floor, and I feel weighed down.

Wisdom reminds me today, though, that the weight comes from inside, not from the pile of bills or the low balance in my checking account. This weight, this listlessness is my response to stress; it is not the stressor itself. When this weight drags me, then, I imagine it here inside. I gather it in. I gather it up. Let's not let our strength be forgotten or given away.

DAY 79

The mind of someone affected by listlessness is filled with nothing but vain distraction. Finally, he is ensnared in worldly things and gradually becomes so grievously caught up in them that he abandons the monastic life altogether.

St. John Cassian, "On the Eight Vices," p. 89

Distraction

FOR A FEW WEEKS, I could not listen to music. For the first time maybe ever, I turned on the news on my car radio. I tried to switch it off, but the constant barrage of breaking news kept me there, as though it were secretly feeding me some kind of emotional or mental opiate. I took and I took and I could not break the habit. I needed to know more, and yet I was wasting away in the sea of the news cycle. And this knowing weighed me down; it followed me into the house when I switched off my car.

After a week away on retreat, where I could not get the news, I was in my car for the first time to drive my son to school. When he got out, I turned on the radio, and the sound of the news voices sliced through me. I quickly changed the channel, and a song I knew came on. The music wrapped around my heart, lifting it, nourishing it, healing it.

There's a place for news and being informed, but there's also a place for music and wonder and prayer and thanksgiving. Too much of the world's constant chatter throws me off balance. Today, I'm reminded that this sort of distraction leads me down a bad path toward listlessness. Prayer, poetry, music, gratitude—these are the cure.

DAY 80

The person who wants to engage fully in spiritual combat and to win the crown of righteousness must try by every means to overcome this beast that assumes such varied forms. He should always keep in mind the words of David: "The Lord has scattered the bones of those who please men" (Ps. 53:5. LXX). He should not do anything with a view to being praised by other people, but should seek God's reward only, always rejecting the thoughts of self-praise that enter his heart, and always regarding himself as nothing before God. In this way he will be freed, with God's help, from the demon of self-esteem.

St. John Cassian, "On the Eight Vices," p. 92

Self-Esteem

I CARE WHAT YOU THINK. I play it off, of course, making it seem as though I'm an outsider. I'm on the edge of things. I'm strange and mysterious. But, really, I'm like everyone else, tired and worn down from the daily rigor of things. It takes work to appear this nonchalant.

I care about these things too much. It is as though my worth depends on what other people think of me, of my family, of my clothing or my profession. The vice of self-esteem is especially hard to grasp, especially now as I reach around the bulk of years I've accumulated under my belt. Have I not, all this time, been trying to elevate my sense of self-esteem? Am I not supposed to think well of myself?

I return to this first thought, though—I care too much what other people think about me and not enough about how I am viewed by the One who made me. Clothing or prestige or honors given mean nothing to my Creator as it pertains to my worth. Why do I let my worth be filtered through the eyes of other people? Why do I allow them to hold such a place of value? How can I set aside those judgments, those false attributes, in favor of God's unwavering care?

DAY 81

Each of the other passions that trouble the soul attacks and tries to overcome the single virtue which is opposed to it, and so it darkens and troubles the soul only partially. But the passion of pride darkens the soul completely and leads to its utter downfall.

St. John Cassian, "On the Eight Vices," p. 92

Pride: Shadowing

SOME DAYS IT FEELS AS though my sense of self is merely an intricate pattern of dominoes I've stacked from one end of the room to the other. Even the gentlest of breezes becomes a hazard. I gather the crowd to witness, to praise, to affirm this creation, but no one can breathe, for a breath can bring it all down. But it must be done in public—this is the scenario pride requires in order to thrive in me.

Perhaps, in fact, there is a part of me that wants those dominoes to fall. It yearns to see it all come to its end, because the thrill of the fall is exciting and briefly satisfying.

I set up the whole system with the purpose of making a show, awaiting the "oohs" and "ahs" the folding of those dominoes will elicit. I imagine them falling one after another, the clicking of the plastic from each tiny fall. I am elated that it all functions smoothly and then, moments later, I am crestfallen by the result. The shadow of the tedious days spent building this self overcasts the entire endeavor. All that work. And for what? Nothing lasting, nothing enduring.

DAY 82

Humility, in its turn, can be achieved only through faith, fear of God, gentleness and the shedding of all possessions. It is by means of these that we attain perfect love, through the grace and compassion of our Lord Jesus Christ, to whom be glory through all the ages.

"On Holy Fathers of Sketis and on Discrimination," p. 93

Pride: Humility

I WANT TO FIGHT OR TAKE my ball and go home. I want to slink away and hide. The sinking feeling that comes from confrontation brings on this fight-or-flight tendency. In those moments when my pride is hurt, I do not know who I am. The sense of self is threatened.

If that sense of self is built only on the things of this world—accomplishments, possessions, connections to power and temporal glory—I am lost. So, instead of leaning on the truth of who I am in the eyes of God, I feel desperate and strike out, or ebb like the tide after a long day in the sun. Neither is particularly satisfying.

When placed in this context, humility feels like a forced position. Backed into a corner, I have no choice but to give up my pride. But in healthy moments, those in which I've arrived at the position from strength and choice, humility is not humiliation, not a feeling but an action, a mindset, a foundation. It is a loving position, a solid position, firm ground on which to stand.

DAY 83

The goal of our profession, as we have said, is the kingdom of God. Its immediate purpose, however, is purity of heart, for without this we cannot reach our goal. We should therefore always have this purpose in mind: and, should it ever happen that for a short time our heart turns aside from the direct path, we must bring it back again at once, guiding our lives regarding our purpose as if it were a carpenter's rule.

"On Holy Fathers of Sketis and on Discrimination," p. 95

Pure in Heart

IN EVERY LITURGY WE SING the Beatitudes. I stumble along, singing what I remember, forgetting much of it. The hymn moves more quickly than my aging brain. I find I am reaching deep for familiar words, as though they are hiding in a cluttered drawer in my kitchen. I paw through grocery lists and paper clips and names of classmates from my grade school years.

"Blessed are the pure in heart, for they shall . . ." and I am stuck, groping for the words while the rest of the congregation sings on. After a few moments, the words come to me, "for they shall see God." Every week when I forget words, I run to catch up, skipping through, dotting in and out. But this time I stay here, in this phrase, "for they shall see God."

What does it mean to see God? Is He hidden, or am I hiding my eyes? If I take my hands away from my face, what keeps me from seeing Him, even then? Blessed are the pure in heart. I stew in this for a long while, even writing it down on the sly while the liturgy continues to wend its way along toward the readings of the day, toward the Creed, toward the blessing of the bread and wine and the offering of the Divine Mysteries. I am floating still, even then as I taste the bread and wine on my lips, knowing full well I am not yet pure in heart—but I yearn for it even so.

DAY 84

Fasts and vigils, the study of Scripture, renouncing possessions and everything worldly are not in themselves perfection, as we have said; they are its tools. For perfection is not to be found in them; it is acquired through them. It is useless, therefore, to boast of our fasting, vigils, poverty, and reading of Scripture when we have not achieved the love of God and our fellow men. Whoever has achieved love has God within himself and his intellect is always with God.

"On Holy Fathers of Sketis and on Discrimination," p. 96

Vigils

TEN MINUTES AFTER MY DAILY reading and fifteen minutes after prayer, I load my children into the car to drive them to school. The sun is pouring in through my windshield. Spring has come. Birds sing. Cars hum along as we inch through the intersection. I should know better than to push the intersection envelope. Usually I wait patiently for the road to be clear. If I am certain I can make it through, I go. I tell my boys they should always wait for this certainty while driving.

But today, I don't wait. I press through. The sun shining, the daily prayer and reading, the promise of spring fade as a car turning right threatens to fill the gap left by the moving traffic. My hands grip the wheel and I move quickly into the open spot, feeling both angry and triumphant. The driver of the other car honks at me, and I shrug. "Idiot," I think to myself, "wait your turn."

Ten minutes after I cut off another driver on the road and fifteen minutes after I forget about it, my kids get out of the car at school. I tell them I love them. And when they close the doors, I pray for them. The disconnect strikes me as I watch the cars ahead jockey for position, horns honking and angry words drifting through open car windows, and I see myself there on display—so close to the vigil, so far from the goal.

DAY 85

When we meditate wisely and continually on the law of God, study psalms and canticles, engage in fasting and vigils, and always bear in mind what is to come—the kingdom of heaven, the Gehenna of fire and all God's works—our wicked thoughts diminish and find no place. But when we devote our time to worldly concerns and to matters of the flesh, to pointless and useless conversation, then these base thoughts multiply in us.

"On Holy Fathers of Sketis and on Discrimination," p. 97

Concerns and Conversations

MOVING FROM ONE SEASON TO another, especially when the season corresponds to Lent, always feels as though it presents opportunities. While some might look on Lent as a time of sacrifice because it involves added prayer, services, almsgiving, and fasting, I like to see it as making space, like spring cleaning or weeding the garden.

When things begin to bloom in the early spring, it's hard to determine what should be pulled up and what should be left behind to expand into that open space. It takes some guidance, good judgment, and patience. Where conversation is concerned, moving into and through Lent means I pay closer attention to the words I speak.

All year I monitor my thoughts and struggles, but during Lent, I like to monitor my words. I enter a time of listening, weeding out the desire to fill every space with talk about the weather, my worry, car trouble, money trouble. Sometimes I talk to dispel my own discomfort with quiet. So today I'll seek out quiet, and where I cannot find it, in places where words and noise and busyness must reside, perhaps I'll bring the quiet with me as a listener.

DAY 86

And this is just what we find; for the power of discrimination, scrutinizing all the thoughts and actions of a man, distinguishes and sets aside everything that is base and not pleasing to God, and keeps him free from delusion.

"On Holy Fathers of Sketis and on Discrimination," p. 99

Lamp of the Eye

I THINK ABOUT CONVERSATIONS BEFORE I have them. I do it to allay my social anxiety around meeting people, talking to people, and my subsequent fear that whatever I say is going to sound incredibly stupid. If I were talking to my therapist about this, she might say, "What's at risk for you to say something stupid? What would it say about you if you say something stupid?" and I might say, "It would mean that people would think I'm a mess."

Honestly, some days I am a mess. I live too much in my head. The real drawback to living too much in my head and to thinking through every conversation is that it causes me to see the real interactions through the fuzzy haze of my preparation. When things go sideways—and they often do—I'm stumbling around, tripping over words and judgments, perhaps even disappointed in myself, in the situation, in the outcome.

What would it look like to clean the lens as I interact with the people around me so that I can truly see the person before me instead of my preconceived idea of that person or my practiced answers to their unasked questions?

DAY 87

Discrimination is also called the "solid food" that "is suitable for those who have their organs of perception trained by practice to discriminate between good and evil" (Heb. 5:14). These passages show very clearly that without the gift of discrimination no virtue can stand or remain firm to the end, for it is the mother of all the virtues and their guardian.

"On Holy Fathers of Sketis and on Discrimination," p. 100

Solid Food

THERE ARE REASONS WE TURN to soup when we're sick. We can usually digest it without taxing the body too much. If we're exhausted, there's not much work involved in the eating of it. The warmth brings comfort, the taste offers a saltiness that encourages us to drink more fluids. These things all help nurse us back to health.

When we do a workout or go for a run, energy-building foods are required, either to prepare us before or to refuel after. These high-energy food choices keep the body in good condition when we are taxing it.

Then, of course, there also are meals meant for the sake of eating them, a pleasure for the palate, good company, fellowship, celebration.

Recognizing the needs of the body and matching the appropriate sustenance is necessary if we're going to be healthy. The same is true of our spiritual lives. What we read, how we pray, the attitude with which we approach liturgy and the Divine Mysteries all factor into how we live and how we fuel ourselves on the journey.

DAY 88

True discrimination comes to us only as a result of true humility, and this in turn is shown by our revealing to our spiritual fathers not only what we do but also what we think, by never trusting our own thoughts, and by following in all things the words of our elders, regarding as good what they have judged to be so.

"On Holy Fathers of Sketis and on Discrimination," p. 103

Telling All

I CONFESS A FEW TIMES A year. I like to get in to see my priest at the very least before each fast. Confession during Lent is especially important to me. There is something freeing about entering into the fast with a nice, clean slate.

When I became Orthodox, I made my first confession. I knew what held me back, which sins were the most bold or highest priority, and I confessed those. After four-plus decades, I knew the condition of my soul and my propensity toward sin. I also confessed that most likely the struggle would continue around those sins. They cannot be dismissed so easily.

So I confess, and though I want to be free of these struggles, truth be told, I know I hold on to some of the things I confess, even after I've professed to give them up. I gather them back into my purse just after absolution while they are still fresh on the floor, having just fallen from my lips. I don't know why I tuck them back into my purse—do I not trust that I am forgiven? Am I counting on some surety that I'll simply do it again? Out of habit or defiance? If this is an attempt at humility, it is, at best, misguided.

What does it look like to leave those sins behind, I wonder?

DAY 89

From all that has been said, we may conclude that nothing leads so surely to salvation as to confess our private thoughts to those fathers most graced with the power of discrimination, and in our pursuit of holiness to be guided by them rather than by our own thoughts and judgment.

"On Holy Fathers of Sketis and on Discrimination," p. 106

Discriminating Spirit

AT THIS MOMENT IN TIME, we hear the word *discrimination* often. On the news, in articles we read, the word is used to describe injustices committed by members of one group of people against another. Whether these injustices are words or deeds, if someone is the victim of discrimination, it means they are suffering at the hands of another merely because of who they are or what they believe.

Of course, we'll hear it in other contexts too from time to time. Someone who has excellent opinions on restaurants or movies or fashion might be said to have "discriminating" tastes. In this case, to be discriminating means that they choose more carefully perhaps than other people. They have high expectations for quality or style.

In the original Latin, the word means "to divide, separate." The Fathers use this word not to describe a way to inflict harm on another person, as in "discriminating against," but rather to encourage choosing well. We are asked to survey our motivations and the choices we have in how to behave in this world. Having done this, when we choose the good, this is the mark of a discriminating spirit.

DAY 90

We should therefore make every effort to acquire for ourselves that gift of discrimination which is able to keep us from excess in either direction.

"On Holy Fathers of Sketis and on Discrimination," p. 107

Excess

I HAVE TO BE CAREFUL WHEN I have something delicious in the house, something sweet especially. I hide it from myself and from the rest of the family to try to store it up, save it, savor it a little at a time. It doesn't usually work.

At first, I blame my family, but it's actually me standing in the kitchen at midnight, taking "just one more bite" to satisfy the sweet tooth that woke me.

I joke that I always think, "If I just eat this right away it won't be here to tempt me!" but there's some truth in the joke. I do believe it in the moment as I stand in bare feet and pajamas staring into the pantry, the freezer, the refrigerator. Call it a failure of self-control or logic, this inclination to overindulge in order to stem a momentary craving isn't healthy or wise. It doesn't lead to fewer temptations, only to a sick feeling in the stomach and creeping attacks of self-recrimination. It's not just the toffee-eating. This is a struggle with trust, scarcity thinking, worry. I sink into excess instead of leaning on building a strong sense of discrimination.

Mark the Ascetic

DAY 91

Introduction by Scott Cairns

EARLY IN THE FIFTH CENTURY, an ascetic by the name of Mark struggled in the desert of Nitria to find his way to prayer. His three works presented in the *Philokalia*—"On the Spiritual Law," "On Those Who Think that They Are Made Righteous by Works," and "Letter to Nicolas the Solitary"—manifest that the athlete's struggle bore abundant fruit.

Known variously as Mark the Monk, Mark the Ascetic, Mark the Faster, Mark the Hermit, he was born in Athens and tonsured by St. John Chrysostom in his fortieth year. The eremite thereafter spent his final sixty years in prayer and in leading others into the prayer of the heart. He knew the Holy Scriptures by heart; he prayed and wrote and ministered to all he came upon—both persons and beasts of the field—by the noetic efficacy of a mind descended into the heart.

Besides those texts gathered in the *Philokalia*, Mark's writings include treatises on baptismal grace and on repentance, as well as profound arguments against Messalianism in general and Nestorius in particular. Capable as Mark was of exposing heresy, his works most clearly manifest a profound self-awareness and humility. "When reading the Holy Scriptures," he writes, "he who is humble and engaged in spiritual work will apply everything to himself and not to someone else." May it be blessed!

DAY 92

May He who inaugurates every good thing inaugurate all that you undertake, so that it may be done with His blessing.

St. Mark the Ascetic, "On the Spiritual Law," p. 110

Every Good Thing

WHEN I WROTE MY FIRST book, an Orthodox friend asked about it. After I finished explaining the premise and the details of the release, he said, "May it be blessed!" And I felt that pronouncement deep in my bones. "Yes," I said, "I hope so."

It takes a shifting in my brain to ask for blessing, whether it is on work, partnering, my parenting, or simply the hours I wander from place to place on these middle-aged feet. What a bold thing to ask!

But these opening thoughts of St. Mark the Ascetic all dwell in the possibility of blessing. He asks that we reside in the truth that we look to God as foundation for our daily lives. In all that we do, all that we say, we hope for every good thing—we hope for God's blessing. Today, I want to make it a point to consider creating space for this simple, though bold, request—may it be blessed! This is a habit worth cultivating.

DAY 93

There is a breaking of the heart which is gentle and makes it deeply penitent, and there is a breaking which is violent and harmful, shattering it completely.

St. Mark the Ascetic, "On the Spiritual Law," p. 111

Heartbreak

HEARTBREAK IS A FACT OF life. While most of us think of dating stories when heartbreak is mentioned, I find it in parenting and friendship, careers and politics, as well. In any situation in which we invest our hearts, we're vulnerable to having the heart broken.

So what's the solution then? To hide the heart away? Never to take a chance and invest the whole of our heart in anything? I don't think it's possible to withhold the heart for one's entire life. It's simply not possible to avoid heartbreak, and I hate that this is true.

But I'm reminded today that there are different sorts of heartbreak. And, in fact, some heartbreak works in our favor over time. When we invest too much or attach wrongly to things (or people) that ultimately move us further away from the best version of ourselves and away from the One who made us, heartbreak can be healing. This sort of heartbreak comes with the gentleness St. Mark suggests. It comes from a place of care, not violence. It has roots in our betterment, our growth. It may still hurt—because how can heartbreak help but hurt?—but in time, and with hope in God, we pray we grow stronger and wiser for it.

DAY 94

At the times when you remember God, increase your prayers, so that when you forget Him, the Lord may remind you.

St. Mark the Ascetic, "On the Spiritual Law," p. 112

Remembering God

How many times will I forget God? And in forgetting God, I forget that I am more than the material I see and feel around me. In forgetting God, I constrain myself to this world. I begin to believe that this world is all I have, or that this is all I am.

Remembering God is remembering myself and the reality of the parts I am not yet able to see, the mystery and the wonder of life. Like every practice, the act of remembering God builds over time. If I practice healthy living by eating well or getting exercise, then on days when I do not eat well or get out for a walk, I still at least remember the feeling I got from it. The feeling boosts me toward choosing wisely next time because the absence of it is a loss.

Remembering God comes more easily as I've grown accustomed to Him, in prayer and thanksgiving, in charity, liturgy, and confession. I need to make a practice of remembering God and let it become part of me so that the absence of that memory leaves a space that yearns to be filled by Him.

DAY 95

God is the source of every virtue, as the sun is of daylight.

St. Mark the Ascetic, "On the Spiritual Law," p. 113

Daylight

HOW MANY THINGS DO I take for granted? Clean water, fresh food, oxygen, and, yes, sunlight. In the winter, I wake in the dark and watch as the skies grow lighter with each child getting up for school, each cup of coffee, each prayer before my icon stand. This time of year, light announces the start of the new day. It shows up early, as though it's excited to make the announcement, eager to spur me into action. *Come now,* it says. *Time to get going.*

In April, I wake in the morning with the springtime daylight, whether blocked by clouds or with sunlight streaming through the windows. It is there, waiting for me. What if today, in the spirit of remembering God, we take the opportunity to give credit to the source of light? Every shaft of sun and every cloud that obscures it should bring to mind the Creator of the sun.

When the light begins to fade, we stand once again before the icons and thank God for this day, for the promise of the return tomorrow of the daylight and the opportunity once again to practice the virtues of this faith life together.

DAY 96

By praying for those who wrong us we overthrow the devil; opposing them we are wounded by him.

St. Mark the Ascetic, "On the Spiritual Law," p. 113

Opposition

THIS VERSE FROM THE BOOK of Matthew rings in my ears—*Love your enemies and pray for those who persecute you.* Most of the time, when I'm feeling the weight of any sort of "enemy," the thing I want least to do is to pray for them, let alone love them. It's an unnatural impulse for me to move toward love when I'm being hurt, and to pray for someone is a loving act in my book.

So, then, what can we make of this instruction from St. Mark, one that echoes so clearly the words of Christ? How can we be expected to pray for someone who wrongs us?

I imagine much has to do with our starting place. It takes some courage to climb out of hiding to offer up prayer. It takes humility to lower my hands from a protective posture, place my palms together, and point my fingers toward God. Even thinking about giving up my defensive posture makes my heart race. I think to myself—what can be gained by reaching out to someone who so willingly hurts me? How can I afford to be that vulnerable?

St. Mark tells me today that to pray for my enemies isn't weakness or giving up, but strength, and courage, and mercy. No one loses when we pray for one another.

DAY 97

Ignorance makes us reject what is beneficial; and when it becomes brazen it strengthens the hold of evil.

St. Mark the Ascetic, "On the Spiritual Law," p. 113

Knowing

TO BE IGNORANT IS TO be uninformed or to lack knowledge. Throw the word around as an insult and it sounds like a synonym for stupid, but being ignorant does not mean we're unable to learn. We simply do not have all the information that is available. To be in the dark is one thing, but to be in the dark and complain about it, all while seated next to the light switch, is another.

There is so much evil we ignore because it's inconvenient or difficult to call it out. We can switch on the light anytime and see what surrounds us in this dark room. We might run our hands over the wall, finding the switch, contemplating the possibilities. We cannot know what we'll see when we turn it on. It may be far worse than we imagine. It may be far better. We have to want to learn the truth. We have to seek for it, all the while feeling for the light.

DAY 98

Distress reminds the wise of God, but crushes those who forget Him.

St. Mark the Ascetic, "On the Spiritual Law," p. 114

Distress

WHEN I AM AFRAID, I call out to God. I beg for help. I shake my head in the face of yet another setback, financial meltdown, emotional break as though I am pushing the weight to the side, or at least shifting it well enough to keep breathing until help arrives.

I go straight to the Jesus Prayer, because it says all I mean in the short lines, "Lord Jesus Christ, Son of God, have mercy on me." In those moments of distress, when there is nothing left for me to do but wait and pray, I go to prayer. And often, it feels like nothing, shouting into the hurricane, whispering into the chaos. But in those moments, I also remind myself that faith is not a totem to ward off bad luck, and prayers are not magic words that fix my life situation. These things are building blocks of a strong and healthy mind, body, and spirit. When I am in distress, it is in remembering God that I am able to push through the rough times. The stress of this world won't crush me, but I remember that only through the grace of God.

DAY 99

Concern yourself with your own sins and not with those of your neighbor; then the workplace of your intellect will not be robbed.

St. Mark the Ascetic, "On the Spiritual Law," p. 114

Workplace

I LOVE THE PICTURE THAT COMES to mind when I consider the "workplace" of my intellect. In this usage, of course, by "intellect" St. Mark means the nous or the "eye of the heart" rather than the logical mind.

If the workplace of my intellect is anything like my writing desk or my laundry room, as those are my usual workplaces these days, then that workplace is a mess. Everything I intend to do, respond to, read later, or file is piled up there. Pens, scrap paper, calendars, Lego sculptures my middle son made for me, all just gather dust. Clutter is apparently the decorating theme in my workplace. To get anything major done, though, I take a day to clear it all out, put everything in its place, at least for now. It doesn't take long before I'm well on my way back to the clutter.

Imagine then what chaos would come if I tried taking on the responsibility of someone else's desktop or laundry room. I don't have the space for it, or the time, or the focus. And yet, often I do I find myself sitting in judgment on someone else's space, use of time, prayer life, shortcomings, sins. Any space I might have cleared for my own work then is filled, crowding me until I am unable to do anything except sit in that judgment seat.

DAY 100

If you want spiritual health, listen to your conscience, do all it tells you, and you will benefit.

St. Mark the Ascetic, "On the Spiritual Law," p. 115

Little Voice

IT'S NOT IN THE BACK of my head, but close to my left ear between cheekbone and temple. The voice doesn't whisper. I can make out all the words easily, though no words are used apart from *you know the right thing* and *do it anyway.*

The voice my conscience uses is warm, personable, and yet strong and solid. *You know the right thing*, it says over and over. *Do it anyway,* it repeats when I tell it in no words at all that I'd rather not, that I'm too tired, that I'm afraid of being rejected or criticized. But it's the right thing to do, to speak, to think, and *do it anyway* is what I need to hear. The voice does not tell me it won't hurt, or that it will all turn out all right. Doing the right thing, saying the right thing, thinking the right thing doesn't always go well. It can be messy and dangerous. That is why I falter the next time I'm faced with making those choices. That hurt, pain, and rejection is what I remember first; the benefits of choosing well get lost in the remembered difficulty.

This is why the voice of our conscience is so vital, and why we must train ourselves to listen to it instead of to the remembered discomfort we carry in our bodies. We do know the right thing, and we know we have to do it anyway.

DAY 101

Understand the words of Holy Scripture by putting them into practice, and do not fill yourself with conceit by expatiating on theoretical ideas.

St. Mark the Ascetic, "On the Spiritual Law," p. 116

Words and Deeds

Bless and do not curse.
Do unto others as you would have them do unto you.
Love one another.
Bear with each other and forgive one another.

THESE INSTRUCTIONS ALL INDICATE ACTIONS. Do this, do not do that. I am amazed at how complicated it all seems in the action but how simple it reads on the page. If someone hurts me with gossip, my impulse is to hit back. If I don't get my way, I lash out. If a group of people has hateful beliefs or values, am I still commanded to love them?

The words given to me in Scripture go against the unspoken rules of societal engagement. *Every man for himself. Get while the getting's good.* To choose to love, forgive, and bless looks like weakness to people who seek power. To serve my neighbor, to care for the sick, to give away my hard-earned money to the poor all sound good in theory and on paper, but in the working out of my daily life, how often will I defer to the status quo? What keeps us from taking the actions in these instructions?

DAY 102

When you observe some thought suggesting that you seek human fame, you can be sure it will bring you disgrace.

St. Mark the Ascetic, "On the Spiritual Law," p. 116

Hard to Hear

I'M STARTING A FILE CALLED "Hard to Hear." I find notes I've written to myself over the years in the margins of this first volume of the *Philokalia*. As I read through the notes now, a trend emerges in them. "Hard to hear!" is one that graces the pages quite often. Generally, the passages so marked have to do with the sense of self. Today it comes in response to the words of St. Mark.

In my case, it's not human fame I want, but affirmation. I collect affirmation to build up the ground on which I stand. I stuff myself with it, my pockets, my purse, my backpack. It makes everything feel more solid and true. That affirmation fades away, the immediate impact fails me over time, but the weight of my desire for it remains.

There's no shame in wanting to be accepted and loved; this is natural. But the temporal nature of fame, affirmation, compliments, or accolades cannot take the place of the deep knowing of myself as beloved of God. If my identity is rooted there, my pockets can be empty, backpack light, and yet the ground will always be firm under my feet—and I will never feel empty.

DAY 103

The intellect is made blind by these three passions: avarice, self-esteem, and sensual pleasure.

St. Mark the Ascetic, "On the Spiritual Law," p. 117

Blind

WHEN MY EYES ARE CLOSED or when it is too dark to see, I can still feel my way around the room. I know the room, each stick of furniture, each pile of books on the floor, light switches on walls, doorknobs and latches. I use my hands to guide me, bumping my hip into the dresser, the bedpost, the windowsill. I am not blind. To walk around in the dark is a choice I make. I can switch on that light, open the curtains, open my eyes.

Blindness of the intellect is like this. It's a choice I make each day to put on a blindfold, to switch off lights, to close blinds and feel my way around the room. Avarice, the love of wealth, blocks out the light. Self-esteem, or thinking only of my own life, my own self, makes windows into walls. Sensual pleasure, choosing only comfort no matter the cost, closes my eyes to the rest of the world.

There is a place, I think, for material things, for paying the bills and having enough to eat. There is a time to choose comfort and a time to think of myself first, to value who I am. But these three things—avarice, self-esteem, and sensual pleasure—will always be temporary fixes to long-term struggles.

DAY 104

He who prays with understanding patiently accepts circumstances, whereas he who resents them has not yet attained pure prayer.

St. Mark the Ascetic, "On the Spiritual Law," p. 118

Pure Prayer

THERE ARE FEW THINGS I can do that are truly self-forgetting. That is, something I do that allows me to truly be in the moment. Most things take work if I'm going to focus. Even watching mindless television or silly movies takes a certain amount of effort. I know as I sit down to binge-watch something that it won't change my situation, but it might numb me against the anxiety of it for a little while. In the end, whatever respite came of that medication evaporates pretty quickly.

Pure prayer seems so intangible and maybe even unattainable, like trying to carry water through the desert using only my cupped hands. The focus must be laser-like. I imagine I must be able to block out all distractions, all temptations, all the rambling thoughts that crop up when I set out to pray. I keep my eyes focused on the water in my hands, one step, two steps. Drops seep through my fingers no matter how tightly I press them together.

The effort is excruciating, but it has this self-forgetting effect as well. The focus, the energy, the task of it, all work toward the worthy end goal.

DAY 105

Just as water and fire cannot be combined, so self-justification and humility exclude one another.

St. Mark the Ascetic, "On the Spiritual Law," p. 119

Full Stop

THE WORST WAY TO START an apology or a confession is this: "I'm sorry, but . . ." Anytime we place "but" in a sentence we negate the first statement with anything that follows. I'm sorry, but he had it coming. I've sinned, but I had a good reason. Even saying something like "I love you, but . . ." gives us cover, as it were. Perhaps we think we can hold these two diverging ideas at the same time. We think it softens the blow, perhaps.

This is evidence of the divide between self-justification and humility. We want to move toward humility and repentance, and at the same time we want to hold fast to whatever brought us here to begin with. I want to be forgiven, but I also want to continue to behave the way I have. I don't want to change.

True humility is the ability to make strong statements without qualifiers. I love you. Full stop. I'm sorry. Full stop. I've sinned. Full stop. If I can learn to do that, and practice making these clear choices, I may finally begin to see progress.

DAY 106

Sin is a blazing fire. The less fuel you give it, the faster it dies down: the more you feed it, the more it burns.

St. Mark the Ascetic, "On the Spiritual Law," p. 119

Warmth

THE FIRST HOUSE WE OWNED had a small fireplace. A functioning wood-burning fireplace in a small Chicago bungalow from the 1900s was quite a find. We would turn off the lights and sit and watch the flames in the winter as snow fell outside. It was beautiful, but it wasn't terribly practical.

The fireplace was so small it did not do much to make the room warmer. In fact, it almost seemed to make the room cooler. We found out that because of the proximity of the fireplace to the thermostat, our heat would turn off and remain off for as long as the fire burned. We were warm if we were close to the fire, but the rest of the room and the house were cold.

Sometimes the sin I build and fan and fuel is like this. It feels warm when I am close to it. I believe in those moments that whatever I'm thinking, saying, doing is keeping me warm, maybe even keeping me alive, but it's an illusion. And sin doesn't stay neatly contained in a brick fireplace. Over time, left to burn or stoked too much, it leaps out from stones and licks the hardwood floors; it catches on the drapery and furniture. It threatens to burn down the whole house.

DAY 107

If you hate rebuke, it shows that the passion in which you are involved is due to your own free choice. But if you welcome rebuke, the passion is due to prepossession.

St. Mark the Ascetic, "On the Spiritual Law," p. 120

Rebuke

TRUE CRITICISM, NO MATTER HOW gently delivered, is painful. I'm beginning to think that perhaps this is the way it ought to be. I always thought what I was after was to mature, so that I could hear criticism and not feel that pain. I thought that in time, with practice and a desire to know myself better, to be honest with myself about my shortcomings, the result would be pain-free. But, of course, it isn't. After all these years, hearing criticism is just as painful as ever.

The reason this real and true criticism hurts is that it is real and true. It points to behaviors or words that come from dark places, deep places, well-fortified places. I might shout at that critic about fairness or tell him he is wrong, but it hurts because I know she is right in her rebuke. In truth, I have probably already given myself that rebuke, already seen the error, already felt the regret of it. I already own that shortcoming but have not yet given it up. The question is whether I'm willing to let it go and trust God with the empty space it leaves, let myself move into whatever is next.

DAY 108

It is the uneven quality of our thoughts that produces changes in our condition. For God assigns to our voluntary thoughts consequences which are appropriate but not necessarily of our choice.

St. Mark the Ascetic, "On the Spiritual Law," p. 121

Uneven

IT'S A LOPSIDED WORLD. ONE side of the body tends to be stronger than the other. One side of the body also tends to hold more tension while the other is more flexible. Part of it is that we favor one side over the other. Left-handed or right-handed, we approach the world reaching out with our stronger side. When we have an injury, the opposite side of the body compensates.

Solid training strategies involve making sure that we pay attention to this and adjust our weight stacks or toe touches to reflect this imbalance. We strengthen the side that is weak; we hold stretches on the tighter areas a little bit longer. We're after symmetry here or as close as we can get.

But there's another technique we use in training. We change the movement suddenly or add elements of imbalance to the movement. When someone is put on a balance ball or wobble board, their world suddenly dips and pulls. The challenge is unfamiliar, and the body has to respond. It's this kind of training that produces the quickest results. It tests us. Uncertainty in our circumstances can be a good teacher. It can show us where we excel and where we need to improve.

DAY 109

A man who is carried away by his thoughts is blinded by them; and while he can see the actual working of sin, he cannot see its causes.

St. Mark the Ascetic, "On the Spiritual Law," p. 121

What We Know

THE COCONUT CAKE RECIPE WAS precise and strangely simple enough. I don't like to cook or bake, usually, but my son wanted this cake, and I thought I'd at least give it a try. Generally, when I make something and it turns out badly, I can point to some reason why. I forgot the timer, I put in too much water, I missed a step. But this time I promise I followed the recipe perfectly. I measured carefully, I whisked when asked to whisk, mixed when told to mix. I baked for the length of time they suggested. I used the right-sized pans.

The recipe was not terribly complicated, but there were a lot of steps. I focused on each step, reading it twice, three times. Still, the cake came out wrong, and I could not see the reason.

As I pored back over the process, I kicked myself for whatever I'd done or not done as I tried to ice the terribly crumbling cake—the icing slid from the sides. It was not until a few days later when I asked a baker friend her thoughts that we figured out where I'd gone wrong. I thought to myself, "I do not know what I do not know," and it works for so many situations I encounter. Sometimes it takes getting out of my head and getting a more informed perspective to see where things go awry.

DAY 110

Everything that happens has a small beginning, and grows the more it is nourished.

St. Mark the Ascetic, "On the Spiritual Law," p. 122

Weeds in Spring

IN THE SUNNY AREAS OF my patio, weeds spring up in the cracks between bricks, pushing them apart if left to spread. Once a week at this time of year I go out there and spend time pulling them up, filling in the space with a small bit of sand to keep it clear.

In the shady spots, it's moss that collects in the cracks. The moss sits on top of the sand mixed with soil, bright green but low to the ground, so I leave it alone. It nurtures itself. There's nothing to take away, nothing to give that it doesn't already gain on its own.

The container garden is fallow this year. After a robust couple of years of active planting, we took up the old dead plants and left the soil alone. Still, the weeds pop up—bluegrass, lambsquarters, dandelion, milkweed. By midsummer we'll see morning glory we did not plant weaving around the railings of the deck. Weeds really are simply plants that spring up where we do not want them. They begin with the same seed smallness, the same nurturing. Their beauty is defined then by intention.

DAY 111

At a time of affliction, expect a provocation to sensual pleasure, for because it relieves the affliction it is readily welcomed.

St. Mark the Ascetic, "On the Spiritual Law," p. 122

Prayer and Fasting and Donuts

TWO COMPETING REMEDIES PUSH THROUGH when things are tough—either prayer and fasting, or donuts and binge-watching. In a perfect world, I'd choose to respond to stress by leaning into prayer and fasting. I'd take some time to settle, breathe slowly and quietly, letting the noise of the city drain away into the background, and nudge my mind back on track when it wanders away. In a perfect world, I'd choose that meager meal of rice and vegetables, prepared lovingly and eaten mindfully while listening to the birds singing.

But this is not a perfect world, and I am not a perfect pilgrim on this road. I am worried about paying the mortgage, about kids with lengthening arms and legs who trip going up the stairs and grow out of their school pants. I am tired all the time, driving around town in a cloud of confusion and street noise. Instead of a quiet meal on my back deck, I choose the drive-thru. Instead of restorative prayer on a long walk, I sit and watch another season of that show I missed last year that everyone was talking about. It does not relieve the affliction, though it might just make it bearable for a time.

DAY 112

Peace is deliverance from the passions, and is not found except through the action of the Holy Spirit.

St. Mark the Ascetic, "On the Spiritual Law," p. 123

Yields and Harvest

NO MATTER WHAT I PLANT each spring, it never looks like the pictures in books or the front of the seed pack. The flowers are there, yes, but they are often crowded instead of orderly. Or perhaps they are choked out by persistent weeds or some other random plant that springs up. Once, a winding pumpkin vine grew from the middle of my stand of tomato plants. I never planted pumpkins. I imagine that came from the birds, the squirrels, the wind.

The pleasure of gardening, I'm discovering, comes from not only the harvest but the process of bringing the harvest to fruition—the tilling, the planting, the nurturing, and the ability to roll with whatever comes. This ability to persevere, and the peace that comes of it, has a supernatural flavor to it. This peace comes from outside of me. I catch a fleeting glimpse of it as I pull up weeds in the heat, with hands sweating inside these gloves, but it is there, and I admit, it is compelling.

DAY 113

A good conscience is found through prayer, and pure prayer through the conscience. Each by nature needs the other.

St. Mark the Ascetic, "On the Spiritual Law," p. 123

Voice of God

THE IMAGE THAT COMES TO mind comes from old cartoons I watched: an angel on one shoulder, a devil on the other. They both give their take on what the character ought to do. The angel's voice is meek and lovely, her halo right and straight, her robe glowing white. The devil speaks in sneers, cool and sarcastic, his horns sharp and red.

But in real life the voices that come are not quite as distinct. The chatter drifts in and out, some words bold, some featherweight. And the images too are complicated, sometimes snatches of glossy magazine photos, sometimes clips from videos, all set on a flicker as they pass through my head while I'm busy doing something else.

To be in dialogue with God is the aim. Pure prayer is this praying without ceasing, this ongoing and edifying dialogue. It means taking time to listen and to hear, to piece together thoughts and images with patience and discernment. No angel, no devil, just focus, waiting, persistence, and listening.

DAY 114

Always do as much good as you can, and at a time of greater good do not turn to a lesser.

St. Mark the Ascetic, "On the Spiritual Law," p. 124

All the Good

TODAY'S WORDS FROM ST. MARK the Ascetic remind me of the instruction I found once while sitting in traffic. The bumper sticker on the car in front of me read, "Do all the good you can." When I got home that day, I looked up the quote and found that it came from John Wesley.

The entire quote is, "Do all the good you can. By all the means you can. In all the ways you can. In all the places you can. At all the times you can. To all the people you can. As long as ever you can." What can I do while sitting in traffic on a rainy spring day? I am trapped here in this line of people.

So, as the words from St. Mark ring in me, I sit in traffic while thunder rumbles and horns honk. I wait for the light to turn green. I move to prayer, for my family, for my struggles with patience. And then I pray too for the man in the car next to me whose eyes are focused straight ahead, whose hands grip the steering wheel, whose story I do not know.

DAY 115

He who relies on theoretical knowledge alone is not yet a faithful servant: a faithful servant is one who expresses his faith in Christ through obedience to His commandments.

St. Mark the Ascetic, "No Righteousness by Works," p. 125

Becoming

BEFORE I CONVERTED TO ORTHODOXY, I read several books. I dove deep into the history of the Faith, into the lives of the saints, into the beauty of the practices, but only in word at first. Books are safe. From the relative quiet of my room I can learn about the entire world.

But entering into the liturgy was different. All the information I had read about Orthodoxy didn't really prepare me for the task of *becoming* Orthodox. Just as reading about flying an airplane or driving a car might give me a sense of the mechanics of the thing, but it's surely no substitute for being in the cockpit or driver's seat. The experience of being physically engaged in this learning is vital.

Using this metaphor, we understand the commandments, then, as action instead of merely principles. We grasp them with our hands, we live them in our hearts. It's all part of this process of *becoming*.

DAY 116

Unexpected trials are sent by God to teach us to practice the ascetic life; and they lead us to repentance even when we are reluctant.

St. Mark the Ascetic, "No Righteousness by Works," p. 126

Compensation

IT BEGAN WITH AN INJURY a year earlier. I fell on the stairs and slammed my right thigh into a step. A large bruise came, and then after it healed, a palm-sized dent in my quadricep. "It'll fill in," the doctor said, and it did, more or less. But the muscle became weak, and this led to leg pain, hip pain, back pain.

When we're injured and the body is thrown for a loop, it compensates any way it can. This compensation keeps us moving, but it costs something too. Without being mindful of that longstanding injury and making efforts to strengthen the muscle that was injured, I compromised the whole chain of movement over time.

This attitude of being reluctant figures in for me. I don't want to do single leg squats every day to overcome the injury. It takes time and focus, patience and practice. So, because I can still move, I move about my day, not making the additional effort, letting the rest of my body do the work.

It is only through developing and keeping a daily practice dedicated to strengthening those weak or injured areas, physically and spiritually, that we can handle the difficulties of this world. If we do the work necessary to help the injured places become strong again, the whole body becomes strong.

DAY 117

Even though knowledge is true, it is still not firmly established if unaccompanied by works. For everything is established by being put into practice.

St. Mark the Ascetic, "No Righteousness by Works," p. 126

Do as I Say

EVEN WHEN I WAS WORKING in fitness, I didn't have the body of a typical personal trainer—at least not the kind you see strolling around the big gyms in town, or in advertisements on television or in magazines. I have an average body for an American woman just entering her fifties, soft in the middle, some aches in my bones. This is not exactly the result of neglect, but maybe a little.

I know how to strengthen my body, how to temper my intake of foods that contribute to the neglect, how to overcome the accompaniments of aging, perennial parenting, and driving around all day instead of walking or running. Knowing these things isn't enough to stave off the long-term effects of neglect. If I want to gain strength, I have to challenge the muscles. If I want to keep my cardiovascular system in good condition, I have to leave my car at home sometimes and walk to the post office instead. If I want to lower the possibility of some age-related ills, I'll need to reach for green and leafy foods, colorful fruits, vibrant vegetables, lean proteins. Just like in the spiritual life, knowing it's the "right" thing isn't enough. I have to put that knowledge into practice.

DAY 118

The self-controlled refrain from gluttony; those who have renounced possessions, from greed; the tranquil, from loquacity; the pure, from self-indulgence; the modest, from unchastity: the self-dependent, from avarice; the gentle, from agitation; the humble, from self-esteem; the obedient, from quarreling; the self-critical, from hypocrisy. Similarly, those who pray are protected from despair: the poor, from having many possessions: confessors of the faith, from its denial: martyrs, from idolatry. Do you see how every virtue that is performed even to the point of death is nothing other than refraining from sin? Now to refrain from sin is a work within our own natural powers, but not something that buys us the kingdom.

St. Mark the Ascetic, "No Righteousness by Works," p. 127

Reaching and Refraining

HOW MANY TIMES DO I reach for the thing in front of me that will hurt me? Even knowing and thinking and struggling as I reach out my arm. I take the thing before me, offered seemingly free of charge—*eat this*, it says.

And in one bite, the bitterness of that choice is evident. I want to put it down, cast it away, far away—but the bite is already taken, already swallowed, already moving the residue of my sin into my bloodstream. I give myself to that poor choice. I swim in the guilt of it, promising to change, to do better next time.

How many times will I reach for it in the future, in a fit of temporary amnesia of the past? I will argue with myself as I wrap my hands around that choice; I will let the memory of my regret seep between my fingers. And then, I will do it anyway.

DAY 119

There is an energy of grace not understood by beginners, and there is also an energy of evil which resembles the truth. It is advisable not to scrutinize these energies too closely, because one may be led astray, and not to condemn them out of hand, because they may contain some truth, but we should lay everything before God in hope, for He knows what is of value in both of them.

St. Mark the Ascetic, "No Righteousness by Works," p. 127

Gathering

IN THE DREAM, I AM gathering fruit that's fallen from a tree in my yard. It looks as though a storm has come through and all the apples were knocked to the patio below. I am sitting on the ground, a brown sack by my knee. I am gathering apples and placing them carefully into the sack, taking time to sort them—this one ripe, this one rotted, this one not yet ready.

But there is another storm coming. I can see clouds building up in the distance. Sounds of thunder rumble overhead, and suddenly, there are flashes of lightning. I open the sack to find that it is mostly empty, and my anxiety rises. Even in my dream, I feel the anxiety in my throat. "But I need these apples," I keep thinking.

I lay the bag open and pile them all in, now indiscriminately, a little panicked. It will be heavier to carry. I may have to drag it up the wooden stairs onto the porch. I'll sort them out later, where it's safe, where it's dry and warm.

DAY 120

The intellect cannot be still unless the body is still also: and the wall between them cannot be demolished without stillness and prayer.

St. Mark the Ascetic, "No Righteousness by Works," p. 128

One Small Stone

EVEN IF IT'S ONLY ONE minute, I'll take it. Even if, in the middle of the crazy busy-ness of this city, this family, this job, this life, I can contact the stillness, I will take it.

Each moment like that is a small stone I take from the wall that already exists between who I am and who I mean to be. I sit with my hands on the cold wall as I switch off the laundry list in my brain, switch off the distractions from outside, from inside, from all around. I dig my fingers into the sun-hardened clay that surrounds each stone. It takes all my focus, all my energy. Sometimes, a stone only loosens a bit around the edges; sometimes, whole stones become dislodged. Sometimes, I arrive at that wall and see that in the intervening time, I've managed to rebuild the torn-down places with my sin.

But even if it's only one minute, one small round stone, I'll take it. I'll throw the stone far from me. And then I'll rub my hands together to make ready for more work, knowing full well it's only a matter of time before the distractions come again.

DAY 121

He whose mind teems with thoughts lacks self-control; and even when they are beneficial, hope is more so.

St. Mark the Ascetic, "No Righteousness by Works," p. 129

Empty Hands

IN THE MOMENTS BEFORE I drop off to sleep every night, I run through a catalogue of the day, the day before, the week before that. I catalogue without words, images in my head about wrongs and injuries, accomplishments, aspirations. Anxiety seeps up through the crevices in my brain and leaks out everywhere. My head aches as I pray or sing to myself without sound, or try in some other way to outpace the thinking.

I have never been able to just turn off my brain, especially at night, when my body is still and the room is quiet. Some nights I stare up at the ceiling, some nights I get up and make a list on paper. The sound of the pen against the paper is soothing; the words come fast and furious. I imagine them pouring through my brain, my heart, my hand, my fingers, and onto the page, where they'll be stored safely until the morning.

I cannot reach out to hold on to hope until I make space for it, until I empty this head and these hands of whatever they are carrying.

DAY 122

When the intellect forgets the purpose of true devotion, then external works of virtue bring no profit.

St. Mark the Ascetic, "No Righteousness by Works," p. 129

Automatic

ONCE THROUGH THE STOPLIGHT AT Ashland and Cortland, I realized I was going the wrong way. I was driving my son to an appointment on the north side of town, and I was heading east—way east of where we were supposed to be. I recalculated in my head and made the first turn possible to get back on track. Given the traffic, now I'd most likely be late.

This was the route I'd take a couple of times a day during the school year. The kids' schools and sports lessons were on this side of the river. It became automatic to leave my garage, turn east in the alley, and then continue south and east, weaving my way through the side streets to avoid all the traffic lights, until, at last, just over the river I hit Clybourn. From there it was a straight shot. But today, I forgot myself, my purpose for the day, my reason for even being in the car.

The spiritual life is like this. When we forget or move automatically, how many times do we suddenly realize we're in the wrong place? How many times do we have to turn around and pick our way through the mounting traffic toward our destination?

There are some times in which moving automatically is beneficial, though, like moving to pray in times of stress or joy without thinking about it. This sort of forgetting builds us, strengthens us, comforts us. It gets us closer to where we need, ultimately, to be.

DAY 123

Grace has been given mystically to those who have been baptized into Christ: and it becomes active within them to the extent that they actively observe the commandments. Grace never ceases to help us secretly: but to do good—as far as lies in our power—depends on us.

St. Mark the Ascetic, "No Righteousness by Works," p. 130

Doing and Being

THE STRUGGLE IS ALL IN my head. The thoughts come fast, this fantasy or that one. I slide into the thinking, the scenario, the worry, the doubt, and I cannot even recall how it happened. I try to force my attention elsewhere, to the trees, the sound of the birds singing, the car in front of me, the story my son is telling as he sits next to me. The thoughts are compelling, though, more compelling than what I'm seeing or hearing, and the thought plays on and on in my head.

When we exit the car, I stretch my legs and take a deep breath. Changing position has done something for me; it's cut off the thinking, the worry, the doubt. My son goes into the house, and I check the mail. The thinking slinks away. I notice it dissipating while I walk the dog later, while I lift weights at the gym, while I make dinner. These acts of "doing" short-circuit the thoughts. These acts of "doing" require my body and my mind and my spirit to work together as nothing else has lately. Sometimes, the work of grace is active, and it requires movement, action, doing.

DAY 124

Again, grace may be hidden in advice given by a neighbor. Sometimes it also accompanies our understanding during reading, and as a natural result teaches our intellect the truth about itself. If, then, we do not hide the talent given to us in this way, we shall enter actively into the joy of the Lord.

St. Mark the Ascetic, "No Righteousness by Works," p. 130

Boats

THERE IS AN OLD JOKE in which a man is sitting on his roof during a flood. He prays to God to save him. A boat comes by and offers assistance, but the man refuses, saying that God will save him. A few hours later a helicopter hovers overhead, and they throw down a rope ladder. He waves them off, saying once again that God will save him. The man dies, and when he reaches heaven he asks God why He did not save him. God replies, "I sent a boat and a helicopter—what more did you need?"

If we are paying attention, and if we are willing to hear and heed the good words we get from what we're reading or the person we're asking, help is there. It seems like such a simple shift to make, such an easy piece of wisdom to take, like boats offered when we're drowning. Yet it takes a certain degree of humility, too. First, we have to admit we're in need, and then we have to ask for help. But further, we have to get in the boat when it comes.

DAY 125

A seed will not grow without earth and water; and a man will not develop without voluntary suffering and divine help.

St. Mark the Ascetic, "No Righteousness by Works," p. 131

This Box

THIS BOX WAS HIDDEN IN a closet for at least three years. When we moved into this house, I must have tucked it into the corner of that closet, thinking I would get to it soon enough. Today I pull it out so I can make room for winter coats that won't need to see the light of day until late fall—maybe October, maybe November.

This box is labeled "Books, other." I slide a sharp knife along the taped seam on top and release the seal. Inside are books, as promised—self-help, old schoolbooks, some notebooks, a journal from years ago when I was pregnant with my youngest. Next to the books, in the margins between the cardboard and the hardcovers, a bag of nails and picture hangers, a screwdriver, a small hammer, and a few packs of seeds—morning glories, sunflowers, Queen Anne's lace. I purchased these when we had a yard in Nashville with enough sun to sustain them, but I never planted them. I simply moved them from place to place, two moves since that sunny Nashville yard.

This box contains histories and hardware, and hope. Those seeds, unplanted and expectant, wait there patiently in the dark, full of promise. Maybe one day, when I have the space for them, a little bit of earth and sun, I'll finally plant them.

DAY 126

Do not refuse to learn, even though you may be very intelligent. For what God provides has more value than our own intelligence.

St. Mark the Ascetic, "No Righteousness by Works," p. 131

Lifelong Learner

MY OLDEST SON TELLS ME that he has plans for the future. He is sixteen, finishing his sophomore year in high school. He has a passion for writing. He says he wants to study English in college, and as I'm about to give him encouragement, he goes on to say he wants to then get a master's degree in creative writing. After that, he continues, he'll finish with a PhD in literature.

"Wow," I said. "You have this all mapped out."

He nodded.

"So you're a perpetual student," I say.

"I guess," he answers. "There's a lot to learn."

There is a lot to learn. I forget this while I'm busy doing all the stuff adults do. This is the stuff that requires me to at least pretend to know what I'm doing—in parenting, writing, driving, cooking, gardening, bill-paying. There's some risk in admitting that I don't know something, or that I don't know the whole of it, at least. And in taking that risk, in adopting the posture of a lifelong learner, I wonder where that will lead.

DAY 127

No one is as good and merciful as the Lord. But even He does not forgive the unrepentant. Many of us feel remorse for our sins, yet we gladly accept their causes.

St. Mark the Ascetic, "No Righteousness by Works," p. 131

Treating the Symptom

IT'S RAINING TODAY, AND RAINING hard. The first spring we were in this house it rained like this. We'd just moved in and had no idea if we might get water in the basement. It was the middle of the day. I was home alone. I went to the basement to investigate a strange sound I'd heard, and it turned out to be a sump pump in a closet. How we missed it before, I don't know.

The sump pump was running strong and loud. I looked out the exterior door that led to a small patio outside, and I saw that the drain was clogged with leaves. A two-inch or so collection of water was trapped in the walled-in patio area, pressing up against the door itself. If I opened the door, the water would rush in. The sump pump helped, but the real cause of the trouble was the clogged drain.

We spent the rest of the day cleaning out the drains so they would function properly and protect us from the possibility of a flooded basement. So now, when the spring comes I check those drains, paying close attention to them. Keeping the cause clear.

DAY 128

We have a love for the causes of involuntary thoughts, and that is why they come. In the case of voluntary thoughts, we clearly have a love not only for the causes but also for the objects with which they are concerned.

St. Mark the Ascetic, "No Righteousness by Works," p. 132

Asking Why

I GET SOMETHING FROM MY FEAR. I get something from my doubt, and my pride, and my envy, too. Whatever it is, I treasure it, and then I consume it. It tastes like candy, sweet on the tongue but always with a bitter finish. When all is said and done, my belly hurts, my head aches. It does me no good. And yet I'll consume it again. I'll hold it in my hot little hand, admiring the look of it, the shape, the color. I will solicit my sin for this terrible reward time after time after time. I will always regret it later.

But the regret isn't quite enough to keep me from doing it again. I mistake that need, that desire, for hunger or thirst. I am wrong about it, but in the moment, I won't remember that.

I will ask myself often, "What do I get from this?" and if I try to answer, "Nothing," I have to call myself a liar. I do get something, or I would not continue to seek it out. The first step in making new choices is to recognize what I am giving up in return.

DAY 129

Pray persistently about everything, and then you will never do anything without God's help.

St. Mark the Ascetic, "No Righteousness by Works," p. 133

Out of Sight, Out of Mind

ONE AND A HALF MONTHS left of the school-carpool shuffle. Chicago-area public schools end their year in mid-June. Six weeks and then I can avoid the twenty-minute route there and back in snaking traffic and constant construction. The boys listen to music on headphones because they can't agree on a song. I listen to nothing except honking and jackhammers, thumping music from the car next to me, sirens in the distance. When I drop them off at school, I pray on the way home for each kid, mine and anyone else's that comes to mind. It's hard to let go of them after shuttling every morning to school. This ride to school offers an easy reminder to pray for them.

It's practice for me for when they grow up and leave home, when they will be loose in the world—floating like balloons, like air, like wind, like leaves. What will remind me to pray when they are gone?

DAY 130

If you want with a few words to benefit one who is eager to learn, speak to him about prayer, right faith, and the patient acceptance of what comes. For all else that is good is found through these.

St. Mark the Ascetic, "No Righteousness by Works," p. 133

Belief and Unbelief

"I DON'T REALLY BELIEVE IN PRAYER," he said. My youngest was worried about something that happened, or didn't happen, or he hoped might happen. He didn't say much about the details, just that he was worried. I told him we could pray about it.

As he comes closer to his teenage years, he's putting on and taking off ideas like overcoats. Some are so very big he is drowning in them. Some fit snugly, pull at his shoulders, cut off the circulation in his hands.

"How come?" I asked him.

"It just seems pointless. I mean, what if you don't get what you pray for?"

"Sometimes you don't," I admitted. "So I try to just pray for help in any situation. We can all use help, right?"

"Sure," he said, "but I still don't believe in prayer."

"Fair enough," I said. "How about I pray and you just listen in?" I told him that if he was simply present for the prayer, maybe we could count that as his "yes." He liked that idea.

I prayed that he would handle whatever might come along really well, and I prayed for the best possible outcome in any case, and this seemed to suit him.

"I'm still worried," he said.

"It happens like that sometimes," I said.

DAY 131

Humility consists, not in condemning our conscience, but in recognizing God's grace and compassion.

St. Mark the Ascetic, "No Righteousness by Works," p. 134

Chief of Sinners

THIS PRAYER COMES UP BEFORE Communion: "I believe, O Lord, and I confess that Thou art truly the Christ, the Son of the Living God, who came into the world to save sinners, of whom I am first."

Each week in liturgy when we arrive at this point, I feel a pang in my chest. Chief of sinners, I think to myself. And it's not that I aim to be the first in this line of those who have sinned; it's just that I recognize, especially in that moment, the depth of my need.

And in that recognition, I feel I have two choices: look to myself as the source of the sin, or look to Christ as the source of my salvation. The first, of course, is a necessary step, but it's only the first step. Without the second part, looking to Christ, I lose track of the point—that He came into the world to save sinners like me. Humility, then, is a posture of gratitude as much as it is a posture of repentance. What does it look like for me to see humility in this way? To adopt the posture of gratitude for forgiveness and healing instead of ruminating on myself as the source of our sin?

DAY 132

To him who hungers after Christ grace is food; to him who is thirsty, a reviving drink; to him who is cold, a garment; to him who is weary, rest; to him who prays, assurance; to him who mourns, consolation.

St. Mark the Ascetic, "No Righteousness by Works," p. 134

Filling Grace

GRACE HAS ALWAYS FELT LIKE an open field, leaving space for what? Forgiveness? Mercy? Something else? Today I wonder if grace is not an absence, a leave-taking, an open field, but rather an active response to a need.

Grace is the energy of God at work, the outpouring of His care for us. If we are hungry for Him, we are given food. If we are thirsty, He is water. When I am worried, He is comfort. He doesn't move away from us when we're in need of grace. God fills the gaps in us with this grace—every pore, every hollow, every need.

This open field, when viewed through this lens, reveals not emptiness, but life and life abundant. Green grasses, wildflowers, honey bees, insects of every kind, animals, trees, bushes, rock, and soil. This field of grace is, indeed, active and alive.

DAY 133

If a man is treated with contempt by someone and yet does not react with anger in either word or thought, it shows he has acquired real knowledge and firm faith in the Lord.

St. Mark the Ascetic, "No Righteousness by Works," p. 135

Nothing Serious

MY REACTION COMES FROM A defensive position. She made a snide remark. He offered a small critique. Nothing serious, nothing close to contempt, just casual talk, just normal ribbing about the condition of my house, my children's clothes or grades, the quality of a piece of work I've done.

My reaction is strong, and it surprises even me with its acidity. The words I offer in return are corrosive and melt the conversation into a puddle on the floor. We can't move anywhere from here without walking through it, having it stick to the soles of our shoes. I tiptoe around it, trying to apologize, to cover my tracks.

And I think, later, if my reactions came from a grounded place, a firm and steady place, how much less painful this life might be.

DAY 134

He who suffers wrong and does not demand any reparation from the man who wronged him, trusts in Christ to make good the loss; and he is rewarded a hundredfold in this world and inherits eternal life (cf Mark 10:30).

St. Mark the Ascetic, "No Righteousness by Works," p. 136

Road Rage

ON A GOOD DAY, I let it go. Someone cuts me off in traffic or slips into a parking space I've been waiting on, and I can brush it off. There's more to life than getting there first or parking close to my destination. I reason it out to myself like this: I'll get more exercise parking in the overflow lot. I'll have more time to get my thoughts together while I sit in this line of cars.

But today is not a good day. Today I'm rushing because I'm late. School is winding down for the year, and I'm playing catch-up on all the things that need finishing before the kids are home. I'm dealing with a home project that went south. I'm contending with a devastating reduction in income when a client decides to bring their writers in house instead of hiring freelancers. Today, I am starting from a deficit, and I feel it in my skin when one more person invades my lane on the highway without signaling.

But it's not "my" lane. It's "our" lane. I try to remind myself of this, and that I don't know this person and their rude driving, and that they don't know the bad day I'm having. So I don't honk or cuss, but I do hang on to the resentment for a little while, even though I know it will seem silly to me to have done so, later.

DAY 135

Acts of kindness and generosity are spoilt by self-esteem, meanness and pleasure, unless these have first been destroyed by fear of God.

St. Mark the Ascetic, "No Righteousness by Works," p. 136

Acts of Service

I TELL PEOPLE THAT DONUTS ARE my love language. Sometimes, I insist instead that my love language is tacos. Well-made tacos are incredible.

I took the phrase "love language" from a book I read a very long time ago. Before I read that book, I was sure that I expressed and experienced love through helping people, "acts of service." What I discovered, though, is that while I do love helping people, it's "thank you" that makes that service valuable to me. My true love language, as it was described in this book, was "words of affirmation." It was a relief in some ways to know this about myself.

But the reality of life is that most of the time we do not get "thank you," and this is true especially in parenting. The gift of the words from St. Mark today is the reminder that to serve one another, though it's not my love language, is still a worthy task; whether I'm affirmed or not is not really the point. As love languages go, I now know that my work is to become multilingual.

DAY 136

Knowledge of created beings is one thing, and knowledge of the divine truth is another. The second surpasses the first just as the sun outshines the moon.

St. Mark the Ascetic, "No Righteousness by Works," p. 137

Sun and Moon

THE MOON HAS NO LIGHT of its own. This is information my middle son gives me as we drive toward the lake. The low-hung moon is almost full, and it is shining. I make a comment about it while driving, as I do with many things as we move through the city. "Look at that bag floating on the air like that!" I say, or "How tall do you suppose that tree is?"

My children give me grief about it—"Pay attention to the road," they moan. But today, instead of complaining, my middle son merely tells me this fact about the moon and its inability to produce light. He's right, of course; I knew that. But I don't say that to him. Instead, I say, "Tell me more about that," and he does.

"The light comes from the sun," he says.

"Yes," I respond.

"And people forget that," he adds.

"We do," I say.

This is the conversation we have as we drive toward the lake, the low-hung moon reflecting the light of night-hidden sun. It's about the moon, but we both know it's not really about the moon.

DAY 137

Knowledge of created beings increases the more we observe the commandments actively: but knowledge of the truth grows the more we hope in Christ.

St. Mark the Ascetic, "No Righteousness by Works," p. 137

Tasting Truth

THIS ROCK, THAT TREE, THE clicking of the clock, the taste of lemon on my lips, sugar on my tongue. The created world is engaging and beautiful. It is also sometimes cruel and punishing. We experience all that is made with our body and brain. All the impulses of our senses relay information into that brain. It affects our heart rate, our mood, our perception of time and reality. We are created beings, like flowers and air, animals and earth.

My head cannot process the idea of divine truth, that thing which is uncreated, without some trouble. It feels outside of me, foreign and elusive. That there is something so very real, yet unknown, is also engaging. I cannot feel it with my calloused fingers, though in the moment, I imagine some small tingling in the fingertips. I cannot hear it with my human hearing, but I can listen for it in between the normal everyday noise. I cannot see it with these aging eyes, but I know it is there, a shelter in the sandstorm. I might have tasted it once, though. It was sweet and fleeting, and I missed the taste the moment it was gone.

DAY 138

He who has come to know the truth does not oppose the afflictions that befall him, for he knows that they lead him to the fear of God.

St. Mark the Ascetic, "No Righteousness by Works," p. 138

Fear of God

JUST BEFORE RECEIVING THE DIVINE Mysteries (Communion) I hear this phrase from the priest: "With the fear of God, with faith and with love, draw near!" It puts us into the proper mind-set for this very holy thing. Everything about this moment is rich with mystery and weight. Drawing near is meant to be this way; I am meant to be awestruck.

How many times in my day do I find myself awestruck? When I witness a great kindness or a terrible injustice? When I see an impossible blue cornflower pushing through the cement cracks? When I realize just how lovely and terrifying it is to belong in a community, in a family, in a church?

It is this belonging that makes affliction even remotely bearable. It is this belonging, and this sense of awe, that allows us to keep moving forward along the road, no matter what comes.

DAY 139

If you wish to make a blameless confession to God do not go over your failings in detail, but firmly resist their renewed attacks.

St. Mark the Ascetic, "No Righteousness by Works," p. 138

Details

I'M ON THE WAY TO confession, and I'm talking to myself, as usual. I'm plotting out my list point by point as I drive. I've been thinking about it for weeks—what I will say, what I will leave out. I've got most of it worked out in my head, so I talk through it out loud as though I am standing there in church, head bowed, describing my latest shortcomings.

I know I will tell my priest I've been thinking too much about all the terrible things that could befall my family, my friends, myself. I know I will tell him that I dwell too often at the edge of despair, as though it were a lake into which I dip a toe on a cold day. I do not want to go in the water, not yet, not now.

I think about explaining each sin in detail—why I did this or that, what drove it, what fuels it—but it feels like this explaining is only meant to make me feel better for those thoughts, those brushes with despair. "I'm sorry, but . . ." echoes in my head, and I throw it away. I move a little further from that lake, not so far that I can't still touch the edge where the water meets the sand, but further than I was before. I don't want to go into the water.

DAY 140

The man who loves God benefits from both praise and blame: if commended for his good actions he grows more zealous, and if reproved for his sins he is brought to repentance. Our outward life should accord with our inner progress, and our prayers to God with our life.

St. Mark the Ascetic, "No Righteousness by Works," p. 139

Communication

WISDOM ABOUT PARENTING SHIFTS WITH the culture. Articles seem to come out every day that conflict with whatever I read just a few weeks earlier. Is spanking effective or abusive? Do we snoop on our children or give them privacy? Is public school better than private school? How much screen time is acceptable?

What does not seem to change is the advice that we have to talk with our children, we have to build the relationship so that it is strong enough to sustain any difficulty that greets us along the way. So we talk with our children when they are wandering off course, but it's equally important to walk alongside when they are on course. Each step of a healthy relationship involves this kind of communication, calls to repentance as well as praise for achievement.

DAY 141

In our ascetic warfare, we can neither rid ourselves of evil thoughts apart from their causes, nor of their causes without ridding ourselves of the thoughts. For if we reject the one without the other, before long the other will involve us in them both at once.

St. Mark the Ascetic, "No Righteousness by Works," p. 140

Beautiful Places

IT IS EASIER TO HAVE the damaging thoughts, to entertain them in my head and let them take up a little bit of space. It's only for a little while, I tell myself. I always go back to repentance, run those thoughts out of town on a rail when I'm feeling stronger or more centered.

But the time during which I allowed the thoughts to take up residence in me leaves a mark, gouges in the floors, holes in the walls, litter left behind. While those thoughts took up residence in me, they treated this space poorly, with no care for the future residents.

And each time I allow the thoughts to come back and mistreat this place, it weakens me. The place becomes run-down, falling apart at the seams. I start to wonder if it's even worth fixing, even worth trying. It's easier to simply let the thoughts come. The more I allow this, the more it shifts my perception of what this place used to look like. I may not even remember, in time, that this was once a beautiful place.

DAY 142

When the devil finds someone preoccupied needlessly with bodily things, he first deprives him of the hard-won fruits of spiritual knowledge, and then cuts off his hope in God.

St. Mark the Ascetic, "No Righteousness by Works," p. 140

Bodily Things

MONEY IS TIGHT. OUR WORK has dried up, and clients have folded or gone elsewhere. It happens like this, in seasons, in cycles. This is a dry season, and we are shuddering under the weight of it. For a week, I do nothing. I sit in the living room and pour out my heart in prayer and desperation. Bills must be paid, food and clothing purchased.

For a week, I worry. It begins to feel like a job. I wake up and worry. I pray and worry. I cry and worry. I look for solutions, but still worry all the while. It's no wonder the feelings of hopelessness begin to win out over anything else.

The worry tells me to stay in bed, avoid the dishes or the laundry, avoid the PTA meeting, the church services, the yard work. When I slip into that hopelessness, I leave all the rest of the breathing parts of my life alone. I let them pant for air on the table. I let them gather dust in the corners.

But these daily, living, bodily things can have a kind of spiritual life force too, if I work at it. Bodily things have their place. I can let them point me to the now or to the eternal. When worry wants to take charge, sweeping the floor becomes a kind of prayer, folding clothes becomes a kind of prayer, caretaking becomes a kind of prayer.

DAY 143

Knowledge of created things helps a man at a time of temptation and listlessness: but at a time of pure prayer it is usually harmful.

St. Mark the Ascetic, "No Righteousness by Works," p. 140

Created Things

THE WORDS "PURE PRAYER" STRIKE me today. What are those times of pure prayer? Morning prayers, liturgy, vespers, those times that are set aside for nothing but the task at hand. So I pray while I drive, while I cook, while I pay bills, while I walk the dog, because I want my prayer to be seamless, "ceaseless" as the apostle Paul has advised. But I must also have these times of pure prayer, times I am focused on praying only, not sneaking in a quick check-in call while doing something else, but rather giving my full attention to the prayer, the steady communication between me and the One who made me.

And it is in these moments I find I am most conflicted, disturbed, distracted. Prayer feels useless, time-wasting, fruitless. I direct my thoughts to the icon before me, the sound of the hymns during liturgy, the waning light in vespers. I nudge my mind back, make the descent into the heart, where all pure prayer resides. My thoughts keep wandering around the room, the street, the to-do list, the car repairs, all the created things that fill my life. I'll guide them back gently each time—*here, here, here, here.*

DAY 144

If someone is not under obedience to you, do not rebuke him to his face for his faults. For that would imply you have authority over him, and are not just giving advice.

St. Mark the Ascetic, "No Righteousness by Works," p. 141

Minding

MY FOUR CHILDREN WERE GOOD at climbing all over the cart at the grocery store when they were little. Back when they were young, we lived in the middle of nowhere, so I had no choice but to load them all in the car and take them to the store with me. As I struggled to put the needed items into the cart and wrangle all the children as well, a kindly-looking older woman whispered to her kindly-looking older friend and pointed at us. She shook her head when she caught me looking. I don't know if her whispering was pity for me or judgment, but I read it as judgment because I was so overwhelmed.

I cried in the car on the way home, and I never forgot that look, that whispering, that feeling of abject hurt, whether she meant it or not.

Years later, while shopping on my own, my kids now old enough to stay home, I spot a woman with children climbing all over her cart. She struggles to put cans of soup in the cart while her boys run up and down the aisle. She catches me looking, and I say, "It's going to be okay. You're doing great. Don't worry," and she starts to cry. I pat her back. I stop the boys running: "Listen to your mom, okay? She's working really hard here." They nod. They'll probably start running again when I leave, but maybe it buys her a few minutes, a deep breath, a chance to remember she's loved.

DAY 145

He who wishes to avoid future troubles should endure his present troubles gladly. For in this way, balancing the one against the other, through small sufferings he will avoid those which are great.

St. Mark the Ascetic, "No Righteousness by Works," p. 141

Enduring Gladly

I DON'T THINK THIS IS ABOUT comparison, but I always seem to land there first. I know the condition of my neighbor because I can see over his fence, into his yard. I see the rusting bikes, the overgrown garden, the broken hinges on his garage door. I know he is too old to move, too old to sell.

I know the condition of my worldwide neighbors, too, because I can see the news reports, the magazine articles about the lack of safe drinking water, public transportation, and basic healthcare, about infant mortality rates, poverty, famine.

Being grateful for where I am, what I have, who is present with me, isn't about comparing my blessings to anyone else's blessings. I don't think this is about comparison, but about grounding. Be here now. Give thanks here. Endure gladly, not because it could be worse but because this is where I am, what I have, who is present with me. This is the life I've been given.

DAY 146

The self-indulgent are distressed by criticism and hardship; those who love God by praise and luxury.

St. Mark the Ascetic, "No Righteousness by Works," p. 142

Softer

IT IS ALMOST SUMMER. MY feet, even throughout the spring, remain socked and shoed. One day after a shower I notice the cracks in my heels from months of simple neglect. My feet are the least of my troubles most of the time. Still, I find the time and money to get a pedicure. I'll indulge this once to celebrate the end of the school year and then wear it out over the summer. Old, dead skin is sloughed off into warm soapy water, nails trimmed, filed, and painted. I choose a muted pink for my toes. It reminds me of the summertime.

The sensation of walking barefoot changes after this. I feel every crack in the wood, every small stone tracked in from the sidewalk. Stripping away the calloused skin has its disadvantages here. There was a kind of protection in these winter feet; I see it now. The softer version may be beautiful to look at, but it is certainly less hardy, like the difference between the hard ground of winter and the soft fragile soil of spring.

DAY 147

When you want to resolve a complex problem, seek God's will in the matter, and you will find a constructive solution.

St. Mark the Ascetic, "No Righteousness by Works," p. 142

Complicated

MY SON SAYS IT'S AN algorithm. He holds the Rubik's cube in his hands, turning and twisting it this way and that. Before long, one side begins to line up colors, then another side, then a third. But the progression of it is not linear; it seems like two blocks forward, one block back. Unlike my strategy to solve all the yellow, then the blue, then the red, he tells me I have to think about it in different terms. He repeats the algorithm statement, and I shake my head. I still don't get it. "It just looks complicated," I say.

"It is a little complicated," he admits, "but it's solvable."

It's like this with most complicated problems, no matter how mundane. The window leaks in the basement every time it rains. It's not the window, really; it's the foundation by the window well. A crack that has been slowly spreading is made worse each time the water gets in. We know how to fix it, though it will take some doing.

We know the root of the issue, and we know the path of the water into the house, just as my son knows the root of the puzzle and the path to take to align the colors. We adopt constructive solutions to complicated problems. It's not simple, but it's solvable.

DAY 148

Every affliction tests our will, showing whether it is inclined to good or evil. This is why an unforeseen affliction is called a test, because it enables a man to test his hidden desires.

St. Mark the Ascetic, "No Righteousness by Works," p. 143

This House

THIS HOUSE WAS BUILT FOR snow and rain, Chicago weather. The specs are based on the climate, the condition of the soil, the location, elevation, population. So when it rains or snows, or late at night when the big trucks drive down the major street close to our house, I don't worry that my house is not steady. I trust the construction of it, the inspectors who have done their job, the upkeep we've managed on it. This house won't fall down around our ears if a storm comes. It's been tested by time and weather.

Now twenty years old, the house shows signs of wear: the roof may need mending, the windows replacing. This is how we know if we're keeping up with repairs, if we're keeping the house solid and dependable. If there is a crack in the foundation, it will show up as water in the basement. There are signs that there is a need, a weakness in the system.

This house was well built for this place.

DAY 149

If a man falls into some sin and does not feel remorse for his offence as he should, he will easily fall into the same net again.

St. Mark the Ascetic, "No Righteousness by Works," p. 144

Tonic

REMORSE, REGRET, REPENTANCE. ONLY ONE feels like an action word. Remorse is a low-lying gnawing in the pit of my stomach. Regret gnaws, too, but it is sharp and immediate. It pierces me at the throat. Things I wish I hadn't said or done are chewed up, swallowed, digested. Regret hits me right away. If I do nothing, it turns into remorse and lives in the lining of my gut.

But repentance is active. I see my choices, I say or do something I wish I hadn't, and I feel sorry about it as I chew. I feel regret as I swallow. I feel remorse and carry it around with me, lead in my belly. In time, if I pay attention to the feeling in my stomach, I hope I learn to turn away from the things that cause the pain and discomfort. I hope that choosing well becomes a kind of tonic to treat me, a habit I foster.

DAY 150

Every word of Christ shows us God's mercy, justice and wisdom and, if we listen gladly, their power enters into us. That is why the unmerciful and the unjust, listening to Christ with repugnance, were not able to understand the wisdom of God, but even crucified Him for teaching it. So, we, too, should ask ourselves whether we listen to Him gladly.

St. Mark the Ascetic, "No Righteousness by Works," p. 144

Source

FROM THE READING TODAY I feel a pull. I want to go to the source, because whatever St. Mark read, I need to read. I need to hear these words, to parse them, to let them sink into my spirit. Today, I feel overwhelmed and maybe angry, too. In this condition, I'm apt to rely on comfort food, comfort television, comfort thoughts.

The reading takes me to the Gospels. I let my fingers page through, and I land on a passage, well read and dog-eared. I see words I underlined years ago in the Gospel of John: "Do not let your hearts be troubled" and "Remain in Me, and I will remain in you." Here, I find passages I have committed to memory because I am so often troubled and so often have felt alone in that anxiety.

But this one jumps from the page: "I have told you this, so that My joy may be in you and that your joy may be complete." I read it over a few times, trying hard to listen gladly, wanting so much for these words to enter in and make their home in me.

DAY 151

We should try to find the dwelling-place and knock with persistent prayer, so that either in this life or at our death the Master may open to us and not say because of our negligence: "I do not know where you come from" (Luke 13:25). Not only ought we to ask and receive, but we should also keep safely what is given; for some people lose what they have received.

St. Mark the Ascetic, "No Righteousness by Works," p. 145

Dwelling Place

IF I ONLY KNEW WHAT the psalmist seems to know when he says in Psalm 84, "How lovely is Your dwelling place, O Lord." This is what comes to mind as I struggle over the words for today. I'm up against a deadline. The dust on my furniture is so thick it seems not even worth tackling anymore. The pantry is empty save for a few boxes of stale cereal. I put everything on hold at home when deadlines loom. This earthly dwelling place is a mess.

I can imagine the place the psalmist knows is the one St. Mark references here, too. The place is bathed in light and clean air, with the presence of God. He so fills the place that there is nowhere sweeter one might go. When I close my eyes, I locate that dwelling place deep in my heart. I knock. I wait. With distractions cropping up all around as I wait, it's tempting to wander away, to move somewhere temporary for shelter, or to look for some food or drink that will satiate me for a time.

When we're tired, hungry, and thirsty, sometimes knocking and waiting feels like too much to ask. But if we knew what the psalmist seems to know, if we knew how lovely this dwelling place really is, how much more inclined would we be to persist?

DAY 152

We are trying to shake off sloth, and laxity, to free ourselves from negligence, and to make every effort to conform to God's will.

St. Mark the Ascetic, "Letter to Nicolas the Solitary," pp. 147–148

Swim

AT THIS POINT IN THE school year, we are limping to the finish line. The sun wakes me early, streaming in through the skylights in my bedroom. I don't mind; I still like getting up early. The boys, though, throw their covers over their heads to stay just a little bit longer in bed. I shake their long teenage legs, uncover their feet and tickle them, cheer them on. "Just one more week, guys!" I say with a little too much enthusiasm. I annoy them awake.

The summer break means freedom, and it is within reach. Everything shifts then. They'll sleep late, slink around the house in pajamas, maybe ride their bikes to the corner store for a snack. They'll drink in the lack of structure for a couple of weeks before choruses of "I'm bored" kick in. We'll drift the whole summer until the school year looms large ahead and catches us by surprise.

Without external forces that determine our days, when left to our own devices, we float along with the current. Sometimes it's good and necessary. Floating can be rest. Floating can be healing. But sometimes we have to swim, get to shore, make some progress toward a goal that we cannot see or touch or feel. We float or we swim to keep from sinking.

DAY 153

This, my son, is how you should begin your life according to God. You should continually and unceasingly call to mind all the blessings which God in His love has bestowed upon you in the past, and still bestows for the salvation of your soul.

St. Mark the Ascetic, "Letter to Nicolas the Solitary," p.148

Lists

THIS CHILD, THIS FAMILY, THIS house, this home. I am keeping depression at bay, just barely. It's sitting on my doorstep. It would like for me to come with it, deep into despair. It asks, "What's the point? Why bother?" and from the other side of the door I recite a list—health, home, family, the smell of new books, the feel of clean water on my hands, the taste of fresh lemon squeezed into my tea. Small things, immense gratitudes.

Each time, I manage to distract myself from the pressures and stressors, new or old, with the list. Sometimes I add things to my list: dirt on my palms after digging up weeds, air in these lungs, breathing without trouble, feet that take me where I need to go, one more slice of bread in the bag, one more dollar in my bank account than expected.

Worry will continue to crop up, depression will continue to knock, despair will lurk in the shadows, but only gratitude offers relief.

DAY 154

Thus, the soul recalls the blessings of God's love which it has received from the moment it came into existence: how it has often been delivered from dangers: how in spite of having often fallen by its own free choice into great evils and sins, it was not justly given up to destruction and death at the hands of the spirits of deception: and how God with long-suffering overlooked its offences and protected it, awaiting its return.

St. Mark the Ascetic, "Letter to Nicolas the Solitary," p. 148

Recollected

OUR SOULS REMEMBER WHY THEY were made. Given the chance, the soul will return to its purpose, its Maker, its essence. We have to give it space and time and permission, but the soul already remembers, and it pines for God. It does.

It's easy for me to forget this because I've stacked my life so full. Not everything that fills my life is bad. What gets in the way of my soul's hope and yearning is often seemingly good and life-giving—relationships, accomplishments, work. And this confuses things even more when my soul speaks up, taps me from inside to tell me it remembers why it was made. I want to put it off, tell it that we'll get to that later. I'm busy doing "life" things now.

Whenever my soul remembers, it is re-collecting, adding back in, rejoining that from which is has been separated. Whether it is by design on my part or by accident, the soul remembers why it was made, why we were made. This is how we recollect that which has been lost.

DAY 155

If a man always thinks in this way and does not forget God's blessings, he encourages and urges himself on to the practice of every virtue and of every righteous work, always ready, always eager to do the will of God.

St. Mark the Ascetic, "Letter to Nicolas the Solitary," p. 149

Eager

ACCORDING TO THE DICTIONARY, SYNONYMS for *eager* include *keen, enthusiastic, avid, fervent, ardent, motivated, wholehearted,* and *dedicated*. Eagerness feels young to me. It feels unrestrained and bursting through blockages. Someone who is eager is active, moving, high-energy.

I don't feel these things today. I struggle to think of the last time I felt eagerness. The weight of life always seems to dampen eagerness before it's had the chance to get anywhere, and I allow that to happen. I invite that weight into the room well ahead of decisions about what to do and how to behave.

I wonder how it might feel to leave behind that heaviness, maybe even just once—to let the eagerness and wholeheartedness enter in, have the floor, fill the air like balloons on a birthday—colorful, celebratory, light.

DAY 156

Do not let yourself be overcome by destructive forgetfulness or by the laziness which paralyzes the intellect and turns it away from life.

St. Mark the Ascetic, "Letter to Nicolas the Solitary," p. 149

Lazy

I WOULDN'T CALL IT LAZINESS. I'D call it procrastinating, and that softens it a bit. "Lazy" is a hard label to shake. "Lazy" is said in a stern voice with a pointed finger. I shrink from the judgment of laziness as I gravitate toward the perceived control of procrastination.

It's a game I play to make it appear that I have things well in hand. I'm procrastinating doing the things I'm meant to do because the list is too long or the deadline is fast approaching, or the sun is out and the sky is clear. I need a break.

What of those times when procrastinating is really just avoidance? To turn away from responsibilities, from doing the right thing or the healthy thing, may feel like a choice to preserve myself; but I wonder how things might be different if, instead, I move forward into it, crawling if I must.

Is this what it means to turn toward life instead of away?

DAY 157

Anger enslaves the intellect, and makes you regard your brother with bestial cruelty.

St. Mark the Ascetic, "Letter to Nicolas the Solitary," p. 149

Shouts and Whispers

A LONG TIME AGO, WHEN I was a young parent, I read an article that suggested we should talk quietly to our children when they are having a meltdown. It seems a perfectly reasonable piece of advice. The shouting, angry child who is waiting for direction from the parent will stop what she's doing to hear the parent. In theory, it sounds wonderful.

In practice, my child did not stop her tantrum. Her brother did not stop his crying. I talked quietly, almost whispering as she shouted. She couldn't hear me, but I found that unlike the child referenced in the article, my kid was not all that interested in hearing me. She only wanted to be heard.

If I'd had the presence of mind to discover this, maybe I might have kept whispering, chosen to wait a little while, continued to whisper. But I didn't. I moved to shouting until all the children were crying. Her anger triggered my anger. I wanted to be heard, too.

At the root of anger, we generally find another emotion, another desire. We have to practice moving that aside for a moment to discover what lies beneath. The heart will continue to whisper even as the anger wants to shout.

DAY 158

Eventually your intellect, at a loss where to turn, is overwhelmed by dejection and laziness and forfeits all its spiritual progress. Then in deep humility it sets out once more on the path of salvation.

St. Mark the Ascetic, "Letter to Nicolas the Solitary," p. 149

Being Lost

WE LIVED IN RURAL TENNESSEE for a few years. My kids were all young then, and our car did not have a GPS. One night, not long after moving there, I got lost driving home. It was a dark winter night, and the twisting roads made it difficult for me to get my bearings. I had all four children in the car with me, and I tried in vain not to let them know how lost I was.

I told them stories. We listened to the radio. We talked about our new house and these long winding roads. We'd been driving around for a long time seeing no other cars, stores, houses, or lights in the distance. I didn't even have a signal on my cell phone to call someone. Then my oldest asked when we'd finally get home, and I noticed the fuel gauge was nearly empty. I pulled over and began to cry. Being lost was hard enough, but being lost on low fuel and in charge of small children was worse.

After a minute, I pulled myself together, put the car back in drive, and made one last effort to find some signs of life. They came a mile down the next road we took—a familiar street, a gas station a bit farther on. We never know how close we are to finding our way if we stop looking for home.

DAY 159

Lacking real knowledge, we still trust solely in the apparent righteousness of our outward way of life, and so lead ourselves astray, trying to please men, pursuing the glory, honor and praise which they offer.

St. Mark the Ascetic, "Letter to Nicolas the Solitary," p. 150

Guidelines

WHEN I AM LOST OR unmoored, I go to the Psalms. Reading the Psalms always helps me find my way They are like signposts, like rest stops. The only psalm I was likely to avoid was Psalm 119 (118 in the Septuagint). It was the word *precepts* that got me. It felt constricting—so many laws, so many commands. When I am lost, I think, I need water or directions from a kind stranger, not more rules and laws.

A friend tells me one day that Psalm 119 is her favorite psalm. She says that she reads the word *precept* not as a strict law but as a guideline or a standard. "God has standards for us," she says, and I like the sound of it. The world's standards are always shifting, like a mirage on the road that I run toward. I need water and directions; the shimmering image promises these things, but as soon as I reach the promise, it vanishes into heat and dust.

What does it look like for me to keep my eyes fixed on the road, to look at the map for the rest stops, for the standards, the guidelines, the true promise?

DAY 160

Pondering, assessing and testing all this, let us realize our situation and correct our way of life while we still have time for repentance and conversion.

St. Mark the Ascetic, "Letter to Nicolas the Solitary," p. 151

Course Correction

IT BOTHERS ME THAT SO many things I read remind me of driving. Once, while I was waiting to pick up my boys at the bus stop, a man knocked on my window and chastised me for driving a big car. I began to argue with him, then stopped. Course correction. I let him tell me what he thought. I thanked him. He left. Why am I so defensive?

Someday, I think, I'll have to drive less often. Someday, I tell myself, I'll walk more, breathe cleaner air. Or I'll sit on the bus and watch people or passing scenery; I'll notice things. When I'm stuck driving, I have to focus on the task of driving. Even listening to music feels distracting sometimes.

There are some things that can wait for someday, some courses that are just what they are because of the timing or the situation. But there are other things that can stand a course correction: my attitude, my responses, my hopes. I can correct those things. These are small choices I can make, decisions for the "now" in the shadow of the "not yet."

DAY 161

Let us perform our good actions with purity, so that they are really good and not mixed with worldly thoughts: otherwise they will be rejected, like a blemished sacrifice, because of our irreverence, negligence and want of real knowledge.

St. Mark the Ascetic, "Letter to Nicolas the Solitary," p. 151

Multitasking

WHILE I WRITE, MY COMPUTER alerts me to new emails. My eyes drift to the little box in the upper righthand corner of my screen. The familiar ding of the alert sounds again. Like a mouse in a maze, I look to the upper righthand corner again, anticipating the little box showing me who is sending the email and what it is about. This one is from an online retailer, the next is from a friend, a third rings through about a work project. Each time the alert sounds, I must pry myself from it and refocus. It takes seconds to acknowledge the email has arrived. It takes longer to sink back into my given task. Before I know it, an hour is gone, and I cannot point to any real progress.

The latest science tells me that multitasking is a lie, ineffective and unsustainable, and this rings true—especially now, as I try to finish this paragraph, this line, this word.

I wonder how much we lose to the distractions, how much time, how much productivity, how much gift.

DAY 162

Try, then, to remember unceasingly all the blessings that have been given to you by God.

St. Mark the Ascetic, "Letter to Nicolas the Solitary," p. 152

Bright Side

GRATITUDE JOURNALS ARE POPULAR. I have one. It lives on my nightstand. I started it about a year ago. I have three entries so far. It isn't that I have nothing to be grateful for, or even that I don't care to acknowledge the blessings. I have and I do. In fact, I think that if I ever had the presence of mind and the gift of follow-through, I might change my bad habit of reserving the nighttime for worry.

As it is, after three days of journaling gratitude, the worry came back with a vengeance at night. I'd sit, pen in hand, and try to write just a few things, a couple of words, even a sketch of something for which I'm grateful. The worry crept in, whispered *Yes, but what about . . .*, and I put down the pen. Why is worry so powerful? Why does it intrude into blessing so easily? As though by embracing gratitude, I am somehow not being vigilant enough. As if being vigilant is enough to stave off the things I'm worried about.

Nighttime may always want worry from me. If that's the case, perhaps daytime ought to be given the opportunity to provide gratitude. I might look ahead for it, hope for it, anticipate it.

DAY 163

It is only right, then, that you should live no longer for yourself, but for Christ, who died for your sake and rose again.

St. Mark the Ascetic, "Letter to Nicolas the Solitary," p. 153

Spotless

When school is in session, I linger over coffee in the morning. I make a list on a bright pink Post-it note of things I need to finish before the bus drops the boys back home.

On the way to the sink with my cup, I pick up a sock three feet from the stairs. I pick up a piece of paper, a graded test that slipped from my youngest child's folder. I kick an area rug back in place, move the dog's bed back to the corner where it belongs, make note of the griminess of the storm door, fingerprints and smudges clouding the view.

With all of this held in balance, I think to myself, *If I lived alone, this place would be spotless.* And there is some truth in it. I deposit the cup in the kitchen, the papers in their place, the sock in the hamper. If I lived alone this place would be spotless, and empty, too. For now, most of my daily tasks I do for someone else, and whether I feel it in the moment or not, there is a gift in it. If I can find that, I may come to see that spotlessness is overrated.

DAY 164

The intellect, renewed by the Spirit through these and similar virtues, discovers within itself the imprint of the divine image, and perceives the spiritual and ineffable beauty of the divine likeness; and so, learning from itself, it attains the rich wisdom of the inner law.

St. Mark the Ascetic, "Letter to Nicolas the Solitary," p. 153

Imprint

THIS LEAF BROKE FREE FROM the tree next door. Probably it was the storm that loosened it. It drifted down to the table on my deck as I sat there in late afternoon, the sun hidden behind one last cloud. The table was wet, the leaf stuck to it, so I pried it away from the glass top, intending to throw it away on the way inside the house. Instead, I studied it a moment, the pattern of veins that carry water from the roots to the trunk, to the branch, to the stem, to the center, and then out to the edges of each leaf until the thing is well fed. This leaf sitting in my palm echoes the vascular pattern on my hand, water for blood, stems for wrists.

In these things, we see the design reverberate in nature, repeating in patterns, like fingerprints left by God as if to remind us that we are made with such great care, such attention to every detail.

DAY 165

While the diabolical tree of bitterness, anger and wrath has its roots kept moist by the foul water of pride, it blossoms and thrives and produces quantities of rotten fruit. Thus, the structure of evil in the soul is impossible to destroy so long as it is rooted firmly in pride.

St. Mark the Ascetic, "Letter to Nicolas the Solitary," p. 154

Roots and Trees

THIS MORNING'S WALK YIELDED OBSERVANCE of the following: one pair of brown loafers, one small muddied plastic soldier, three rotted apples—half eaten. Down the block there is a dwarf apple tree. This stash might have been the work of a neighborhood raccoon. I stop to look closely at the apples, something one would not often see in the middle of a Chicago neighborhood. The core of each apple is brown and soft. I poke them with a stick and find them mealy, falling apart.

The tree itself is planted in a patch of green between the sidewalk and the street which has been subjected to construction by the water company for the last three months. The water company tears up the road, then repaves, tears up again and repaves. I wonder if this has any effect on it.

When I look at the leaves, I can see that they are yellowed, the remaining fruit hanging already ripening though they are not large at all. Too much water causes a plant stress. The tree is drowning; the fruit shows us this.

DAY 166

Call to mind who He is; and what He became for our sakes. Reflect first on the sublime light of His Divinity revealed to the essences above (in so far as they can receive it) and glorified in the heavens by all spiritual beings: angels, archangels, thrones, dominions, principalities, authorities, cherubim and seraphim, and the spiritual powers whose names we do not know, as the Apostle hints (cf. Eph. 1:21).

St. Mark the Ascetic, "Letter to Nicolas the Solitary," p. 155

Context

THE FURTHER I DRIFT, THE more difficult it is to see the shore. When I am sailing along the coastline, navigating is a matter of wind, speed, a general sense of movement with the passing scenery. Following the shore gives me context; it tells me, generally, where I am in relation to land.

If I were a better navigator, I might not need to sail along the shore. I might be able to sail the ocean, pinpointing my position in the bigger picture, using the stars to guide me. Or maybe I'd be fortunate enough to have technology to tell me exactly where I was at any given moment. But technology fails, and sometimes the stars are hidden. Seeing landmarks reminds me of where I am in the world, just as remembering and looking for the landmarks of the One who made me reminds me of who I am in this life.

DAY 167

The Logos became man, so that man might become Logos.

St. Mark the Ascetic, "Letter to Nicolas the Solitary," p. 155

Logos

When I have too many words, I stutter. They crowd in my mouth, fresh from my brain. They want equal time. They want to pour out and flood the place. When I have too many words, I sometimes have to choke them back down, or chew a few and spit them out.

Maybe we are all made of words—all the cells, all the amino acids, all the bones, muscles, sinew, heart and brain, lungs and blood. We are made of words, and words are made of God. If this is so, then all of life is infused with God.

All of us are living, walking, breathing icons of the One most holy and pure Logos. What kind of stunning thought is that? God as Word, spoken before time began, speaking the world into being, speaking the shape of animals, speaking the form of mankind, breathing life into everything.

So many words rushing out, no stuttering at all.

DAY 168

In His great love for man He became like us, so that through every virtue we might become like Him.

St. Mark the Ascetic, "Letter to Nicolas the Solitary," p. 155

Burdening and Unburdening

COMPASSION COMES TO MIND. THE word, meaning "to suffer with," feels appropriate here. That Christ would become like us—with wound-prone flesh, temptation, grief, to know what it feels like in our very skin—is a profound act. In His place, I'd rise above and stay far from the injury. Self-protection doesn't cancel out the drive for compassion, but it does hamper it.

He became like us not for Himself, not merely to experience our suffering, but to take it on, to carry it. Even now, on days when I am bent over from the weight of life, I know He is urging me to set it down, straighten up, stretch my arms, and open my heart. Even now, He suffers with us. We are never alone in the suffering.

DAY 169

If, therefore, you continually recall this with all your heart, the passion of bitterness, anger and wrath will not master you. For when the foundations constructed of the passion of pride are sapped through this recalling of Christ's humiliation, the whole perverse edifice of anger, wrath and resentment automatically collapses.

St. Mark the Ascetic, "Letter to Nicolas the Solitary," p. 156

Water

WATER FINDS A WAY. WATER carves canyons into pure rock. It presses out from its banks, eating away the fleshy clay. It rises up from cracks in the foundation of a house. We may not even know the crack was there. Perhaps the foundation was poured well enough, but it didn't cure as it was meant to cure. Over time, the house settles and the crack develops. The water seeps in quietly, under and around, shifting sand and soil. Left unchecked, the crack will widen, and the foundation will falter.

It's a good reminder today that water isn't the trouble here. It's the foundation. Water finds a way because that is how water behaves. It's up to us to repair a poorly poured foundation, but first I should recognize that it's broken. Sometimes we can only see it when the water comes in.

DAY 170

For when the soul has been overlaid by pernicious forgetfulness, by destructive laziness, and by ignorance, the mother and nurse of every vice, the afflicted intellect in its blindness is readily enchained by everything that is seen, thought or heard.

St. Mark the Ascetic, "Letter to Nicolas the Solitary," p. 157

Pernicious Forgetfulness

According to *Webster's Dictionary*, *pernicious* means "having a harmful effect, especially in a gradual or subtle way." It's a slow slide, making choices or avoiding choices moment after moment, until finally I look up and see that I've made a mess of things.

The school year is like this for me, which is why the summer feels like such a gift. I start out with good intentions, permission slips signed, buy the notebooks, new shoes and haircuts all around. By the second week, I've let this commitment slide, and then that one. I shirk the attempts at routine. I push the timing of the school bus until I'm driving them every day because it's "easier." But it isn't easier; commitments still must be kept, dinners made, work done. I make things more difficult by not paying attention, by not following through, by letting myself slip down that slow slide of forgetting.

In the summer, when school is out, I put it aside. I make promises to myself that I'll do better next year, and I mean it. By the time the autumn comes, I'll most likely have forgotten all those promises.

DAY 171

They should make every effort to seek the company of experienced spiritual fathers and to be guided by them. For it is dangerous to isolate oneself completely, relying on one's own judgment, the dark shroud enveloping the soul in murk.

St. Mark the Ascetic, "Letter to Nicolas the Solitary," p. 158

Own Devices

THE ANSWER IS YES. I would hide out in the mountains, in a cave, in a lonely cabin, away from everyone and everything. I would build a quiet life, cold water and stale bread, a small fire for warmth, in the company of the birds and the stars. At least, this is what my soul tells me when the roar of the subway drifts in through the windows along with the cars honking, the dog barking, the children arguing in another room.

I would hide out. I would pray. I would write. I would sew my own clothes and eat twigs and berries. It sounds ideal. My hands and face would age with the land. Perhaps I would not even own a mirror, seeing my reflection only in a clear stream while hiking. My hair might be wild, my eyes bright, my soul at rest.

But then there is the world, and the responsibility of being a part of this family, this community, this citizenry. I would miss this. And liturgy, voices singing the troparion together, incense and handshakes and kisses on both cheeks from friends. And confession, the feel of the epitrachelion on my head as I receive absolution, blessing. I would miss it.

DAY 172

If then you wish to conquer these three passions and easily to put to flight the hordes of the demonic Philistines, enter within yourself through prayer and with the help of God.

St. Mark the Ascetic, "Letter to Nicolas the Solitary," p. 159

Entering In

WIDE AWAKE AS I LIE in bed, I stare at the ceiling. I go through a running list of all the missteps and mistakes from the day. I go through a running list of everything I should do tomorrow. I push into next week, next month, next year. The worry creeps in next to me, whispering *more, more, more.*

Here's the deep breath. Now, sitting up with pillows propped behind me, I switch on the light and read a little to take my mind off things, to move my brain into neutral, to push worry further away so that I can have more room in the bed, so that I can stop the whispers of *more, more, more.*

My reading choice, poetry by John O'Donohue. Poetry forces me to slow down, read each word, each phrase. I cannot skim this work because every part of it figures into the flavor and the feel. With this slowing of the frantic pace, I find my mind calms. I put my hand over my now slowing heart. This benediction helps me to enter in:

And so may a slow
Wind work these words
Of love around you,
An invisible cloak
To mind your life.

DAY 173

Take up the weapons of righteousness that are directly opposed to them: mindfulness of God, for this is the cause of all blessings: the light of spiritual knowledge, through which the soul awakens from its slumber and drives out of itself the darkness of ignorance, and true ardor, which makes the soul eager for salvation.

St. Mark the Ascetic, "Letter to Nicolas the Solitary," p. 159

Mindful

I TRY TO USE A COMPUTER program to narrow my focus when I need to get work done. I tell it what I want to see and what I don't want to see. It's a sort of digital "Do Not Disturb" sign. The message is for no one else but me. I have to force myself into that narrow focus; otherwise I'll travel all kinds of rabbit trails.

I often wish I had a program in my brain to do this for me when I'm praying. I wish I could narrow my focus, look only to God, think these words, utter them with my lips moving, breathing deeply. The moment I begin, though, sirens blare outside, car engines roar, kids call from downstairs, the phone rings, and even if I ignore all those things, thoughts still pester me—great new ideas, lines from poems, song titles I've been trying to remember for weeks, the name of the doctor I need to contact, the permission slip I neglected to fill out, the dishes that can't wait, the laundry that is bound to mildew if I don't move it now.

My soul is eager for salvation; my mind is eager for productivity; my body is exhausted from the struggle. I may only glean one or two good minutes in prayer, moments in which I can touch my fingers and then my lips to my icons, moments in which I can whisper the Jesus Prayer, my mind in complete agreement with my soul.

Hesychios the Priest

DAY 174

Introduction by Cameron Alexander Lawrence

A MAN WHO WANDERED INTO THE Sinai desert. A man who became a monk, an abbot, a spiritual teacher. Beyond these things, we don't know much about the life of St. Hesychios the Priest—the seventh-century author of *On Watchfulness and Holiness*, a collection of 203 sayings that exhort us to adopt a simple, constant refrain: the name of Jesus Christ, the heart's deepest prayer.

Once thought to have been written by a different person altogether—the fifth-century Hesychius of Jerusalem—these sayings reveal not the details of the saint's life, but the heart of a man who sought to fulfill his vocation of dying to the world. How fitting, then, that the story we, in our biography-obsessed culture, might long to know is now "hidden with Christ in God" (Col. 3:3).

What remains is a witness to the power and efficacy of the Jesus Prayer in helping us attain stillness, the illumination of our hearts, and oneness with the Lord. Again and again, with the vision of a poet, St. Hesychios compels us to give ourselves over to the pursuit of humility—not as an end in itself, but as a means of apprehending God's presence within. In these sayings, we begin to see that the Son of God is not only the torch guiding us, nor merely the moon's serene light, but the sun burning in full brightness, revealing all truth (see Saying 166).

What led St. Hesychios into the desert, we don't know. But we can safely assume that one motive undergirded all the years of his life there: a hunger to know God, even as he was known by Him. Let us listen carefully to this humble servant and learn watchfulness. Let us, by the prayers of St. Hesychios, pay attention and draw ever closer to the light.

DAY 175

Watchfulness is a way embracing every virtue, every commandment. It is the heart's stillness and, when free from mental images, it is the guarding of the intellect.

St. Hesychios the Priest, "On Watchfulness and Holiness," p. 162

Heart's Stillness

I WOULD BUY AND READ A parenting book called *Constant Vigilance*. For me, this is what makes being a parent most exhausting. I expected that when the kids got older, I'd feel inclined to relax a bit, but so far, that hasn't happened.

The vigilance shifts; the focus widens and then narrows and then widens again. I may never stop feeling that I pay strict attention to the dangers of the world where my children are concerned. At the end of the day, if I feel as though I've done all I can, I turn it over to God. I'm filing my report for the day, as if "constant vigilance" were my job description.

But I don't stop worrying whether I've done enough. My downfall is neglecting to embrace that stillness of the heart. I am suspicious of it. I push it aside, thinking it means I'm not doing my job. I'm shirking something if I let myself feel stillness or peace. So my task now, at the end of each day, is to file the report, as is my habit, and then to let the night shift take over. I cannot be constantly vigilant. It's not possible, and it's not healthy.

DAY 176

Watchfulness is a continual fixing and halting of thought at the entrance to the heart.

St. Hesychios the Priest, "On Watchfulness and Holiness," p. 163

Entrances

JUST THIS ONCE, I DECIDE to take a little bit longer at the icon on the way into liturgy. Usually there's a pileup behind me, fellow parishioners trying to get inside before the Great Entrance. But today, it's quiet. I'm early and have no kids with me. I take my time with the icon, pressing my forehead to it as I've seen some of the older women do. I imagine something in me opening and waiting for further instructions. They do not come, at least as far as I can tell.

For the rest of liturgy, I think about entrances, finding them, unlocking them, knowing when to go in and when to wait. I think about all those years I was arriving to church a little bit late, kids in tow, waiting in the hallway where the narthex meets the nave, waiting for the right moment to make the noisy move to the chairs in the back where we like to sit. Once we are in, settled and ready, I can relax a little, find the place in my prayer book, close my eyes, and let the place enter in with sound and feel and scent. It's tempting to think this is the gift—the settling part—but it really does begin with the entrance.

DAY 177

Continuity of attention produces inner stability; inner stability produces a natural intensification of watchfulness; and this intensification gradually and in due measure gives contemplative insight into spiritual warfare.

St. Hesychios the Priest, "On Watchfulness and Holiness," p. 163

Continuity

LOOKING FOR SOMETHING TO DO with his hands, my middle son explores knitting, card tricks, guitar playing. He tells me it relaxes him to do this work. It helps him steady his ever-buzzing mind in a way that nothing else can. He says the most difficult part is the learning. Whether it's choosing the needles and yarn for the task, casting on, knitting a gauge swatch; or tuning the strings, reading the chords, strumming or picking to make the sound he wants—this part of the process takes a different kind of focus than the work of producing a song or a sweater.

This is like the continuity of attention described here: building up the resources, the ability to cultivate watchfulness so that we can even begin to feel that inner stability. And that inner stability allows us to enter into an entirely new experience. We now see the world with a new perspective. We can put our hand, then, to producing something beautiful.

DAY 178

Much water makes up the sea. But extreme watchfulness and the Prayer of Jesus Christ, undistracted by thoughts, are the necessary basis for inner vigilance and unfathomable stillness of soul, for the deeps of secret and singular contemplation, for the humility that knows and assesses, for rectitude and love. This watchfulness and this Prayer must be intense, concentrated and unremitting.

St. Hesychios the Priest, "On Watchfulness and Holiness," p. 164

Unremitting

Unremitting: Relentless, incessant, continual, constant, continuous, uninterrupted, unbroken, sustained, unshakable, unceasing, endless, persistent, perpetual. So many words for this one word. Even in the heat of summer it makes me think of snow.

Unlike rain, snow falls and falls, building and accumulating. While the rain saturates, the snow blankets, wraps, creates weight on top of the soil before it melts and sinks into the earth. I think about this unremitting stuff as I launch into prayer that is bound to be interrupted in less than the time it took to sit down, open my prayer book, and come back to some quiet in myself. I think about the snow falling as a way in, as it were. One flake after another, large, white, and fluffy, lying delicately on top of the thin layer that makes itself a foundation, an insulation against the sidewalk, the garden, the parked cars that line my street.

I'll think of the snow falling, even in the heat of this June day, and let the prayer rise in me, build up, take up space where the interruptions want to rush in. And in that thinking, that visualization, I'll try to remember to let the peace of that prayer reside there as long as possible, until everything warms again, until the snow melts and sinks into the earth, giving comfort to whatever needs watering deep under the surface.

DAY 179

One type of watchfulness consists in closely scrutinizing every mental image or provocation: for only by means of a mental image can Satan fabricate an evil thought and insinuate this into the intellect to lead it astray.

St. Hesychios the Priest, "On Watchfulness and Holiness," p. 164

Wandering

I CAN USUALLY TRACE A MEANDERING thought process. It's connected somehow in my brain, though often it seems random that I start out thinking about the light on the walls of the church and end up remembering an episode of a television show I watched a year ago. I become so distracted by that memory, trying to remember the name of the main character, what happened in the previous episodes, how the trouble resolved in the next few episodes.

But it started with the light that came pouring into the windows. I admired it and was reminded of something else, something related but not exact. Then it's the trees outside my bedroom window, a bill I forgot to pay, the sheets I left in the dryer that trigger the scene in that show I used to watch, and I wander there in the memory of it for a while.

The memory, the show, the wandering, none of it is "evil" really, but it takes me away from this present moment. It takes me away from the church, from the community of worshippers, from the sounds that echo around me.

My brain sometimes needs nudging back to this present moment. "Live here, be here," I say to it sometimes. I guide my thoughts back, though they are often resistant, and I am often worn out trying.

DAY 180

A second type of watchfulness consists in freeing the heart from all thoughts, keeping it profoundly silent and still, and in praying.

St. Hesychios the Priest, "On Watchfulness and Holiness," p. 164

Listening and Hearing

WHEN I'M DRIVING AND TRYING to find a street or a parking place, or if I'm lost, I need quiet. "Shh," I tell my kids, "I can't see where I'm going." It's as though my eyes and ears are connected in that moment in a way that only a mystic could know. The kids think I'm crazy, but I turn off the radio, turn off the conversation, turn off my own chatter both in my head and out loud.

When the quiet comes, I can finally think straight.

At our house in Tennessee, out in the middle of nowhere, the nights were so quiet, it was sometimes unnerving. In that sort of quiet I began to hear everything, leaves blowing, the house settling. An owl hooting would make me leap out of my skin. That sort of quiet had the opposite effect. I became fixated on the absence of noise. My thoughts raced, that inner voice making up stories about the silence, about the dark.

When the quiet comes, my thoughts fill in the gaps.

DAY 181

A third type consists in continually and humbly calling upon the Lord Jesus Christ for help.

St. Hesychios the Priest, "On Watchfulness and Holiness," p. 165

Lord, Have Mercy

WHEN WORDS ARE INADEQUATE, I beg for mercy from the only One who is able to grant it. How often these days I'm faced with troubling news, whether it's personal or public, and I can only say "Lord, have mercy" with lips barely parted, breath hardly spared. I repeat it over and over as though it had some cumulative power that way, as if there were some measuring point that once hit will solve the problem at hand, refill the loss, smooth out the road ahead.

I wonder what it might feel like to make this a frontline response rather than a last-ditch effort. Instead of falling back after trying to advance by reason or argument, what if this movement toward prayer is our fortification? This calling out to God, this prayer without ceasing, "Lord, have mercy" with lips barely parted and breath hardly spared, makes us strong even as it keeps us humble.

DAY 182

A fourth type is always to have the thought of death in one's mind.

St. Hesychios the Priest, "On Watchfulness and Holiness," p. 165

Deathbed

When I last saw my friend Debbi, she was on her deathbed. I didn't know it then, but I think maybe she knew it. Debbi was struggling with her illness. It had taken its toll on her body but not her spirit. She still spoke of God's love the day we met, which was a week before she died. She ministered to me, though I was there to help support her.

She wanted to pray with me. She put her soft hands on mine. We closed our eyes. She reached out to God as if He was in the very room, and of course, He was. She spoke to Him as though He was the dearest friend, a most trusted brother, a perfect parent. And of course, He is.

She did not talk about dying that day, but the prayer revealed it in not so many words. It had been on her mind, I think, for a long time. I was angry that she was sick, that she was dying. I could not think of what to say when we met that day on her deathbed. Even now as I consider it, I am struck by her beauty, by her strength, by her friendship, and by her immense and evident love of God, even as she faced her own death.

DAY 183

These types of watchfulness, my child, act like doorkeepers and bar entry to evil thoughts.

St. Hesychios the Priest, "On Watchfulness and Holiness," p. 165

Doorkeepers

WHEN I'M NOT HOME, MY middle son won't answer the door. He says he doesn't answer the door because he doesn't want to stop whatever he's doing, but when I press him on it, he also says that he's uncomfortable. The intercom crackles when the person outside speaks. The only real way to see who is out there is to open the door and look down the long gangway to the fence.

Once, while I was out, he did answer the door. The dog barked the whole time he was trying to understand what the person outside was saying. I was expecting a package, so he had no choice but to buzz them in to find out who it was and what they wanted. It was the middle of the day, and he was home with his brothers.

The man at the door was selling something, and my son didn't know how to tell him to go. At thirteen, he's awkward already with people, but here he felt trapped and vulnerable. He spent a few minutes trying to say "no" to whatever the man was selling before my oldest son came and asked the man to leave.

And now he won't answer the door without someone there to fend off the uninvited. We are the doorkeepers for him, as *nepsis* is the doorkeeper for our thought life.

DAY 184

When we have to some extent cut off the causes of the passions, we should devote our time to spiritual contemplation: for if we fail to do this we shall easily revert to the fleshly passions, and so achieve nothing but the complete darkening of our intellect and its reversion to material things.

St. Hesychios the Priest, "On Watchfulness and Holiness," p. 165

Small Floods

THE SOUND OF RUNNING WATER woke me. I stumbled down to the family room in our finished basement to find the water pump for the fish tank dangling loose. It had broken free at some point in the night and flooded the corner of the room. The first thing I did was shut off the water, though the temptation to try to get the standing water up was strong. We'd had small floods like this before. The longer the water sits on the hardwood floor, the more saturated the wood becomes, but if the source of the flood isn't dealt with, all the Shop Vac work in the world won't help.

So, I go first to the source to shut off the flow of water, then work to dry out the flooded areas. I vacuum the carpet, put fans in place to dry it out, try to repair the problem that caused the problem.

A few days later, I hear a noise from downstairs and I see, once again, the floor is flooded with tank water. It's not the pump this time, but another, smaller problem. The amount of water was less, but the damage was deeper, because the hardwood was already compromised. It is this smaller flood that makes things worse. The wood has not yet had time to recover.

Our devotion to being watchful must be daily. Checking for the integrity of the systems, not relying on any kind of fail-safe. When we slip, we stop what we're doing and attend to the trouble, and we remain watchful, even when it appears we're on the right path.

DAY 185

If we have not attained prayer that is free from thoughts, we have no weapon to fight with. By this prayer, I mean the prayer which is ever active in the inner shrine of the soul, and which by invoking Christ scourges and sears our secret enemy.

St. Hesychios the Priest, "On Watchfulness and Holiness," p. 165

Shrine

SOMETIMES I LOSE WORDS. IT feels impossible for me to string together a sentence. When I begin in prayer, it's all words, read from my prayer book or from lists of names of those I want to remember. One prayer, one name, one event leads to another, like a web that never seems to stop adding strands. I feel, at that moment, two conflicting impulses:

Stop praying or

Never stop praying.

The first is easy. I turn on the radio, pick up a book, check my email inbox. The second is less tangible. It feels like water running through my fingers as I wash my hands. It feels like opening my chest, letting the air come in, cool and free. "Here is my heart," I want to say, "come and see."

This is the moment when I make the choice to recognize that prayer is ongoing, never-ending, heart-exposing. In that position, I am vulnerable, but willing. Prayer lives in that shrine, open to the world, ever present. It is not ruled by words, by sentences, by logic, by prayer books, or by lists. And that's a comfort with prayer's intangible, water-running ways.

DAY 186

It is impossible to find the Red Sea among the stars or to walk this earth without breathing air; so too it is impossible to cleanse our heart from impassioned thoughts and to expel its spiritual enemies without the frequent invocation of Jesus Christ.

St. Hesychios the Priest, "On Watchfulness and Holiness," p. 166

Autonomy

When my son wants to know how to find something on his computer, I move to put my hands on the keyboard and he bats them away. "Just *tell* me," he says, but I can't. I'm better at figuring these things out by doing rather than telling. He's adamant, so I give in. I try to find words to describe the file location, the box to tick, the password or the username. After three or four tries, I finally tell him that I have to just do it. I can't tell him how to do it. He relents.

There is something about putting my fingers on the keys that clicks something in my brain. I narrate as he watches my movements. One, two clicks and I'm in. This is where the file lives, I say. This is where you'll find the password. This is how you toggle from one place to another. I can't tell you how to do it without actually doing it as I tell you. This is the word and the deed, the idea and the action.

DAY 187

In other words, the incensive power, although God-given as a weapon, or, a bow against evil thoughts, can be turned the other way and used to destroy good thoughts as well, for it destroys whatever it is directed against. I have seen a spirited dog destroying equally both wolves and sheep.

St. Hesychios the Priest, "On Watchfulness and Holiness," p. 167

Fire

WHEN I READ THE WORD *incensive*, it conjures up fire in my head, even though *incense* might have jumped out at me first. But no, fire comes to mind, and anger too, maybe. If one is "incensed," she is enraged.

So, when St. Hesychios speaks of taming my thought life with an incensive power, I am reminded of fire. It gives warmth, heating the cold bones of this house on frigid days, or it can burn the bones of this same house to the ground, leaving nothing behind.

To know that this fire is here, within me, is frankly a little disturbing. Maybe that was the point St. Hesychios wanted to make. We hold within us the ability to preserve our life or to destroy it. We're building a fire in the forest to light the dark, to keep us from freezing to death in the wild. But we must tend that fire once it's lit. We're meant to be discerning about this process, to stay vigilant, to be good stewards of the fire—feed but don't overfeed, tame but don't smother.

DAY 188

The task of moral judgment is always to prompt the soul's incensive power to engage in inner warfare and to make us self-critical.

St. Hesychios the Priest, "On Watchfulness and Holiness," p. 168

Judgment

I THINK ABOUT ALL THE THINGS I love about other people that I hate about myself. I love Paula's kindness. I hate my stinginess. I love Karen's thoughtfulness. I hate my self-centeredness.

I can find examples, too, of things I hate about other people and love about myself. I hate the way the man on the train yelled at his son. I hate injustice and prejudice.

But we can replace the word "love" here with "value." I value those qualities I see in my friends. I love them because I value them. They are important to me. Those things I see that I love, I can only love because I have experienced them. I could only love them and give them value because I had the ability to access those traits as well.

The same is true of judgment. How can I judge someone for bad behavior unless I know the depth of my own sin? I recognize the destructive power of a trait because I recognize it in myself. It's a humbling idea. The work we need to do to follow Christ always begins in our own hearts first.

DAY 189

The task of wisdom is to prompt the intelligence to strict watchfulness, constancy, and spiritual contemplation.

St. Hesychios the Priest, "On Watchfulness and Holiness," p. 168

Sentinel

MY BACK HURTS THINKING OF standing at the door and watching. The pain resides in my lower back and climbs up my spine to the upper back. My shoulders round forward, protective. I want to roll forward, stretch that spine, fall to the floor, take a nap.

When we stand, though, and train ourselves to watch, to patrol, to be vigilant, do we grow stronger? Do we, at some point, look at the clock and wonder how we lasted so long? Do my legs, my core and spine grow strong, engaged, working almost without effort?

I don't know. I hope so. It feels as though I always quit when my back begins to throb from the constant work this requires. I begin to wonder, when the fatigue turns to pain, if this job is really meant for me. Perhaps there is another way, I think. Perhaps this is not at all necessary. I bargain with myself. I'm a good person. I'm mostly all right. Everyone slips from time to time.

It's in those bargaining moments that the return to prayer is vital. I want to push through the saccharine sweet-talk of the bargaining and return to the steady call of prayer, to recommit to standing watch again. This is true sweetness.

DAY 190

The task of righteousness is to direct the appetitive aspect of the soul towards holiness and towards God.

St. Hesychios the Priest, "On Watchfulness and Holiness," p. 168

Hungry

WHEN I'M WORKING ON SOMETHING that requires all my attention in the morning, I forget to eat lunch. By two, my hands are shaking. My body is reminding me that food is something I need to combat my low blood sugar, even if I don't feel hungry in that moment.

My hands shake until I get the food down, until my body has begun to process the fats, the proteins, the sugars. Sometimes, I'll break into a cold sweat as I transition back to acceptable blood sugar levels. I don't eat because I don't feel hungry, and I don't feel hungry because I'm focused on other things.

So many other things fill my waking hours when my prayer life is concerned. Could the sense of righteousness, then, become the shaking hands, alerting me to my spiritual needs? What does this look like when I cannot get in touch with a hunger for God?

DAY 191

Fortitude's task is to govern the five senses and to keep them always under control, so that through them neither our inner self, the heart, nor our outer self, the body, is defiled.

St. Hesychios the Priest, "On Watchfulness and Holiness," p. 168

Fortitude

THE FIRST RESULT IN MY online search for *fortitude* is a site for a television show about a town by that name. The fictional place is in the Arctic. It boasts a "tight-knit community" and was peaceful until a research scientist is murdered. Isn't that always the way?

I imagine the town is called Fortitude because the word is used to embody traits like courage and endurance. Living somewhere with a harsh climate requires this fortitude, as does living in community, close-knit or otherwise, especially when the unexpected arises.

Do we build fortitude the way we build muscle strength? Do we develop it, over time, the way I develop thicker skin on the bottoms of my feet when I walk barefoot in the summer? Or perhaps it's always here within us, something we tap into when we need it, like a survival instinct.

In this thinking, fortitude is not so much something we aim for, but rather something we possess. It protects us from the outside elements, but also from the injuries we can do to ourselves. What does it mean for us to become aware of this force? To become aware of the threats to our safety and wellness, whether it is from the harsh climate around us or the harsh climate within us already.

DAY 192

Let us learn humility from Christ, humiliation from David, and from Peter to shed tears over what has happened; but let us also learn to avoid the despair of Samson, Judas, and that wisest of men, Solomon.

St. Hesychios the Priest, "On Watchfulness and Holiness," p. 169

Humiliation and Despair

HERE'S SOMETHING I'LL CONFESS TO you. I still don't know how to greet clergy without feeling foolish or awkward. Once, a priest I didn't know reached to help me try to bring my bag up some steps, and I thought I was supposed to kiss his hand first. It was a bizarre moment. I still shake my head when I remember it.

I have asked friends who are priests or deacons. I have asked for advice from friends who have been Orthodox a long time. Every single person has a slightly different answer for me. Like many things in Orthodoxy, there does not seem to be a consensus on how to "do it right."

So, each time I'm unable to avoid meeting a member of the clergy (apart from my own priest, who knows my quirky nature where this is concerned), I panic. That's not the worst thing. Everyone panics from time to time when we do something weird, awkward, or just wrong. My trouble is that I carry the resulting embarrassment around with me. I've carried the first attempts and fails for years now. They sit at the edge of my brain and nibble on my thoughts so that every time I'm supposed to do this thing, I'm flummoxed. I panic again. I make more weird or arbitrary greeting choices. It becomes a cycle that leads to despair. It makes me question every greeting, every interaction, every touch or word.

DAY 193

Let your soul, then, trust in Christ, let it call on Him and never fear: for it fights, not alone, but with the aid of a mighty King, Jesus Christ, Creator of all that is, both bodiless and embodied, visible and invisible.

St. Hesychios the Priest, "On Watchfulness and Holiness," p. 169

Piloting

FROM WHERE I SIT ON this 747, with the ground so far below, the clouds grazing the wing as we move, it feels like magic. I do not know how the engine operates, only that at this moment, it is operating. I do not know how the aerodynamics work, the mass of this huge metal bird fighting the pull of gravity.

Lift, force, thrust, drag. These are just words on a page. I trust in the knowledge of the scientists and engineers who discovered this. I trust in the people who manufactured this plane. I trust in the skill and training of the flight crew. I buy my ticket, take my seat, and trust.

Time and history prove this to be a safe way to travel from one place to another. And I am not left to my own devices here. I am in good hands. My role is clear. I could sit in my seat and question the pilot, the takeoff, the weather, the structure of the plane. There are moments, fleeting moments, in which I do just that. The wave of worry washes over me when turbulence hits, or when I hear a noise that seems not quite right. It is then that I ask myself about trust, remind myself that I'm not here alone, that I've got someone piloting up front who knows this route, this plane, this process, far better than I do.

DAY 194

The more the rain falls on the earth, the softer it makes it: similarly, Christ's holy name gladdens the earth of our heart the more we call upon it.

St. Hesychios the Priest, "On Watchfulness and Holiness," p. 169

Absence

IN THE SUMMER, I MAKE any excuse possible to get out of driving. The weather is warm enough for me to walk most places, and I no longer have the daily task of driving kids to school.

What I miss from that daily drive to school, though, is prayer. I use that time stuck in traffic in my dented Honda Pilot to pray. I pray for my family first, then my priest, my godmother, her family, my friends, their families, anyone who comes to mind. It's become such a habit that every time I pull out of the garage to drive anywhere I fall into prayer.

The absence of that daily prayer is striking when I've gone a day or two without it. It hits me all at once as I start the car the next time I have the chance. It floods back to me. I've been missing this, I think to myself.

DAY 195

Just as it is impossible for fire and water to pass through the same pipe together, so it is impossible for sin to enter the heart without first knocking at its door in the form of a fantasy provoked by the devil.

St. Hesychios the Priest, "On Watchfulness and Holiness," p. 170

Dressed as Friends

EVERY ONE OF MY DEMONS comes dressed as a friend. I'm trying to imagine how I should handle a situation, a conversation, a confrontation. I envision it, role-play it in my head, consider the people who will be part of it, try to think about what they'd say or do.

It's not a bad practice. It's actually helpful in most circumstances. But when I'm stressed, when I'm most afraid, or especially when I'm teetering on the point of sin, it's not helpful at all. I am thinking too far in the future. I am planning for circumstances that have not happened and may never happen.

In those fantasies, my demons visit me, dressed as a friend. They tell me I'm doing the right thing, though I know that's not true. They help me reason away my misgivings. Or else they tell me lies about myself, degrade my value in the eyes of the ones I love, in the eyes of the One who made me. They tell me that if I do not think this way, I'm wrong or bad. They say it's for my own good.

It is then that I should break away. I have to say, even aloud sometimes, "You are not my friend," and turn away. I have to move to prayer, to repentance, to shut the door to my heart to these things that aim to tear me apart.

DAY 196

Let your model for stillness of heart be the man who holds a mirror into which he looks. Then you will see both good and evil imprinted on your heart.

St. Hesychios the Priest, "On Watchfulness and Holiness," p. 171

Lacking

THE MUSIC IS SWEETER WITH my eyes closed. I can focus on the words, the cadence, the echo of the choir's voices. With my eyes closed, the music feels as though it can pierce my skin, enter into my bloodstream, move through my beating heart. I open my eyes after a minute or two, worried that my fellow parishioners will think I've fallen asleep standing up. I just listen better with my eyes closed.

This is as still as I can be, immersed in liturgy and surrounded by the sound of music, the scent of incense, the prayer of the people. And this is where, in that stillness, I am faced, most often, with the condition of my heart, the state of my soul. Distraction finds a way in—every sin I cover up, every obligation I've avoided this week. Liturgy holds up a mirror to me each week. In the stillness of that place, in the prayer, in the fellowship, in the mysteries, I am asking how I might be worthy and finding myself lacking. And yet, I keep returning and I keep receiving and I keep practicing and praying and moving toward the One who made me.

DAY 197

Watchfulness is a graceful and radiant virtue when guided by Thee, Christ our God, and accompanied by the alertness and deep humility of the human intellect.

St. Hesychios the Priest, "On Watchfulness and Holiness," p. 171

Keeping Watch

FOR A FULL WEEK, WE battled the stomach flu in our house. First, it was my oldest kid. It began in the middle of the night, as these things do, vomiting for several hours followed by a fever, and then a day later, on the mend. The cycle was about 24 hours, and the incubation appeared to be about the same, so as soon as one person was recovering, the next would fall.

I was unable to sleep after that first night. I was just waiting for the next inevitable victim to begin his or her bout with the illness.

And my vigilance was validated as I was up each night with another vomiting patient, doing laundry, once even catching vomit in my hands before it hit the blanket. We do things like this as caregivers, and though no one really likes doing it, I find some strange grace in it too.

In the middle of the week, I was up with my third kid as he snoozed on the couch with newly clean covers and clothing. I listened to his soft breathing, a little bit raspy still from throwing up. Still, I know he slept with some measure of peace, knowing that I was there, ready for whatever was next in the terrible sickness. I was there, keeping watch.

DAY 198

An intellect that does not neglect its inner struggle will find that—along with the other blessings which come from always keeping a guard on the heart—the five bodily senses, too, are freed from all external evil influences. For while the intellect is wholly attentive to its own virtue and watchfulness and longs to enjoy holy thoughts, it does not allow itself to be plundered and carried away when vain material thoughts approach it through the senses.

St. Hesychios the Priest, "On Watchfulness and Holiness," p. 171

Connected

BEING ON THE EDGE OF turning fifty ignited some never-before-experienced desire to go for a run. In fact, it ignited the desire to run a 5K race. I cannot explain it, really, except to say that though I never have enjoyed running, I thought if I had any impulse to run a race, it's now or never.

After my first trial run, which was more fast walking than anything else, my hip began to hurt. I didn't choose the right shoes for running, and something about my gait on the long, fast walk caused an issue at the hip.

Later the same week, as I eased the hip pain, my middle back began to ache. Muscles operate as a team, so when one area of the body is injured, other areas wake up and do double duty. By the end of the week, I was lying flat on the floor, trying to give all the muscles a break and straighten things out.

Our body systems are connected, and our spirit systems are connected as well. When we neglect one part of our spiritual lives, other parts suffer. When we strengthen those parts, our entire system is affected. All things work together for the whole of us.

DAY 199

Guard your mind and you will not be harassed by temptations. But if you fail to guard it, accept patiently whatever trial comes.

St. Hesychios the Priest, "On Watchfulness and Holiness," p. 172

Be Prepared

BEFORE HE RUSHED OUT THE door in only a light jacket, I told my son to put on a warmer coat. He decided against it. He told me that he was "fine" and that I shouldn't worry so much. He's thirteen now, so I let him go. He should know how to dress for the weather by now.

When he got home that day after walking from the bus stop, his hands and face were ice. I'm not much for "I told you so," but I made an exception this time. He should know better and he does know better, but he still chose to ignore my advice and do things his own way. He maintained in the face of my "told you so" talk that he was fine with his decision. He had no regrets, though his chattering teeth told another story.

Part of our process of maturing means that we take responsibility for our choices. When we choose poorly, we suffer the consequences. What's worse for me in this situation is not so much suffering the consequences but admitting that I made a bad choice at all.

DAY 200

He who does not know the truth cannot truly have faith; for by nature knowledge precedes faith. What is said in Scripture is said not solely for us to understand, but also for us to act upon.

St. Hesychios the Priest, "On Watchfulness and Holiness," p. 172

Light and Heat

FROM WHERE I STAND IN my usual spot at liturgy, I can watch people enter the church, venerate the icon near the door, and move to the icon that resides near me to offer veneration. My favorite fellow parishioners to watch as they enter are the young children. They have their own grasp of the ritual, crossing themselves with clumsy toddler arms, kissing the stand of the icon with more piety than I ever can muster myself. It's humbling to watch.

All the children are eternally curious about the candles, but one small guy in particular catches my attention every week. He reaches for the candles, and his mother pulls back his hand. He reaches again and again. She whispers something into his delicate ear. It makes no difference to him. He wants to touch that flame, and one week, he finds a way to do it while his mother venerates the icon before them. He cries out in pain. She calmly comforts him, calmly walks to the restroom to survey his mild injury, calmly brings him back in when all is restored. His eyes are a little red still from crying. He eyes the candle now, but he does not reach for it, because he knows—not because he was told, but because he felt for himself—the full power of the flame, the light and the heat.

DAY 201

We should therefore set about our task, for by doing so and advancing steadily we will find that hope in God, sure faith, inner knowledge, release from temptations, gifts of grace, heart-felt confession and prolonged tears come to the faithful through prayer.

St. Hesychios the Priest, "On Watchfulness and Holiness," p. 172

Running

SIGNING UP FOR THAT 5K race seemed like such a good idea at the time. Despite years of saying that I am not a runner and the fact that generally I do not enjoy running, I signed up for the race. I regretted it almost immediately. The reality as I set to the training was that my knees hurt, my lung capacity was far worse than I anticipated, and the oft-mentioned "runner's high" was elusive or nonexistent for me.

But each week, I walked a bit further, alternating a block of running here and there. Each week I took notice of my improvement and my pains in my knees, my hips, my lungs. Each week I was sure I would decide to sleep in on the day of the race instead of making good on my promise to myself to just "try it."

I cannot say that the training has made me into a runner, but I can say that it has helped me to know the value of a steady pace, a regular rhythm, and the power of persistence. If there is no other upside to it all, this would be enough.

DAY 202

Dispassion and humility lead to spiritual knowledge. Without them, no one can see God.

St. Hesychios the Priest, "On Watchfulness and Holiness," p. 174

Fire and Ice

FIRE AND ICE, HOT AND cold. To be passionate about something these days is to show interest, to pursue, to seek after with all one's heart perhaps. When passionate, we are on fire.

To be dispassionate these days is viewed as to be cold towards, calculated, removed from. When we are dispassionate, we are all ice.

But the Church Fathers would not have understood the concepts this way. The passions were fire, yes, but that sort of fire consumes all, burns fingers, chokes the soul with its black smoke, stings the eyes, making us blind. This sort of passion can burn until there is nothing left of us.

To be dispassionate, then, is ice, yes. It is stepping back from the flame, feeling the heat but remaining far enough away to see our way through. To have this sort of dispassion feels like cool water when the heat is too much. We become clear-eyed and calm before the heat of the flames.

DAY 203

Who in this generation is completely free from impassioned thoughts and has been granted uninterrupted, pure, and spiritual prayer? Yet this is the mark of the inner monk.

St. Hesychios the Priest, "On Watchfulness and Holiness," p. 175

Cookies

MY INNER MONK WANTS COOKIES. Chocolate chip with walnuts, like the ones my grandma kept in the yellow Tupperware container she had on her kitchen counter when we'd come to visit. My inner monk is tired of being vigilant, tired of policing my thoughts, sweeping the floor clean every night, carrying the baggage I've accumulated over the years.

It's hard to miss the fact that I am not free from impassioned thoughts, and that next to nothing at this point in my life is uninterrupted. I begin to think that perhaps this idea that I can tap into some underground stream of quiet, solitude, peace, and prayer is ridiculous. It feels ridiculous.

If I have this inner monk, she is hungry. She knows that green vegetables and lean meats are needed, but right now, she only wants cookies.

DAY 204

Many passions are hidden in the soul; they can be checked only when their causes are revealed.

St. Hesychios the Priest, "On Watchfulness and Holiness," p. 175

Monsters

IF THERE ARE MONSTERS UNDER my bed, I put them there. I crafted them from dirt and lint and thoughts I had in my worst moments. I made them from words and images I've gathered over the years. Nothing came to me *ex nihilo*. Nothing came to me from nothing.

The monsters under my bed or in my closet or tucked away in desk drawers I no longer dare to open are all made by me, and yes, they do haunt in the night. They do whisper in the cold, and in the fever, and in the weaknesses.

And only prayer can dispel them.

But prayer only comes when I remember that first, *I* made them. No matter how large they have grown, no matter how strong they seem, I made these monsters.

This is the start of revelation. Lights on. Having a look under the bed, and remembering.

They are not invincible. I am not alone in my fight against them.

DAY 205

Humility and ascetic hardship free a man from all sin, for the one cuts out the passions of the soul, the other those of the body.

St. Hesychios the Priest, "On Watchfulness and Holiness," p. 175

Soul and Body

JUST BEFORE RECEIVING COMMUNION EACH week, I say this prayer alongside my fellow travelers at liturgy: "May the communion of Thy Holy Mysteries be neither to my judgment nor to my condemnation, O Lord, but to the healing of soul and body."

And I am struck by the last words in the prayer—soul and body. I can feel something rise up each time I say that prayer—anticipation and some trepidation too. I am not worthy to partake, and I am so in need of this nourishment. It surprises me each time I say those words and have that mixed feeling climb up from my gut. I wonder in those moments when I might approach the cup with any kind of confidence. Maybe never. Maybe that's the correct response.

Still, it reminds me that I am not merely a body with a soul, or a soul with a body, but both at once, body and soul intertwined and inseparable in this worldly life.

DAY 206

Just as someone who wounds the heart of a plant withers it completely, so too sin, when it wounds a man's heart, withers it completely. We must watch for such moments, because brigands are always at work.

St. Hesychios the Priest, "On Watchfulness and Holiness," p. 175

To Fight

OF COURSE, THERE IS STRUGGLE. It's a constant theme in the writings of the church fathers. But this word jumps out today: *brigands*. I look it up, as I'm a lover of words and want to know what makes them what they are today.

Brigands, from the Italian *brigare*, "to brawl, fight."

It is one thing to struggle, to push along, rolling that giant boulder up a hill, like Sisyphus. It is another to fight, but the word *brawl* offers up some rather heavy imagery. There's a sense of utter abandon to violence, of beating to a pulp without concern or care for the outcome. This is something. This is a wounding that leads to death, or at least disfigurement, disability, disaster.

This is the warning we take from these readings—that those who want us to quit the fight, leave the struggle, choose the path of least resistance, are the same who would see us beaten and left to die.

I did not realize until now that I was in this sort of fight.

DAY 207

Unexpected trials are sent by God to teach us to practice the ascetic life.

St. Hesychios the Priest, "On Watchfulness and Holiness," p. 176

Functional Fitness

TO GET OUT OF TRAFFIC on the main road, I turn onto a little cut-through street called Kingsbury. It will take me quickly from traffic jam to traffic jam, but oddly enough I'll get where I'm going more quickly than by staying on the main roads.

At this time of day, I will see a line of men and women running along the road carrying sandbags or sometimes heavy chains in their hands. My son asks what they are doing, and I answer, "functional fitness." In this sort of training, the participant is not static, pushing or pulling weights in a stack on a machine. She is not stationary, running nowhere on a treadmill. In this sort of training, we have to avoid potholes, cars honking, other runners, weather. In this training, we're given external weight to carry; it shifts as we shift. This variable resistance helps the body to build quicker reflexes, stronger connections, and a stable core of strength because of what is unexpected. We keep the body guessing, and that builds it up.

Where we come close to this in our non-monastic lives is in the daily tasks of prayer and fasting, taking charge of our thoughts and actions. We're not given the advantage of controlling our circumstances all the time. We're not locked away from the world. We are in it, running alongside the traffic, rain or shine, carrying whatever heavy thing we happen to have been given to carry that day. It builds us up. It keeps us going.

DAY 208

Just as when light is absent, all things are dark and gloomy, so when humility is absent, all our efforts to please God are vain and pointless.

St. Hesychios the Priest, "On Watchfulness and Holiness," p. 176

Without Light

OUR EYES ADJUST TO THE dark. It takes time and some patience, but we adjust, and what was once impenetrable darkness becomes inky outlines of familiar objects. Our eyes find the light, pupils opening wide like the aperture of a lens on a camera.

We cannot see in the dark, but we can sometimes see just enough to get by. So we go on like that, feeling our way around the room, finding the light wherever it happens to be. If we're in the dark for a while, we start to get proficient at it, and maybe if left to our own devices, we might even think this is how we're meant to live, that light is just a luxury, or a myth we heard about in stories a long time ago.

I wonder if we can forget humility the way we might forget the light. I wonder if we become so reliant on what we "know" or what we have "always known" that we brush the desire for light aside. Perhaps there have been times in which I've walked by a lamp, or a closed blind on a window, and never even considered raising it, thinking, "Why bother?"

DAY 209

Just as salt seasons our bread and other food and keeps certain meats from spoiling for quite a time, so the spiritual sweetness and marvelous working which result from the guarding of the intellect effect something similar.

St. Hesychios the Priest, "On Watchfulness and Holiness," p. 177

Seasoning

SOMETIMES I CHEW HIMALAYAN SEA salt when I have blood taken. When I'm confronting my fear of needles, it raises my blood pressure enough to keep me upright.

The salt is pink, smaller than the rock salt we use to melt the snow on our sidewalks in the rough Chicago winters. It's larger than the kosher salt I sprinkle on the homemade soft pretzels we make in the summers.

The taste of salt on my lips finds me after a long run on a cold day. The taste of salt greets my tongue from the chips I eat in the car on my way home from picking up kids at school. They've had a long day. I've had a long day. We eat the chips, letting crumbs fall wherever they might. They lick their fingers, wipe them on their pants, the grease and salt leaving marks on their jeans.

I think to myself, "I will miss these days," and I mean it, too.

We don't often consider how prevalent a thing is—moments of quiet or chaos or companionship, these things that sustain us, that "season" our lives—until it is no longer there. We can tell immediately if salt is absent where it ought to be. We miss it immediately.

DAY 210

To invoke Jesus continually with a sweet longing is to fill the heart in its great attentiveness with joy and tranquility.

St. Hesychios the Priest, "On Watchfulness and Holiness," p. 177

Invoke

INVOKE COMES FROM THE LATIN *invocare*, "to call." The definitions listed under the word reflect this: *to call on, to declare, to appeal to, to call earnestly.*

I don't think about the Jesus Prayer anymore; I just pray it. I pray it automatically when I get into the car, when I drop a kid someplace, when I wake in the morning, when I go to sleep at night, when I do the dishes, when I can't think of words to write. Wherever there are open spaces in my heart and head, I pray the Jesus Prayer. It fills those places as water fills parched earth, sinking into the cracks, making barren land fecund again.

And even as I pray without thinking about it, I am earnest in the prayer. I call out, I declare, I appeal to. I call earnestly, because I am always in need of God, always feel I'm in too short supply, parched earth that cannot even begin to be filled with my efforts.

DAY 211

Watchfulness and the Jesus Prayer, as I have said, mutually reinforce one another; for close attentiveness goes with constant prayer, while prayer goes with close watchfulness and attentiveness of intellect.

St. Hesychios the Priest, "On Watchfulness and Holiness," p. 178

Vigilant

EVERY NOISE IS A DISTRACTION when I'm trying to finish something. I attempt to block out the birdsong, the doorbell, the cars honking or dog barking, but my attention is pulled away from the task at hand at every turn. I think we train ourselves like this, for better or for worse. As a parent, I know I have become acutely aware of sounds, cries, coughs in the night.

During that most recent family-wide bout with a stomach bug, I jolted awake whenever I heard a certain kind of cough coming from the kids' rooms. I'd jump from my bed and run to them, springing into action as needed. It's a kind of superpower, maybe.

But when I need to focus, I have to let those sounds, those distractions fade. I have to let them exist, let them continue as I move my attention to where it needs to be. This, too, becomes a kind of superpower. Listening to that which needs my complete focus as it says quietly "here, here, here" amid the many other voices around me.

DAY 212

Just as it is impossible to fight battles without weapons, or to swim a great sea with clothes on, or to live without breathing, so without humility and the constant prayer to Christ it is impossible to master the art of inward spiritual warfare or to set about it and pursue it skillfully.

St. Hesychios the Priest, "On Watchfulness and Holiness," p. 179

Prepared

WHAT'S STRIKING ON THE LIST here today:

Weapons for battle
Proper (and improper) swimming attire
Air

Being prepared is not simply a list of what to take with us, what to put in our pocket or retrieve from the closet, but a combination of all these things. We ready ourselves in the ways we can, wearing the clothes for the weather outside and choosing the weapon we'll need in what St. Hesychios calls a battle. Both make perfect sense.

But the reminder that we need air to breathe stops me mid-sentence. Unlike the other two, we cannot store up air, or choose to breathe or not breathe. Prayer, then, is the clothing and the weapon with which we are armed. Perhaps then, the air we need comes from this practice of prayer. The gift of air is the humility that comes of being ready, of keeping our eyes on God, our lips moving with prayer.

DAY 213

For just as coal engenders a flame, or a flame lights a candle, so will God, who from our baptism dwells in our heart, kindle our mind to contemplation when He finds it free from the winds of evil and protected by the guarding of the intellect.

St. Hesychios the Priest, "On Watchfulness and Holiness," p. 180

Flammable

THE FIREWOOD WAS WET. IT had been a few days since heavy rain, and I thought certainly it was dry enough. But no amount of kindling or fire-starters would entice the wood to catch. It might smoke a bit, maybe the edges would light, but the heart of the wood was too damp to keep the flame. A telltale sizzle let me know in no uncertain terms that the heat I was trying to force on the wood was just pushing out the wet, turning it to steam and smothering the flame before it could take hold.

We recognize this truth that we are, in some way, flammable. But that heart inside this chest has been underwater at times, drowned in despair or loneliness, fear, doubt, or injury. We worry that no amount of kindling or fire-starters will get the wood to catch. We may hear the steam hiss as the heat presses us, the water being squeezed out, drying us out so that the fire will, at last, burn again.

DAY 214

The Old Testament is an icon of outward bodily asceticism. The Holy Gospel, or New Testament, is an icon of attentiveness, that is, of purity of heart.

St. Hesychios the Priest, "On Watchfulness and Holiness," p. 181

The Old and the New

WHEN WE ARE NEW TO the world, our bodies are awkward in it. Arms flail, legs kick, noises escape our lips as crying or cooing. This is how we all begin, as bodies in need, spirit without words.

That first smile or laugh in response to a parent or sibling or friend makes connections. I wonder if this is what St. Hesychios calls the purity of heart. It speaks to us, draws us together, drops pieces into place. Babies can pierce the veneer of our grown-up selves. There is power in this relationship, the old and the new, body and spirit, purity of heart reaching into the world from the newborn arms.

DAY 215

This is the path of true spiritual wisdom. In great watchfulness and fervent desire travel along it with the Jesus Prayer, with humility and concentration, keeping the lips of both the senses and the intellect silent, self-controlled in food and drink and in all things of a seductive nature; travel along it with a mind trained in understanding, and with God's help it will teach you things you had not hoped for; it will give you knowledge, enlightenment and instruction of a kind to which your intellect was impervious while you were still walking in the murk of passions and dark deeds, sunk in forgetfulness and in the confusion of chaos.

St. Hesychios the Priest, "On Watchfulness and Holiness," p. 182

Moment by Moment

WHAT ABOUT THE NOW? I think to myself.

I've been running the list in my head—things to do, things to fix, to say, to avoid. If I am deep into the thoughts about what might happen, I am paralyzed with anxiety. I don't want to get out of bed. I don't want to leave the house. "What could happen?" rings in my ears, and the answer I give is always dire. So many bad things *could* happen.

"What has happened?" whispers too, from somewhere inside. It is soft but persistent, making its way to my own lips. "What has happened" is always humiliating, always shame-filled. So many difficult things *have* happened.

But what about the now?

Get out of your head, out of the dark past, out of the murky future. Sit. Be quiet. Drink some water. Eat some bread. Taste and see.

DAY 216

The soul's true peace lies in the gentle name of Jesus and in its emptying itself of impassioned thoughts.

St. Hesychios the Priest, "On Watchfulness and Holiness," p. 183

Emptying

EVERYTHING IS ABOUT FILLING, ACCUMULATING, acquiring. We get a bigger living space, and the first thing we do is to fill it. We fill our shelves, cabinets, closets, refrigerator, and pantry. To be empty in any of these spaces means we are in need. A voice in our head, on the radio, or on the television tells us that we need more. Billboards along the road, flyers that come in the mail, emails by the dozens crop up and remind us of what we are missing. They tell us that being empty means need, and that this need can be best filled with things the world can offer.

Emptying is a terrifying idea to us. To empty means to give away, to release, to give up, to let go, to put aside. And yet I am oddly attracted to emptying. Pouring out all that has accumulated in my head, my heart, my hands, clearing away the clutter so that peace can enter in and take up residence in me. Emptying looks attractive now, necessary.

DAY 217

So long as we concentrate our attention on the intellect, we are enlightened; but when we are not attentive to it we are in darkness.

St. Hesychios the Priest, "On Watchfulness and Holiness," p. 184

To Sit in the Dark

IT CREPT IN ON ME as I was reading. One moment the sun was out, shining in through the big window at the front of the house; then I found myself squinting at my book. I took off my glasses, rubbed my eyes, yawned, and wondered about the time.

The light had retreated, the dark crept in, as natural as anything. I put down my book and closed my eyes. It was quiet with the kids all out at friends' houses. I could fall asleep like this. It would be easy.

But I don't want to sleep. What I want is to read. I get so little time of quiet like this. I want to finish this book of poetry and one about prayer, too. There will be time for resting the body; this is work for the mind and the spirit. And so, begrudging my body's inclination to sleep, I stand up. I stretch. I turn on the light. Then return to my book about poetry, about prayer, letting in the light.

DAY 218

A traveler setting out on a long, difficult and arduous journey and foreseeing that he may lose his way when he comes back, will put up signs and guideposts along his path to make his return simpler. The watchful man, foreseeing this same thing, will use sacred texts to guide him.

St. Hesychios the Priest, "On Watchfulness and Holiness," p. 185

Breadcrumbs and Signposts

MAPMAKING IS AN ART. MAP-FOLLOWING is an art too. I think about the way the landscape has changed even in the short amount of time I've been in this neighborhood. I can give directions to my house using street signs and highways, and I can direct too by pointing out the landmarks in the area.

But sometimes those landmarks are more like breadcrumbs scattered to mark the trail: the bodega on the corner closes, the building across the street is torn down, the big tree that used to mark the space in front of my house was struck by lightning and then made into mulch by the city while I was away one summer.

The landscape changes, eaten up by developers, house builders, renovators, and nature, too. The mapmakers have to scramble to change. The map-followers have to sort through what is old and what is new. It's a matter of timing, paying attention, and choosing markers that will endure no matter the culture or the weather.

If this mapmaking, this map-following, this faith life is an art, I hope it is a dance. Perhaps a traveler's tango.

DAY 219

Just as it is impossible to cross the sea without a boat, so it is impossible to repulse the provocation of an evil thought without invoking Jesus Christ.

St. Hesychios the Priest, "On Watchfulness and Holiness," p. 186

Crossing the Sea

THE WORLD IS SHRINKING. I can take a plane to see my friends across the country or across the ocean. At one time, we were limited by our transportation options. It took months to get from one place to another, and so most people stayed where they were born; they lived and worked and dwelt in the known places. It was the explorers and adventurers who took to the ships to sail to the unknown places.

Now the impossible is possible. Now we have the means to reach places that were once inaccessible. It still takes courage to board the plane, the train, the boat, but we have the means.

The coming of Christ into our midst has had the same effect. What once felt impossible to cross, to bridge, to reach, is now possible. The name of Jesus is available to us; we have the means. We can be transported. We can be changed.

DAY 220

Contemplation and spiritual knowledge are indeed the guides and agents of the ascetic life; for when the mind is raised up by them it becomes indifferent to sensual pleasures and to other material attractions, regarding them as worthless.

St. Hesychios the Priest, "On Watchfulness and Holiness," p. 187

Guides

TODAY I'M PONDERING THE DIFFERENCE between a guide and a map. I have a map in my car, folded quietly in my glove compartment. It's nearly obsolete now that my car offers its own guidance system. The guidance system in my car tells me where to turn, how far to go to the next stopping point, what the traffic is like, what detours I may encounter.

The map is static and unchanging. The lines on this paper will remain as they are now no matter how the road changes. It can guide me only so far, and that guidance relies on my ability to read it well enough to take advantage of its wisdom.

Guides are interactive, offering wisdom I may not have even thought to consider. Contemplative texts are like this, dynamic and living, saying "look here" or "look away" when I am most in need of direction.

DAY 221

To human beings it seems hard and difficult to still the mind so that it rests from all thought. Indeed, to enclose what is bodiless within the limits of the body does demand toil and struggle, not only from the uninitiated but also from those experienced in inner immaterial warfare.

St. Hesychios the Priest, "On Watchfulness and Holiness," p. 188

Still

IT IS STILL SUMMER. I remind myself of this, though internally I'm already thinking ahead to the start of the school year. The needs are already making lists in my head: four children, four schools, four different start dates, four different spring breaks, homework requirements, assignment notebooks, new pants and shoes for boys whose feet and legs seem to grow overnight.

When the list starts to overwhelm me, I take a deep breath, hold it a moment, blow it out through pursed lips. It helps a little. It sounds like exasperation to anyone within earshot, but it's not that so much as it is a reminder to breathe. When the list starts to overwhelm, my instinct is to hold my breath, as if I'm hiding and must be quiet to keep from giving away my hiding place.

Hiding won't help, but breathing will. That gives small comfort, momentary stillness, a break from the list-making. We're more than the sum of our lists.

DAY 222

If the soul has Christ with it, it will not be disgraced by its enemies even at death, when it rises to heaven's entrance: but then, as now, it will boldly confront them.

St. Hesychios the Priest, "On Watchfulness and Holiness," p. 188

Protector

I AM REMINDED TODAY OF A line in the prayer of Saint Patrick: "May Christ shield me today. Christ with me, Christ before me, Christ behind me, Christ in me, Christ beneath me, Christ above me, Christ on my right, Christ on my left, Christ when I lie down, Christ when I sit, Christ when I stand."

This prayer coupled with the excerpt from St. Hesychios paints an image of protection in my mind. When Christ is with us, He is with us completely. We are surrounded and immersed and infused with Him. It feels protective. It feels safe. We have nothing to fear when Christ is with us like this.

DAY 223

We will travel the road of repentance correctly if, as we begin to give attention to the intellect, we combine humility with watchfulness, and prayer with the power to rebut evil thoughts. In this way, we will adorn the chamber of our heart with the holy and venerable name of Jesus Christ as with a lighted lamp, and will sweep our heart clean of wickedness, purifying and embellishing it.

St. Hesychios the Priest, "On Watchfulness and Holiness," p. 189

Altar

WE PLACE THE HOME ALTAR, the icon corner, within sight for good reason. I'm easily distracted by family needs, advertisements, housework, career decisions. I walk past the row of icons constantly, taking time to greet them, even for a moment. A slight nod, a sheepish apology for my lack of attention to my prayer life. Some days I'm better than others.

Today I lit candles, something I often neglect because of the time or effort, and I was surprised at how different the room felt. There was suddenly a small flickering in the icon corner. When I passed by it seemed to call to me. *There is a light here,* it seemed to say, *come and see.* And so I did, and I let go, for a moment, the family needs, advertisements, housework, career decisions, and it was good.

Tomorrow, it may be different. I may neglect this part again. Some days I'm doing better than others.

DAY 224

Most of us do not realize that all evil thoughts are but images of material and worldly things. Yet if we persist in watchful prayer, this will rid our mind of all such images; it will also make it conscious both of the devices of our enemies and of the great benefit of prayer and watchfulness.

St. Hesychios the Priest, "On Watchfulness and Holiness," p. 189

Watchful Prayer

SOME THINGS WE DO WITHOUT thinking. We breathe, if we are healthy, without thinking about it. When we're ill, congested, compromised, breaking down, we have to consider our breathing. We take steps to improve the conditions, heal the lungs, soothe the throat, clear the congestion.

The sort of watchfulness in prayer described by St. Hesychios assumes that we are always in a state of illness. We are not able to live without prayer, without watchfulness. The idea that I live in a state of chronic illness on this front is exhausting.

Will there be moments in which I will be able to relax the vigilance, to breathe without any trouble at all? To not worry about pollution, or sinusitis, or a threat of pneumonia?

DAY 225

A true monk is one who has achieved watchfulness; and he who is truly watchful is a monk in his heart.

St. Hesychios the Priest, "On Watchfulness and Holiness," p. 190

The First Run

THINKING BACK ON IT, THAT first run was a disaster. Panting and sweating, I'd gone about a mile, mostly walking. My chest hurt after only a few minutes of "running" down the path. I felt like an idiot on the running track, stopping every tenth of a mile just to keep from falling over.

I didn't know I was so deconditioned. I thought I was doing pretty well for an almost-fifty-year-old. That day on the running path was an eye-opener. I nearly quit, thinking that the modest goal of running one 5K race was not worth this kind of work. I didn't quit.

The second run was better. The third was worse. The fourth and fifth were mediocre. The sixth showed vast improvement. The seventh, eighth, ninth, and tenth were average. I was surging one week and retreating the next, feeling failure, reveling in improvement, rising and falling, and on and on. I did not realize that over time I'd developed a habit of running. "I've never been a runner," or "I hate running," I had said in the past. I may quit after this race and never run again, but those old statements will never be true again.

Habits show who we are. The habit of prayer makes us watchful; the habit of watchfulness leads us to prayer.

DAY 226

Human life extends cyclically through years, months, weeks, days and nights, hours and minutes. Through these periods, we should extend our ascetic labors—our watchfulness, our prayer, our sweetness of heart, our diligent stillness—until our departure from this life.

St. Hesychios the Priest, "On Watchfulness and Holiness," p. 190

The In-Between

AUGUST ALWAYS FEELS TRANSITIONAL. THE summer is ending; the fall is not yet begun. In this in-between space, I find myself floating. The list of things to do when fall comes is a series of scribbled notes on the back of envelopes on the countertop, or candy wrappers from my car, or receipts from my purse.

One day soon, when the next season solidifies, I'll take those notes and make a proper list, take action, check those to-do lines off one at a time.

But I don't want to leave this floating just yet. Today I'll practice staying present in the sweetness of summer and set aside the looming list of back to school, back to work, back to heavy sweaters and heated rooms. Each season has its own rhythm. The in-between, the transitional times, are no different.

DAY 227

The fruit starts in the flower; and the guarding of the intellect begins with self-control in food and drink, the rejection of all evil thoughts and abstention from them, and stillness of heart.

St. Hesychios the Priest, "On Watchfulness and Holiness," p. 190

First Fruits

MY URBAN GARDENING FRIENDS SUGGESTED I try to grow tomatoes. They know I'm eager to try despite my poor gardening skills. The tomato plants don't need much room to grow. The sunlight is ample on my back deck. I buy plants already begun from the nursery down the street. It doesn't take long for the small buds to begin to form in the center of the delicate pale yellow flowers on the vine. I am attentive to the plants, watering them, but not too much, pruning away dead areas, keeping them out of the windy spots on the deck.

The tiny fruits grow daily on the vine in the summer heat, the sunlight lending its hand, the water coming daily from my own hand. When they reach a harvestable place, I'm called away. It is the summer; there are sports and parties and short trips out of town.

In my absence, the plants left untended fall prey to the elements, not the least of which is the cadre of squirrels I'd kept at bay with a barking dog or chicken wire. When I wasn't paying attention, they scaled the wire, broke in, ate all the first fruits.

DAY 228

Stones form the foundation of a house; but the foundation of sanctity—and its roof—is the holy and venerable name of our Lord Jesus Christ. A foolish captain can easily wreck his ship during a storm, dismissing the sailors, throwing the sails and oars into the sea, and going to sleep himself; but the soul can be sent to the bottom even more swiftly by the demons if it neglects watchfulness and does not call upon the name of Jesus Christ when they begin their provocations.

St. Hesychios the Priest, "On Watchfulness and Holiness," p. 192

After the Fast

IT ISN'T THE ABSENCE OF something that bothers me while fasting. I rarely think about what I am missing from my plate. What bothers me during fasting times is that I lose the thread of why I'm fasting at all. I might reach for a non-fasting food without thinking, pull my hand away quickly, and then reset my brain. "I'm not eating this right now," I will tell myself.

But why?

It helps to have children who were not raised Orthodox, who ask me every day of every fast, "But why?"

And most days, I cannot articulate it well enough for them, for me, for anyone.

The words today from the *Philokalia* offer some imagery that helps. When they ask me next, "But why?" I will say, because we're building something for after the fast. This fasting is foundation work. We keep it close, we pay attention to something easily forgotten in a place where food is abundant and diverse. This is the thread; we're building something eternal that manifests now and continues after the fast.

DAY 229

The sun cannot shine without light; nor can the heart be cleansed of the stain of destructive thoughts without invoking in prayer the name of Jesus. This being the case, we should use that name as we do our own breath. For that name is light, while evil thoughts are darkness; it is God and Master, while evil thoughts are slaves and demons.

St. Hesychios the Priest, "On Watchfulness and Holiness," p. 192

Light and Breath

EVERY BIT OF LIFE ON earth is fueled by the sun. This planet, placed at this perfect distance from the sun, sustains life because of the light from our neighborhood star. Without this star, we would cease to exist.

So, too, are we sustained by the oxygen here on earth, invisible, powerful, vital. Without clean air to breathe, we cannot live.

Without the name of Jesus on our lips, we are apt to shrivel to nothing or gasp for air when we're confronted with the trials in this life. How does it change our view of things, difficulties and sufferings, when we remember that we have light and breath that sustains and nurtures us?

DAY 230

Let us hold fast, therefore, to prayer and humility, for together with watchfulness they act like a burning sword against the demons. If we do this, we shall daily and hourly be able to celebrate a secret festival of joy within our hearts.

St. Hesychios the Priest, "On Watchfulness and Holiness," p. 193

Herding Cats

PRAYER, HUMILITY, WATCHFULNESS. IT SEEMS simple enough when it's written down as a list. Pray every day, be humble, pay attention.

But what if my prayer becomes empty?

What if humility slips away from me without my noticing?

What if I grow weary and cannot stay awake?

When I read this passage, I can only think of the expression I use when I talk about parenting my kids when they were younger, or my failed attempts to keep the house running smoothly, or my constant struggle to keep up with my writing projects or work-related tasks. It's like herding cats. You get one thing in line, and then another one wanders off the path.

And sometimes our prayer does feel empty, and our humility slips, and we're weary and cannot stay awake.

But there is that feeling that comes when we are happily in the herding "zone," what St. Hesychios described as a "secret joy." We know that feeling in moments; we remember it well enough in our bones to keep at it, to pray again, to realign ourselves, to wake up, to pay attention.

DAY 231

In this way the soul can attain in the Lord that state of beauty, loveliness and integrity in which it was created by God in the beginning. As Antony, the great servant of God, said, "Holiness is achieved when the intellect is in its natural state."

St. Hesychios the Priest, "On Watchfulness and Holiness," p. 194

Forest and Trees

I ONCE GOT LOST WHILE WALKING the wooded grounds at the Abbey of Gethsemani. I had no map, only the direction of the monk at the abbey. I was there for a silent retreat and wanted to visit the hermitage of Thomas Merton, who had lived there.

The path seemed easy enough to follow. It was midday and summertime. I thought I'd pray my way there, through the forest, through the trees. Somewhere in all my prayer and wandering I must have made a wrong turn, and I lost the path. I found myself wandering through the thickening branches, drenched in sweat. I was beginning to feel a little desperate pushing through branch after branch, down a steepening slope, when I noticed the light. Shafts of sun were streaming through the branches, casting light on the slope, glittering on leaves like gold. I caught it there for just a moment. Stopped in my tracks. Sat down on the ground and got my breath. This is why I came.

I never found the hermitage, but I did find the road back to the abbey—and the reason I was in the forest to begin with.

DAY 232

Letters cannot be written on air; they have to be inscribed on some material if they are to have any permanence. Similarly, we should weld our hard-won watchfulness to the Jesus Prayer, so that this watchfulness may always be attached to Him and may through Him remain with us forever.

St. Hesychios the Priest, "On Watchfulness and Holiness," p. 195

By Heart

I AM WORKING THROUGH THE WORDS of a short poem by Emily Dickinson, trying to come to know them by heart. I master one line and then another line slips out of my head, and no matter how much I try to grasp the next word in that sentence, it slides away from me. I can remember full days of my childhood, like the feel of old sand on the floor from shaking out my clothes after we spent the day at the lake house my grandparents owned, but I cannot remember seven lines from a poem I love. I just cannot wrap my hands around the words. There is nothing tangible in them for me.

I have this trouble with prayer, too, keeping my eyes glued to my prayer book every morning or every liturgy. The one prayer I know by heart is the Jesus Prayer. I can wrap my arms around it, and it seems to wrap arms around me, too. I wonder what it is that anchors this prayer to me like this?

DAY 233

With your breathing combine watchfulness and the name of Jesus, or humility and the unremitting study of death. Both may confer great blessing.

St. Hesychios the Priest, "On Watchfulness and Holiness," p. 196

Study of Death

THIS IS ALL TEMPORARY. THAT is as much study of death as I can handle most days. The car with its rust and engine that has begun making a strange noise. The house with shingles falling away after a storm. And the trees in the yard, the dirt under my feet, the air I breathe? All temporary, changing, earthbound.

When the stress levels make sleeping impossible, when the mounting list of things to fix or arrange worms its way into my thought life, my prayer life, my family life—this is when I remind myself that it is all temporary. Only God is eternal. So I look for Him and I pray without ceasing. Sometimes the name of Jesus is the only word I can muster to anchor myself to something that is unchanging.

DAY 234

When clouds are scattered the air is clear; and when the fantasies of passion are scattered by Jesus Christ, the sun of righteousness, bright and star-like intellections are born in the heart, for the heart is then illumined by Jesus.

St. Hesychios the Priest, "On Watchfulness and Holiness," p. 197

Cloudy

IT'S EASY TO TELL WHEN fall is coming in this city. Normally clear and sunny days begin to form a cloud-skin. I wake up in the morning to a diffuse light in my room instead of bright sunshine. Even the birds seem to know it's nearly here. Their song is silent, as though they are already making plans for the colder weather. It sneaks up on me some years, but it always happens.

The opposite is true of winter to spring. Days that are mostly dark in the morning grow gradually lighter, until one day I wake again with the sun on my face. That clearing, that bright light that wakes me, reminds me that all things are new again. There will still be cloudy days, dark and rainy and cold, but the newness, the promise that the sun is still there and waiting, is usually enough.

DAY 235

Come, then, you who long in spirit to see days of blessing, follow me towards that union attained through the guarding of the intellect; and I, in the Lord, will instruct you in your task on earth and the angelic life.

St. Hesychios the Priest, "On Watchfulness and Holiness," p. 197

Days of Blessing

ALL I NEED TO KEEP me afloat is for one good thing to happen after a string of bad things, one day of blessing in a mess of a week. I go through cycles in which it seems as though calamity is my only constant. I can feel far from the days of blessing that St. Hesychios speaks of here, but I imagine that perhaps they are just on the horizon.

If I keep my eyes trained there, looking ahead and not behind—watching for the rise of the road, the rest stop ahead, instead of worrying about the bandits that may be hiding up the road, expecting potholes and wrong turns—I may find that blessing yet.

DAY 236

Just as the angels do not concern themselves with property and money, so those who have purified the soul's vision and who have attained the state of holiness are not troubled by the evil ploys of the demons. And just as the richness that comes from moving closer to God is evident in the angels, so love and intense longing for God is evident in those who have become angelic and gaze upwards towards the divine.

St. Hesychios the Priest, "On Watchfulness and Holiness," p. 198

Sunflowers

THREE YEARS AGO, THE HOUSE a few doors away burned down. We woke to the sound of sirens one Sunday morning. At 7 AM on that summer day, it was already 85 degrees.

We sat on our deck and watched the firemen work at the rear of the house. We'd heard from our other neighbor that everyone got out, but the house was beyond help. They put out the flames. The street was filled with soot. The immediate neighbors on either side had smoke damage. One lost his vinyl siding to the heat.

Within a week, the house with the fire was torn down, excavated to the basement level, and then filled in again. Now, an empty lot sits on that place, all rocks and cement bits. Weeds pop up in the spring and linger in the summer.

But today as I walked past, I saw that the large plant in the middle of the lot had bloomed. Sunflowers. Rather than long gangly stock stems of the large-head variety, this was bush-like, with blooms the size of my palm. I could not get close, though I wanted to, as I was blocked by the fence that still stands on the property, all that remains of what was once there.

Property and money are tangible but temporary, at best. Sometimes what rises from destruction can surprise us. Blooms come in unlikely places.

Neilos the Ascetic

DAY 237

Introduction by Fr. Kaleeg Hainsworth

THERE ARE TWO VERSIONS OF saints. The first is the version we think we know—"so and so is awesome and is just like me, so I will choose him as my patron!" This is natural. Humans are experts at making God and His saints into their own image. Anyone who has wrestled with God and their faith over a lifetime will aver that a great deal of what passes as "Orthodoxy" is in this category.

Then there is the actual saint—with his own culture, caught up in his own controversy, and with no loyalty whatsoever to our imaginary vision of him. Ever met a living saint or heard a story of someone who has? I have. It never goes the way you think it will. These men and women are living in discipleship to a holiness that is wild, not of this world, free from our opinions, and thus feels humbling. Meeting a saint, for real, will challenge our basic assumptions about God and the Church every time.

St Neilos the Ascetic is not our Orthodox buddy, probably not at all the version of him we imagine. He started out married with two children. At some point in his marriage, he had a conversation with his wife and decided to leave with his eldest son to the Sinai monastery (one does wonder what that conversation was like!). Eventually, his wife took their other child and went to live in a different monastery.

The choice of the Sinai monastery, at that time in history, was a difficult one. I remember seeing an icon once from the time of St. Neilos that was painted with the blood of the murdered monks of Sinai. A lone monk had arrived from a trip to find all his friends murdered by a group of bandits. After this he did what few modern, Western persons would think of doing—he collected the blood-soaked sand and painted an icon of Christ with it. Hardcore, and as good a description of the life and times of the Sinai monastery (which survives to this day) as I can offer. But St. Neilos thrived in the ascetic traditions, of which he became a master, and selections of which we read here.

DAY 238

If the rewards of virtue are restricted to this present life, then one is engaged in a contest where no prizes are ever offered, wrestling all one's life for no return but the toil and the sweat.

St. Neilos the Ascetic, "Ascetic Discourse," p. 201

This Present Life

How do I know if I'm getting ahead? My kids are clothed and fed, the car is running, dishes done, floor clean, the rent is paid, the pantry is stocked, the bank account is not overdrawn, the dog is well behaved, the yard is raked. I feel a small amount of accomplishment. I bask in the quiet of the day knowing that each of these things on my list is checked off. We're fine, I think to myself. We're fine.

But what endures? What will each of these tasks mean in the long run, in the life after this?

I remind myself that the work I do now, the thoughts I have, the words I read and write, the children I raise, the house I keep all have deeper implications. I may not ever know what those might be. I may leave this life not knowing, but the impulse to do better and be better, so long as it is rooted in Christ, means something more than mere toil and sweat for earthly rewards.

DAY 239

He taught us that the true philosopher must renounce all life's pleasures, mastering pains and passions, and paying scant attention to the body: he must not overvalue even his soul, but must readily lay it down when holiness demands.

St. Neilos the Ascetic, "Ascetic Discourse," p. 201

Chief of Sinners

FROM WHERE I SIT IN my safe, warm home, I can easily argue with whomever I want through the miracle of my laptop. Life, politics, religion—conflict is always stirring someplace. I have a peek into it. I have a pass to play there. Words fire like bullets from guns making damage I cannot see. Who wants that?

A stranger, angry as we disagreed, told me all about his works of charity. He challenged me, "What have *you* done to serve the poor?" And I struggled with the answer, building my case in my head first with all the acts of charity, monetary and otherwise, and I began to type my list. The knot at the pit of my stomach, the one that rose when we began to argue, tightened, rose to my throat; tears came to my eyes. I erased the screed.

"Not enough," I said, and the knot left my throat, but the tears stayed because I knew it was true. "I am the chief of sinners," I added, and I meant it.

DAY 240

For philosophy is a state of moral integrity combined with a doctrine of true knowledge concerning reality.

St. Neilos the Ascetic, "Ascetic Discourse," p. 201

Piece by Piece

*I*NTEGRITY MEANS "THE STATE OF being whole," but there's more to the definition. It means being whole but also being undivided. Reality takes me apart. I have pieces of myself scattered all over the place, schedules on the countertops, commitments in the trees. Putting all those pieces back together to a state of being whole is a task that makes my eyes burn. When faced with it, I want to lie down on the floor amid the dropped cereal from this morning's breakfast and the dust bunnies I've avoided the entire summer.

In my best moments, I think I can conquer this divided *me*. I can pull all these parts together, whip them into shape, dress them in finery, and face the world again. In my worst moments, I recognize the truth of my situation. I may be divided for a long time yet.

There will come a time when the parts will again be put into place, making me whole again. It won't come through wishing or sheer force of will, but through prayer and patience and gathering myself piece by piece.

DAY 241

Some were impervious or dead to the coarser passions; they had so firmly repudiated all traces of them from the start that now, through daily asceticism and perseverance, they had acquired inner stability and did not even have fantasies of them in their dreams. In short, they were lights shining in darkness; they were fixed stars illuminating the jet-black night of life; they were harbor walls unshaken by storms. They showed everyone how simple it is to escape unharmed from the provocations of the passions.

St. Neilos the Ascetic, "Ascetic Discourse," p. 202

Simple but Not Easy

SO MANY THINGS ARE SIMPLE, but not necessarily easy. Climbing a tree is simple—scale the trunk, grab a branch, arm over arm, leg up here, and leg up there until you find a place. Still, it takes strength and perseverance and hands that can grasp, legs that can lift the body. It's a simple task, but not an easy one.

Driving a car is simple—one pedal for the gas, one for the brake, a steering wheel to turn. When you're on the road with other cars, though, or in an unknown place, the simple act of driving isn't at all easy.

The example of the saints who struggled as we struggle simply shows us it can be done. We have the tools, the mechanical necessities, the ability, the time, the inclination. It can be done, and it may be a simple process, but it is not easy. We've never been promised otherwise.

DAY 242

Because of our material concerns and shameful acquisitiveness, we have blunted the edge of true asceticism.

St. Neilos the Ascetic, "Ascetic Discourse," p. 202

Safety Net

It's always while I'm in traffic—whether it's heavy car traffic, or waiting-in-line traffic, or getting-the-kids-out-the-door-to-school traffic, or clutter-in-my-house traffic. The anxiety hits me when people or things or events crowd in toward me, pressing in like walls closing. I want to run away to somewhere quiet and safe.

And maybe I go. Maybe we take a vacation away from the walls closing in, to somewhere wide open and wild, with bird-song instead of cars honking or alarms ringing. Maybe we spend a week there, no television, no radio, no internet, just enough creature comfort to make us remember how soft our lives are back home. We still have a safety net. We have somewhere to land.

What does asceticism look like for the modern life, the city dweller, the middle ground? Is what we do enough to become sharp again?

DAY 243

So, we no longer pursue plainness and simplicity of life. We no longer value stillness, which helps to free us from past defilement, but prefer a whole host of things which distract us uselessly from our true goal.

St. Neilos the Ascetic, "Ascetic Discourse," p. 203

Advertising

ADVERTISING WORKS ON ME. THE algorithms that drive the ads on social media are tuned perfectly to my moods and inclinations. I admit, I click more often than I should. I buy more often than I should.

I am trying to fill something with each click, each purchase. I have some emptiness inside that speaks to me day in and day out. My first response is to avoid my responsibilities, watch too many episodes of this show or that. My next response is a constant refresh on social media to fill the empty places with sound and stuff. Each refresh promises to fill the empty place, but nothing ever works.

The last-ditch effort is to click and then buy. It feels like filling, but it's temporary. Everything worldly is temporary. I forget, and then I remember. I've got it all wrong.

Stillness isn't an emptiness. Stillness isn't a condition that needs curing.

DAY 244

Thus, like so many others, we look on the ascetic way as a means of gain, and follow the once unworldly life of blessedness merely in order to avoid hard work through a feigned piety, and to gain greater scope for indulging in illusory pleasures.

St. Neilos the Ascetic, "Ascetic Discourse," p. 203

Giving and Giving Up

EVERY DAY WHILE DRIVING IN Chicago I see someone on the street asking for change. I keep a small stash of coins in the door of my car for this purpose. I have it to give, at least in this meager amount. I don't even feel the absence of those quarters and dimes.

I pray as I drive, as I clean, as I work out. I have the time to spare because it fits neatly there during tasks like this. I don't have to give up my "free" time for that prayer. It's convenient.

While fasting, I sometimes think about the bonus of reassessing my dietary habits. I think more about the weight loss and less about the spiritual gains.

But in all these things, I wonder what it might look like for me to look at giving and giving up in order to grow closer to the One who made me rather than as a means to gain something. These practices are not meant to fill, but to empty—the heart, the belly, the reliance on material goods.

It's daunting to approach prayer, fasting, and almsgiving like this. I wonder what it would look like to do it anyway.

DAY 245

They do not realize that indulgence in gluttony leads only to further hunger, and that they should satisfy the needs of the body only with whatever food is at hand, thus quelling their shameful and disordered appetites.

St. Neilos the Ascetic, "Ascetic Discourse," p. 204

Appetites

MY YOUNGEST THREW UP AT school last year during a class party. He was quite proud of the fact that he drank five cans of soda, despite throwing up in the trash can immediately afterward.

We don't generally have soda pop in the house, so when he gets the chance to have it, he guzzles it quickly, taking in as much as he can before the door closes on that opportunity. We talk about moderation, we talk about self-control, we talk about the damage this sort of thinking does to the heart, the spirit, the body. He doesn't really care. He can only think about what he's missing in those moments, and then he takes a direct path to alleviate this. He's a child. He'll grow out of it.

It makes me think about the things I rush toward, guzzle down, or hoard to compensate for some perceived missing piece—affirmation? money? It's never enough, and I find myself coming up hungry again every single time. How will I grow out of that, I wonder?

DAY 246

It is difficult to treat those who suffer from chronic diseases. For how can you explain the value of health to people who have never enjoyed it, but have been sickly from birth?

St. Neilos the Ascetic, "Ascetic Discourse," p. 205

Chronic

IT TOOK YEARS FOR ME to get my chronic pain diagnosed. The simplest explanation for why it took me so long even to ask a doctor about it is that I didn't realize this was not normal. I thought most people in their mid-thirties probably slept poorly, legs and hips aching all night, constant pain in the upper and mid-back, arms, thighs, neck. I thought that this was just what the body feels like approaching middle age. I thought that most people were so severely fatigued around 3 PM that they had to lie down and rest to get through the rest of the day. This was my normal.

It brings to mind the story of Plato's cave. Those people who sit in a cave, seeing shadows cast by the sun but never the sun itself. They begin to believe that the shadows are all; the sun does not even register. Even witnesses coming back to tell them the truth, that the sun makes the shadows possible, won't move them from the dark.

So what comes first? Feeling the sun on my face to know it is there? Or believing it exists enough to stand up and leave the safety of my cave?

DAY 247

As for ourselves, who claim to have renounced worldly life and its desires in our longing for holiness, and who profess to follow Christ, why do we entangle ourselves once more in worldly distractions? Why do we wrongly build again what we have rightly torn down?

St. Neilos the Ascetic, "Ascetic Discourse," p. 205

Worldly Life

THEN THERE ARE THOSE OF us who are fully immersed in the worldly life. We have chosen to live in the world with school meetings and board meetings, with rising and plummeting interest rates on mortgages and credit cards and car payments. I know there must be a way to straddle this life and the one St. Neilos describes, but I cannot see it from here.

St. Neilos's words are meant as an admonition and an encouragement, I'm sure, but when I read them all I can think is that if those who have turned away from the worldly life struggle with tearing down structures and then rebuilding them, what chance do I have?

What comes to me, though, is the desire to ask why I rebuild after tearing down that which works against me. I don't have the ability to block out the world—I am in it by choice—but I do have the ability to question my response to the world, to ask myself why I turn back again and again to practices, choices, words, and thoughts that destroy the good work that comes from prayer, liturgy, fasting, and charity.

DAY 248

Why do we attach such value to material things, seeing that we have been taught to despise them? Why do we cling to money and possessions, and disperse our intellect among a host of useless cares?

St. Neilos the Ascetic, "Ascetic Discourse," p. 206

Feel Better

IT'S NOT MOVING INTO MY first apartment that stands out in my memory, but the first trip to the grocery store to stock my own kitchen. It was now my responsibility to fill those empty shelves and the bare refrigerator and freezer. I was buying for myself. I answered only to myself.

Every aisle was an opportunity. I knew what I should eat, but I also knew what I liked to eat, and so I chose that more times than not. Having the ability to choose, for better or worse, is a great responsibility. Now that I'm older, most of the time, I'll opt for the better choice, the food I ought to buy. Sometimes, though, I still choose things I like, food that seems to medicate some emotional problem. It feels better, at least for a short time.

DAY 249

Attachment to worldly things is a grave obstacle to those who are striving after holiness, and often brings ruin to both soul and body.

St. Neilos the Ascetic, "Ascetic Discourse," p. 207

The Gift Remains in Motion

SOME DAYS, I THINK I want to sell everything and clear out the place.

Years ago, I read a book called *The Gift: Creativity and the Artist in the Modern World* by Lewis Hyde. The start of the book centers on the history of giving gifts in different cultures. He tells stories of how early cultures viewed giving gifts to one another. In those times, the idea of gift-giving was not about accumulation but about community. Across various populations, the true nature of a gift was that it would remain in motion. Once a gift stopped moving, it was no longer a gift.

It's hard for me to look around the stuffed closets and storage spaces in my own life and see the gift in each of these things. I have wedding gifts from twenty-five years ago that I have never used. I simply packed them in a box move after move, feeling no connection, no value apart from knowing when it arrived in my house. What would it look like for me to put this gift back into motion?

DAY 250

Why, then, do we abandon the service of God and devote ourselves entirely to empty trivialities? For it is God who supplies us with all that we need.

St. Neilos the Ascetic, "Ascetic Discourse," p. 207

Empty Trivialities

THIS IS THE WEEK WHEN the daytime gets quiet again. All the kids are back in school. The house feels empty.

Rather than simply appreciate the silence, I start to fill it up, with sound and work and getting organized. At the start of this silent day, I imagine all the things I will get done. By noon, I'm already discouraged by my lack of productivity. By three, I'm back to the carpool, and I feel like a failure. Time compresses like this.

At some point, not long from now, I won't be waiting for school to start or to end. I want to begin to practice slowing down, letting the silence fill me, instead of trying to be productive or organized. It might prepare me for something lasting, something eternal.

DAY 251

All this shows that we should seek holiness, not clothing, food and drink. Strange though all these things may seem, they are by no means impossible.

St. Neilos the Ascetic, "Ascetic Discourse," p. 208

Provisions

CAN I STORE PRAYER? CAN I stock it on shelves in the back of the closet for days when I'm too busy to pray? Too stressed to turn to the One who made me?

I'm inclined to say that I can't store it up, though I wish I could have jars of prayer, comfort, reassurance, lining the shelves in my basement, stacked up on the floor of the closet, ready and waiting. I cannot store it up and open a jar when I need it. Prayer is quotidian, daily, seeping into dry skin like water.

What I can do is practice. I can do this daily act, create a habit, travel along in the groove of it so that when I need it most, I am not shuffling through the overstuffed closets but find that it is already in my hand, open and ready.

DAY 252

Why do we abandon hope in God and rely on the strength of our own arm, ascribing the gifts of God's providence to the work of our hands?

St. Neilos the Ascetic, "Ascetic Discourse," p. 208

I Do It

IN THE BABY BOOK MY mom kept for me, she has notated my first words—"Mama," "Daddy," "Baba"—and my first sentence: "I do it." My mom would pour the milk in my cup, and I'd grab it away from her. "I do it," I'd tell her. She would try to dress me, and I would say, "I do it."

Even now, as an adult, I have this impulse. Things go south on a project, and I pick up the slack. An assignment isn't finished by another writer, and I throw in on it. The kids' attempt to clean up the mess in the kitchen misses the mark, and I redo it. Someone forgets a notebook or school project, and I save the day.

It feels good to save the day. It feels good, too, to rest and rely on other people from time to time. For someone like me who likes to be in control, who likes to jump in and save the day, faith is a terrifying act of trust. But I realize now, in faith and in life, how often I am in need, how often I cannot do it, how often I need to rest and rely on God, and how vital that act is to my faith life.

DAY 253

What will our fate be, and how shall we escape condemnation, if we are constantly occupied with these bodily needs, and never stand upright or straighten our legs, so as to raise ourselves from the ground? For our two legs together carry the whole mass of the body, and by crouching a little we are able to spring upwards; and in the same way our faculty of discrimination, after stooping to attend to the needs of the body, can once more look upwards unimpeded, separating itself from all worldly thoughts.

St. Neilos the Ascetic, "Ascetic Discourse," p. 209

Posture

IT'S GRAVITY, OR STARING AT my phone, or just being tired all the time, but probably gravity. My stooped posture began when I was in the eighth grade, a result of being shy and growing tall rather quickly. I pulled myself inward, bodily, hiding, making myself small.

Now, years later, the evidence of that hiding is in the tight muscles of those shoulders, the stretched ligaments, the weakness of the rotator cuff. All these things plus staring at my phone, plus being tired all the time, plus gravity, weigh in. Standing upright, then, is work. It does not come naturally anymore. Left alone, I'd stay in this posture. Left with no other calling or recourse or responsibility, I'd continue to fold inward, body and now spirit hiding. But it's time to look upward. Lift the heart and head toward the One who made me.

DAY 254

But improbable details are often included in a story because of the deeper truth they signify. Thus, the intellect in each of us resides within like a king, while the reason acts as doorkeeper of the senses.

St. Neilos the Ascetic, "Ascetic Discourse," p. 210

Architecture

THE FEAST OF MY PATRON saint is September 11. I was welcomed into the Orthodox faith only a few days from this date several years ago. The date already carries a heaviness because of the events on this day in the United States in 2001. There is a significance to the date, then, historical and heart-related too.

My patron saint, Theodora of Vasta, is said to have lain down her life to fight for the safety of the people in her village. The story we tell is that her dying words were, "Let my body become a church, my hair a forest of trees, and my blood a spring to water them." On that spot where she is said to have died, a church was built. Trees grew around and through the walls of the building, making it an architectural miracle. An underground spring was found later, explaining how the roots of the trees were fed. It's considered miraculous, even by architects' and engineers' standards.

We build and we hope. Even in the face of fear, God tells us it's safe to build and to hope.

DAY 255

Through our anxiety about worldly things we hinder the soul from enjoying divine blessings and we bestow on the flesh greater care and comfort than are good for it.

St. Neilos the Ascetic, "Ascetic Discourse," p. 211

Far

HOW FAR DO I GET from home before I begin to worry that I've left the door unlocked or the stove on? Not far.

A block or two into a trip to the museum, or the beach, or the movie theater, I begin to wonder about the place I just left.

It happens, too, with my children. I drop them off, go about a block or two, feel their absence, wonder about the vast myriad of things that happen in the world, in this city, in this time.

So many reasons to worry. So many reasons to fear.

How far do I get into the muddy pit of fear before I decide to move to prayer, to reach up and take a hand offered and pull myself out? Not far, I hope. Not far.

DAY 256

Men such as Elijah and Elisha became what they were through their courage, perseverance and indifference to the things of this life. They practiced frugality: by being content with little they reached a state in which they wanted nothing, and so came to resemble the bodiless angels.

St. Neilos the Ascetic, "Ascetic Discourse," p. 212

Longing and Contentment

IF I WERE IN THE wilderness, not surrounded by advertising and traffic, but instead with trees and mountains and ocean, would I long only for God?

In my heart, I believe it. In my heart, especially when the city presses in, I believe it's true. I believe that I would long for God more readily. I reach for that impossible thing, to be in a clear open space where only what is God-made is evident.

I cannot go to the wilderness. Not now, maybe never for more than a few days, a week or two. If only there's a way to put my hands on that longing, to wrap it in my ribcage, to keep it close, then there must be a way through the forest of traffic, the pothole-heavy hills of this city, the noise and the exhaust.

Contentment doesn't come in longing for a better place, from hoping for a better setting, a clearer view of the mountains and ocean. If there is anything we can glean from this passage today, it is this. Contentment comes in longing for God, no matter what our location or circumstances.

DAY 257

We are apt to say that in sickness the body needs some relief. But is it not much better to die rather than do something unworthy of our vocation? In any case, if God wishes us to go on living, either He will give our body enough strength to bear the pain of the illness, and will reward us for our courage: or else He will find some way to relieve the pain, for the Fountain of Wisdom never lacks a remedy.

St. Neilos the Ascetic, "Ascetic Discourse," p. 214

Respiratory

AFTER WEEKS OF PRACTICE, GETTING up and dressed in workout clothes, I head out the door to run in the morning. One day, my chest is tight, my throat shows signs of soreness. I have a cold coming on. But I'm in the habit, hitting a stride, in the groove, so I go.

It's all about following through.

Three days later, the cough is rough, I slept poorly because of the congestion, my head aches, my body aches. Getting out of bed is difficult. Getting dressed is difficult. I only want to fall back into the warm bed, and so I do.

My system is already working. I forget this sometimes when I'm sick. What presents in the head cold isn't the virus, but the body fighting the virus. It tells me to rest. It tells me that it's hard at work. My respiratory system needs me to cooperate now.

A good, healthy habit won't be broken with a day or two of rest. Still, I know it will take some doing to get me back up and out the door again once the head clears, once the chest clears. It's this struggle I want to pay attention to—learning when to stop to rest, and then to start again. It's all about the follow-through.

DAY 258

Let us seek the wilderness and so draw after us the people who now shun us. For Scripture praises those who leave the cities and dwell in the rocks, and are like the dove (cf. Jer. 48:28).

St. Neilos the Ascetic, "Ascetic Discourse," p. 214

Dwelling in the Rocks

IT IS A HEART ISSUE, not a location issue. I have become so comfortable. I have become accustomed to the easy way, the heat and the air conditioning. But this is a heart issue, not a house issue—not about heat or air, about soft linens on the bed, about a well-tuned car, being well dressed or well fed.

What is nagging at this heart that stirs when I read these words?

Where is the wilderness?

This is the place that endures when all the "cities" are destroyed. Those cities live in the heart. I build them. I guard them.

If I make my dwelling in the rocks, I give up the comfort and choose the struggle instead. If I make my dwelling in the rocks, God promises shelter, promises strength, promises hope. It's a heart issue, not a location issue.

DAY 259

For holiness is held in higher honor than wealth; and the life of stillness wins greater fame than a large fortune.

St. Neilos the Ascetic, "Ascetic Discourse," p. 214

The Quiet Game

I'D WAGER THAT MOST ANY grown-up, at one time or another, has tried to convince a child that the "quiet game" is a real thing. In fact, the job to convince the child is not only that there is a game there, but indeed, that it is a much better option than, say, the "run around the house screaming" game or the "sing the most annoying song you can think of over and over while on a long car ride" game.

It's a tough sell. I don't think it has ever worked for me. Still, as grown-ups around children, we all try it. The desperate longing for some quiet while parenting or caregiving is a strong motivator.

In the middle of all the loud, we can see how a moment of quiet becomes valuable. We'll do all we can to get to that place.

DAY 260

To master any art requires time and much instruction; can the art of arts alone be mastered without being learnt?

St. Neilos the Ascetic, "Ascetic Discourse," p. 215

Ten Thousand Hours

MONKS WERE PROBABLY NOT WHO Malcolm Gladwell had in mind when he described his "ten thousand hours" theory in his book *Outliers*. Gladwell theorized that it takes ten thousand hours of dedicated practice to develop the skill to be considered expert at something. Ten thousand hours of singing, dancing, computer-coding, lumberjacking, writing, accounting, and perhaps, yes, prayer too.

I find myself doing the math to figure out how many hours of prayer I have practiced. How many more I will need to practice. And what, then, would it mean to be considered an expert in prayer? Will it mean that I have less struggle? Fewer moments of doubt? That I will no longer lose my temper with my children? Will it grant me some ability to choose the good? To hope more often? To breathe more deeply? To seek after God with all my heart, mind, and soul, finally and completely?

DAY 261

First, we must struggle against our own passions, watching and keeping in mind the course of the battle; and then on the basis of personal experience we can advise others about this warfare, and render victory easier for them by describing the tactics beforehand.

St. Neilos the Ascetic, "Ascetic Discourse," p. 216

Everything Works for Five Minutes

IF I EVER WRITE A parenting book, I already know I'll call it *Everything Works for Five Minutes*. My point being that we try things, we hope for the best, and it usually works—at least for five minutes at a time.

I joke that I can't write a book about parenting, though, until my kids are well grown, and maybe not before they have children of their own and we know that they turned out all right, too.

By my best reckoning, I can write a book about parenting in about fifty more years. By then, I'll have a track record. I'll know if whatever I did in my stumbling along in raising these little humans will have been for the better or the worse. Right now, I know that everything works for five minutes. That's all I know.

DAY 262

Experience shows that the task of guiding others should be undertaken by someone who is equable and has no personal advantage in view. For such a person, having tasted stillness and contemplation, and begun in some measure to be inwardly at peace, will not choose to entangle his intellect with bodily cares: he will not want to turn it away from knowledge and drag it down from the spiritual to the material.

St. Neilos the Ascetic, "Ascetic Discourse," p. 218

Searching for Fr. Zosima

MY CONFESSION HERE IS THAT despite some advice and admonition from my poet friend, Scott, I have not yet finished reading *The Brothers Karamazov* after years of trying. I've gotten about halfway through. I intend to finish it, when time and life and my poor weary brain allow. The first chapters stick with me, though—in particular, the character of Fr. Zosima, the elderly monk and spiritual father to Alyosha.

Mystical and wise, he transcends the ordinary life. That I read these few chapters before becoming Orthodox means that I went into it hoping I might find my own Fr. Zosima. It would be awfully helpful.

The reality is that we don't usually find one perfect, easily accessed *starets* or *geronda*, ready to dispense advice on cue. Instead, we build relationships with ordinary humans who are sometimes poets, sometimes parents, sometimes priests who are wise, yes, but often struggling, as we all do. And these relationships are powerful and life-giving. You'll know these people by their humility, by their love of God, by their caretaking, by their kindness.

DAY 263

Let no one imagine that to be a spiritual guide is an excuse for ease and self-indulgence, for nothing is so demanding as the charge of souls.

St. Neilos the Ascetic, "Ascetic Discourse," p. 219

Caregiving

THE FIRST FEW DAYS AFTER I became a parent for the first time, I would look at my daughter and wonder, "Who left this baby here with me?" I felt incredibly unqualified to have such a great responsibility.

Being responsible for another human is a daunting task, whether it's a child, an elderly parent, a sick loved one, a grieving friend. Anyone in need who turns to us for advice, care, comfort, puts their trust in us. And it feels as though we are mostly undeserving of that trust. We will fail, we will make mistakes, we will sometimes cause more pain in the care we give.

It's hard work. It's worthy work. Though we feel unprepared and unworthy at times, we should not turn away from it. We must be mindful of that trust, but not afraid of it.

DAY 264

The spiritual director must also possess knowledge of all the devices of the enemy, so that he can forewarn those under his charge about snares of which they are unaware, thus enabling them to gain victory without difficulty. Such a person is rare and not easily found.

St. Neilos the Ascetic, "Ascetic Discourse," p. 220

Guides

ONE OF MY FAVORITE FRIENDS is a therapist and an avid reader. Her library is beautiful, shelves sagging with books about the body, the mind, the spirit. Once, while we were having coffee, she told me about a book she loved and began to quote a line she remembered from it. She stopped, frustrated that she couldn't get the wording just right. She stood up, walked to one of the beautiful, sagging shelves, and ran her fingers along the row of books. She pulled a book down, opened it, and thumbed through a moment until she came to the very place in the book she needed.

I was dumbfounded. I can barely find my shoes and car keys most days. She remembered the name of the book, the shelf where the book lived, and even the paragraph where the quote lay waiting to be rediscovered and passed along to me.

A good guide remembers the terrain, the tools, and the best way to navigate. That moment crystallized to me the essence of her gifts. She is an excellent guide.

DAY 265

My aim in saying all this is not to discourage people from assuming the spiritual direction of beginners, but to urge them first to acquire the inward state needed for so great a task, and not to undertake it without adequate preparation.

St. Neilos the Ascetic, "Ascetic Discourse," p. 221

Training

WHEN I WANTED TO HIRE a personal trainer to lose the last of the baby weight I'd gained over the years, I knew I wanted to work with a woman. I asked to work with someone who could identify with me, someone who knew the struggle of motherhood and baby weight. "It would help if she doesn't have a perfect body," I said.

After some confused looks, the gym sent me to a woman who looked to be in her mid-twenties, muscled and thin. She had a wide smile and a friendly disposition. She told me she was not a parent but she had "lots of experience" training women like me. In the end, I didn't feel heard or safe or well cared-for or understood, and I stopped working with her.

I wanted a woman like me to train me, because I needed someone to whom I didn't feel I'd have to explain myself or my situation. It's tender work, vulnerable work. I needed someone who understood that and could draw from a deeper well. Sometimes we can identify who we need and when we need them. In those moments, wisdom means being able to articulate it and search for the right teacher and the right time.

DAY 266

In the spiritual life, more than anywhere else, the proper order and sequence must be observed from the start. Guests at a dinner may not like the introductory dishes and may feel more attracted by what comes later, but they are forced to comply with the order of the courses.

St. Neilos the Ascetic, "Ascetic Discourse," p. 222

Order

GENERALLY, WE LEARN TO CRAWL, then stand, then walk, then run. Most of us know someone who will say they skipped this order, went straight to running from crawling, spoke in full sentences as soon as words came to the shore of their lips. It happens.

But most of us follow the pattern, working from the ground up, the cycle continuing as we learn new things—into adolescence, into adulthood, into our later years. We crawl. We stand. We walk. We run. And in these stages, too, we fall, we fail, we falter. The progress feels, at times, slow and impossible. When we're still crawling, we want to be running; we want to skip over the next round of failures that takes us further toward the goal. The goal seems too far away; our time seems too short.

No matter where we are in the order of things, we're working against gravity pulling us down. Every bit of progress is a move forward. Every failing is another opportunity to stand up and try again.

DAY 267

But what if someone, not from any choice of his own, is obliged to accept one or two disciples, and so to become the spiritual director of others as well? First, let him examine himself carefully, to see whether he can teach them through his actions rather than his words, setting his own life before them as a model of holiness. He must take care that, through copying him, they do not obscure the beauty of holiness with the ugliness of sin.

St. Neilos the Ascetic, "Ascetic Discourse," p. 223

Lead and Follow

WHEN I WAS A HIGH school senior, my friend and I became Girl Scout troop leaders. The younger grades needed leaders and we were long-time Scouts, so they let us take a bunch of sixth graders and teach them things for a few months.

We did some badge work. We did some teaching about the principles of the Girl Scouts, but mostly we sat in meetings and talked about what was happening in their lives—and about camping. We talked a great deal about camping: when we'd go, what we'd pack, what we'd do there.

But we never actually went camping. My friend and I never got our act together enough for that. We were already very focused on graduating, moving into whatever life had for us next. We were not really equipped to lead these girls at all. We liked the idea of the authority, we liked the idea of teaching, but the troop began to dissolve as the weeks wore on. We had nothing of substance to offer these girls, who needed, more than anything else, something of substance from us. We were still so pliable ourselves, still finding our form, still watery around the edges.

DAY 268

The constant influence of a good example marks other souls with its own impress, so long as they are not completely stubborn and insensitive.

St. Neilos the Ascetic, "Ascetic Discourse," p. 224

Soul Friends

DO YOU HAVE THOSE DEEP soul friends? Those friends who might live far away, but the moment they speak on the phone you feel as though they are in the room with you? Those friends who know the very insides of your heart and your brain, who can speak truth that hurts and can then bandage and heal the wound?

The very best soul friends are wise, without perhaps even knowing they are so wise. They say things that make me later gasp aloud as I ponder them. They know without having to ask. They offer water on hot, dry days without a second of hesitation. Love increases in these friendships, never diminishes.

This is my aim, to find and hold fast to these people. I'm a better human, a better mother, a better spouse, a better friend, when I am in relationship with these soul friends. Like calls to like, deep calls to deep, soul calls to soul.

DAY 269

For, after being tamed and taught to graze like cattle, the passions can become savage once more through our negligence and regain the ferocity of wild beasts.

St. Neilos the Ascetic, "Ascetic Discourse," p. 225

Wild Things

JUST WHEN I FEEL I am doing well with my thought life, the wild things come raging back. I move from a place of peace, in a pasture contemplating the beauty of the blue sky, the summer day, when the late-day sun lowers on the horizon and it turns cold. The birdsong is replaced with deep growling from the growing dark.

I know this fear rising in my throat. I remember how far I've gone into the darkness of my thinking, how close I have come to the bite of these wild things, savage and persistent. I can only hold them off for a while before my arms grow tired and my legs weak.

Here I must remember that these passions are my own, not actually wild things at all, but beasts I have already tamed. Here I must remember to stand up straight, use eye contact and a strong voice, herd them back to the places they belong. There's no new action to learn, only a course of action I already know, already have mastered.

DAY 270

Every shameful thought formed in the mind is a secret idol. If it is disgraceful to disclose such thoughts to others, it is also dangerous to set them as an idol in a secret place: and it is even more dangerous to search for images that have already been made to disappear, since our mind readily inclines towards a passion that we have previously expelled, and we are drawn towards it by sensual pleasure.

St. Neilos the Ascetic, "Ascetic Discourse," p. 226

Holding Back

I SOMETIMES MISS THE OLD WOOD confessionals we used when I was growing up Catholic. I miss the curtain and the screen that stood between me and the priest. I miss being able to choose which priest I'd go to each week. I mixed it up to keep that "anonymous" advantage, though I'm sure each priest knew exactly who I was.

At least at that time, I felt I could confess without holding back. Now I choose my words carefully, because I cannot choose my priest; I cannot hide behind a curtain or a screen. There is no comfort of a chair into which I might slump if I'm losing my courage. There is no pretense of anonymity.

But there are moments in which I can, finally, after much consternation, pull out that hidden thought, hidden idol, hidden action, and lay it on the table, next to the cross I kissed when I arrived, next to the embossed silver-covered Gospel book I kissed too. "Here," I say to myself, to my father confessor, to my Savior, "take this now, I don't want to carry it anymore."

DAY 271

From this we may understand that virtue is a thing most delicately balanced, and that if neglected it quickly turns into its opposite.

St. Neilos the Ascetic, "Ascetic Discourse," p. 226

Cairns

AT A WRITING RETREAT A few years ago, I went searching for a quiet place to sit outside and write. The courtyard by my room was crowded. The patio outside of the dining hall was too sunny for me to see my screen. After some looking, I found a space away from people, away from the blazing New Mexico sun—a small bench next to a few trees to hide me, just enough, from the pathway I took to get here. As I readied myself to write, I noticed a stack of small rocks at the edge of a group of plants. A bit further, I spied another stack of rocks, "cairns," I thought to myself. Little rock altars built from things scattered. They were just rocks, related but individual, at one time. Human hands did this, grouping them in this way, a testimony of some sort, a mile marker, a message.

So, as with many things in the life of the spirit, we gather, stack, balance, and breathe, and hope we have done well enough to keep them standing despite the elements.

DAY 272

When pursuing the spiritual way, therefore, we should not be influenced by the pleasures of eating or the allurements of sensuality, but should consider where they both end up.

St. Neilos the Ascetic, "Ascetic Discourse," p. 227

Fleeting

YOUTH IS TEMPORARY. THE BOOK of Ecclesiastes calls it "fleeting." The Book of Proverbs tells me the same thing of beauty. "Temporary" at least has some weight to it. Something can be temporary and still taste sweet on the tongue. I can remember that taste years later. The very best ice cream sundae, a first kiss, a long run on a cool day. I can remember these things in my body and in my mind, sometimes even pining for a return to those days, that moment, that temporary feeling.

Fleeting, though, is even less than temporary. It's a passerby. It's a blip on the radar. Beauty and youth and this perfect meal are fleeting, replaced quickly by another ice cream sundae, another first kiss, another long run on a cool day.

What is most distressing to me about the nature of these things is my desire to hold fast to them. I try to tuck those fleeting moments into my pockets, press them into books like flowers from a field I passed once. I try to keep going back to youth, to some previous beauty, to the taste of that one exquisite dessert.

Instead, I wonder how it might look to let fleeting things go, and hold on, instead, to what is eternal.

DAY 273

What seems reasonable and convincing to the inexperienced is not necessarily correct. The skilled craftsman judges things quite differently from the unskilled man, for the first is guided by precise knowledge, the second by what seems to him probable.

St. Neilos the Ascetic, "Ascetic Discourse," p. 228

Possible and Probable

THE PICTURE I SHOW THE hairstylist seems straightforward to me. "This is what I want," I say to her, "but I don't want to have to work hard on making it look like this every day." She looks at the picture and then at my head. I imagine she's looking for a way to tell me that it's not possible given my hair texture, my head shape, my reluctance to use more than one hair-care product at a time.

We do the same thing with our house builders, furniture makers, clothing manufacturers, and sometimes, our spiritual leaders. We want something very specific, and we want it quickly, with easy-to-follow directions and not a lot of maintenance to make it look stunning. It's possible, but not likely.

Real change, true progress, deep and abiding spirit lives are sometimes messy for a very long time. Directions might be confusing or difficult to follow. The scenery can be dull, unlike anything we might see in a magazine. Listening to a skilled craftsman, taking his advice when we don't have the experience required, might be the only way to get to where we want to go.

DAY 274

Those who have only just renounced the world find stillness hard to practice, for memory now has time to stir up all the filth that is within them, whereas previously it had no chance to do this because of their many preoccupations.

St. Neilos the Ascetic, "Ascetic Discourse," p. 229

Filling Silences

THE FIRST TEN MINUTES OF writing today were perfect. I got settled at my desk, listened to the birdsong outside, the absence of cars honking or the train passing. I opened my laptop, ready to work, and I drew a blank. I lay down on the bed to try to read and promptly fell asleep. When I woke, I thought, "I just needed some rest—this is a good thing."

But the page remained blank for hours after that. I drank tea. I met some friends for dinner. I took a walk and returned to the page, still blank, still waiting for me to fill it.

Then the voices started in, the "what ifs", the "I should have knowns." By the end of the day, I was convinced I had no words to give the blank page. Those voices are always there, no matter where I am or what I'm trying to accomplish. I thought solitude and silence would quiet those voices, but sometimes it only seems to make space for more voices. They simply fill in those places that silence and solitude created.

DAY 275

The intellect of someone who has lately withdrawn from sin is like a body that has begun to recover from a protracted illness: when the physical organism is in this state, something quite trivial is enough to cause a relapse, since it has not yet fully regained its strength.

St. Neilos the Ascetic, "Ascetic Discourse," p. 231

Relapse

AFTER HER ILLNESS A FEW years ago, my mom was fragile. The time spent in the hospital with a rare blood disorder had affected every part of her body. Moving was difficult; her strength was sapped. She had trouble getting up from a chair, getting in and out of the car, loading the dishwasher.

And she was susceptible to every virus. Her immune system was compromised for a long time after she was released, so much so that she developed complications from a virus at home and had to get further treatment. All these things wore her down physically, yes, but it also wore on her spirit, her emotions, her ability to cope.

What illness does, too, is shine a light on our fragility. It makes us aware of how far we have yet to go. When we get to the path of recovery, relapse may be around each corner, but healing is always waiting just up the road.

DAY 276

Before we are properly trained, then, we should avoid the agitation of city life and keep our minds far from all distracting noise.

St. Neilos the Ascetic, "Ascetic Discourse," p. 232

Fireworks

It's early October in Chicago, and yet I can hear sounds and lights of fireworks outside at night. I look at the calendar wondering if there is some obscure holiday I've missed. Nothing jumps out immediately. It may not be anything at all—a birthday, a good day on the job, anything that needs celebrating with bursts of fireworks from the vacant lot near my house.

The noise didn't wake me. I'm awake already, sitting, thinking, worrying. I'm rehearsing conversations I need to have this week or next. I'm rolling around the list of chores, errands, writing ideas. I'm listening to the elevated train roll by a few blocks away.

I sometimes think that if only I lived somewhere quiet again, as we did a few years ago in Tennessee, I'd sleep better, but I know it's not true. It wasn't true back then; why would it change now? The nights are noisy in the city, but the noise in my head is worse.

DAY 277

For the provocations or the passions begin with trivial fantasies, creeping up unnoticed like an ant; but eventually the passions grow to an enormous size and their attack is as dangerous as a lion's.

St. Neilos the Ascetic, "Ascetic Discourse," p. 233

Small but Persistent

WHAT WOKE ME WAS THE sound of water running. It was too early for anyone to be up and in the shower, so I went downstairs and saw the kitchen floor covered in an inch or so of standing water. The water line from the refrigerator to the sink had burst.

I turned it off under the sink, and then we set to cleaning up. It didn't look that bad. What we didn't realize is that the line had burst just after we went to bed, and the water had been running for hours. What we also didn't know was that the line had apparently had a steady leak, probably for months, so that when it broke, the wood under the refrigerator was already saturated. The standing water on the kitchen floor was just the surface of the problem. The real damage was in the finished basement, where most of the water found its way—running along the cabinets, through the ceiling, cascading down the walls, into the carpet, into the bookcases, into the couch.

The damage began with the constant dripping over a length of time. Small but persistent habits, thoughts, and actions are powerful, whether they are meant to harm or to heal.

DAY 278

It is a terrible thing when the force of habit holds us fast, not allowing us to rise to the state of virtue which we possessed initially. For habit leads to a set disposition, and this in turn becomes what may be called 'second nature'; and it is hard to shift and alter nature.

St. Neilos the Ascetic, "Ascetic Discourse," p. 236

Losing Ground

BY THE END OF THE summer, my dog could get through most of our daily walk without too much drama. He had begun to trust me more, looking to me when we saw other dogs, people, cars. I'm inclined to celebrate this training as a success except that I remember we've been here before. I remember what it was like when we went without taking him on long walks in the winter last year. He hated the cold, so we just went to the backyard when he needed to go out. It took all spring and summer to get back to this point, trusting, watching, making progress.

As we get closer to the return of cold weather, I can already see his reluctance to go outside and already feel my own reluctance to take the time. School in full swing, more layers to keep warm, errands piling up, workload increasing, it's easier to just take him a few steps outside than make the effort of a real walk.

We'll lose ground. I already know this. We'll remember our old habits, fall into old patterns. They are familiar, offer false comfort, false security. This is where I make a choice to fight against the easy thing.

DAY 279

As well as nursing and feeding these passions, gluttony also destroys everything good. Once it gains the upper hand, it drives out self-control, moderation, courage, fortitude and all the other virtues.

St. Neilos the Ascetic, "Ascetic Discourse," p. 239

Medicating

FOOD AS MEDICINE OR FOOD as medicating. Am I eating to heal myself from the inside, as sustenance, as a cure? Or am I choosing something that I think will make me feel better for the moment? It feels as though these are the decisions I make every single day. I am paralyzed with indecision while in the grocery store aisles, in the line at the bakery, looking at the menu while at lunch with a friend.

Is this what I need, or is this what I want—and why can't I want what I need?

When I am tired of the struggle, I throw out the questioning, I throw out the discernment, and just choose to medicate with what feels good in that one moment. Later, I regret it. I always regret it.

The regret is worse than the momentary relief from the struggle. It rumbles in my brain and my belly, nagging and poking. The struggle is worthy; I don't want to forget that.

DAY 280

All of us, then, who long to make spiritual progress should strive to imitate the holiness of the saints. Let us rid ourselves of enslavement to the body's demands and pursue freedom.

St. Neilos the Ascetic, "Ascetic Discourse," p. 241

Run

IF THERE IS ANYTHING I take from the lives of the saints, it is that we are surrounded, supported; arms are ready to take us in when we need it most. We have only to ask. Long-gone saints leave their fingerprints in the stories, miracles, and wonders. We tell and retell, and remember and hope, and fall and get back up.

When the telling is not enough, I need to go to warm, living humans, with voices on the phone to tell me to keep going, don't quit, pursue progress rather than perfection.

When I don't want to finish the book, I don't want to run the race, I don't want to get back up, it's these voices, the living saints I choose so carefully to spur me on, that point me to Christ. I tell them I don't want to run anymore.

"Go," they say, "do it anyway. Call me after. I'm here. I'm on your side. You're not alone."

DAY 281

We do not appreciate how much better the blessings of the spiritual world are than the tawdry attractions of this present world, which dazzle us with their specious glory and draw all our desire to them; in the absence of what is better, what is worse will take its place and be held in honor.

St. Neilos the Ascetic, "Ascetic Discourse," p. 242

Shortsighted

COMMON SENSE TELLS ME TO take what I can get. A bird in the hand and all that. I do not know exactly what I am missing—I suppose that much is true. The thing is, I know I am missing something, and that feels important.

I can try to live this life feeling as though I am already complete, but I'm in for a disappointment. Or I can admit that I am, at best, on the road to completion. The temptation, always, is to try to fill up the empty space with something or someone who is less than worthy—food that does not nourish, people who take without giving, time-consuming tasks that jam that sacred empty place with anything I can get my hands on just to feel some kind of satisfaction for a little while.

DAY 282

Those who travel by sea, when overtaken by a storm, do not worry about their merchandise but throw it into the waters with their own hands, considering their property less important than their life.

St. Neilos the Ascetic, "Ascetic Discourse," p. 243

Setting Apart

WE ARE PACKING UP OUR house in Tennessee this month, ready to turn over the place and most of the furnishings to a new owner who has more time and money to keep it up. Because we've been renting it long distance for so long, we'd already removed most of the personal things, keeping generic art on the walls, furniture that is sturdy but absent any personal value to us.

We did take the books in our library, and in one locking closet we kept several bins—some clothing we kept there for our visits, paperwork and a box of knick-knacks left over from when we lived there as a family.

In some ways, it was an easy time of packing, all our true belongings so carefully set apart from the rest of the contents of the house. We found ourselves scouring the rooms, the walls, the other closets, the attic, just to be sure we hadn't missed anything, but we came up empty. This is what years of preparation, separation, setting apart had yielded. We had been making ready for this moment, it seems, for a long time. Though our property was still there in a sense, our lives had moved on from this place.

DAY 283

A cloak measured to fit the body is both necessary and in good taste; while one which is too long, getting entangled in our feet and dragging on the ground, not only looks unsightly, but also proves a hindrance in every kind of work. Similarly, possessions superfluous to our bodily needs are an obstacle to virtue, and are strongly condemned by those capable of understanding the true nature of things.

St. Neilos the Ascetic, "Ascetic Discourse," p. 245

Fitting

TWICE A YEAR I CLEAN out my closet, taking everything out of drawers and off the shelves that hold most of my clothing. I place the contents on my bed, spreading it out and sorting by type: T-shirts, pants, dress clothes, coats. It seems as though anything on the bottom of the stack tends to be the least-worn item.

Some articles of clothing, like the bottom-of-the-stack clothes, are easy to part with, moving right to the "donate" pile, or the "throw away" pile if they're in bad shape. But other things are more difficult—this shirt with a tear at the shoulder that I got from a concert, this pair of jeans long worn and long loved that they just don't make in this style anymore.

I find a lot of my trouble comes from changing styles. I like what I liked five years ago, sometimes ten. Times change, styles change, my body changes, yet I remain committed to T-shirts and jeans in the older fashion.

As I get older, I realize that I no longer shun fashion trends because they are fashion trends and I want to be different, but rather because I want what I wear to fit the life I have, the work I do, the body I have now.

DAY 284

We should remain, then, within the limits imposed by our basic needs and strive with all our power not to exceed them.

St. Neilos the Ascetic, "Ascetic Discourse," p. 246

One Hundred Things

MY ARTIST FRIEND HAS A goal to own only one hundred things. He's a minimalist, and I am in awe of his progress. I envy it, truth be told. I often think about the end of my life, how I'd like to live, how I'd like to be. The idea of owning only one hundred things makes me take a deep breath, feeling the space in my lungs inflate, breaking free after years of shallow breathing.

And those deep breaths also sometimes hurt a bit. The air is colder than I expect. The years of shallow breathing come because of the crowded nature of my life. I fill it up—this hand cream I saw advertised, this jacket I thought I really needed, this car that has room to seat seven plus a dog—all things that will have to go in favor of a minimalist goal.

But instead of thinking of what I will not have, I wonder what it might look like to consider what I would take with me: this photograph of my children, this book that changed my life, this journal to record my griefs and joys, a warm coat, a soft blanket, a pillow for my head, and all the memories I can carry.

DAY 285

Let us cure the passion of avarice through voluntary poverty. By embracing solitude let us avoid meeting those who do us no good, for the company of frivolous people is harmful and undermines our state of peace.

St. Neilos the Ascetic, "Ascetic Discourse," p. 247

Food Drive

A FRIEND OF MINE HELPS RUN a food pantry a few times a year. She tells me they prefer donations of money to actual canned goods or stable shelf products because given the chance, most people will simply go through their cabinets and give the food they bought but didn't really want to eat.

I know it's true, because cream of mushroom soup always went into the basket first from my house, then artichoke hearts I bought for a recipe and never used, one of the seven cans of tomato paste. I don't know why I can't remember not to buy tomato paste.

It's striking when I realize that we give first from our unwanted store of overabundance. It's not at all sacrificial, not in the least any kind of voluntary poverty.

Strangely enough, though we might hold on to only the food we want and give away whatever is frivolous, we sometimes prefer to hold on to people we may not want. I wonder if it is some fear of loss that keeps us in the relationships with people who, as St. Neilos says, do us no good. It's another example of things the Fathers say that are hard to hear and hard to heed, as well. Hope springs eternal. People change. God is always working. And perhaps the lesson here is just that. He is always working, whether I am in relationship with them or not.

DAY 286

Once we have learnt to train our body, let us also train our intellect in true devotion.

St. Neilos the Ascetic, "Ascetic Discourse," p. 248

Endurance

FIRST, I TRAIN FOR ENDURANCE. It's the least fun part of running, but I'm a beginner, so I start there. At this point, I'm not even running at all, really. It's more a sort of fast walk, followed by a couple of almost run-like movements. My body feels awkward in this, arms and legs pumping through space, feet slapping the pavement. I try to forget about what I might look like as I go through the motions of learning to run.

I stop frequently, rest and stretch and drink water even though it's already cold outside. My lungs are not cooperating. My legs are complaining after only a mile or so. I finish the three miles I've got slated for today. I'm training for endurance, so this means that while I may not have achieved the fastest time or the prettiest form, I have completed the task I've set for myself today. In two days, I'll work on strength. In four days, it will be speed. These promise me harder work but for a shorter period of time, a shorter distance. But first, I train for endurance.

DAY 287

In short, beginners try to train their body, while the more advanced attempt to restrain the impulses of their intelligence, so that its workings may accord solely with the teachings of wisdom, and no worldly fantasy may distract it from thoughts about God.

St. Neilos the Ascetic, "Ascetic Discourse," p. 248

Drifting

MY THOUGHT LIFE IS WORSE now than it has been in the past. I drift into imaginary conversations while I drive or work out or cook. I have always done a version of this, trying to think ahead about who I might talk with, what we might talk about, how I might conduct myself.

In the best moments of this practice, I'm rehearsing so that I can function in the world. In my worst moments, I'm trying to escape this present moment. The drive is boring or the workout is difficult or the cooking is a disaster. Or it might be a wider problem, not momentary at all—my heart is injured, my head is foggy, I am fearful, I am overwhelmed and feel I'm failing, so I invent another scenario in which I am confident and in control.

The reality floods back at the next stoplight; the invention, the fantasy fades. It has always ebbed and flowed for me, but now it's worse than it has been for years. Perhaps it is because there is more at stake the longer I live, the closer I grow to my Creator, the more strongly I feel His hand on mine. This is an anchor, a mooring. I cannot afford the drifting.

DAY 288

Each passion, when active within someone whom it controls, holds his intelligence in chains: why, then, cannot zeal for holiness keep our mind free from everything else?

St. Neilos the Ascetic, "Ascetic Discourse," p. 249

Impatient

I AM FRUSTRATED BY MY PROGRESS: two steps forward and one step back. I feel impatient. In dreams, sometimes I am running someplace, eager to get there and held back by some imaginary force. I struggle against the unseen arms that hold me back. I press forward as though my feet were becoming glued to the ground. Each step moves me forward, but only a bit.

I wake from those dreams drenched in sweat, heart pounding. These are stress dreams, I'm told. The stress, this embodied fear, might be related to ordinary failings in housework, career, parenting, or partnering, or the dreams may speak to that deeper yearning that has been stirring. Reaching toward God as I run. Maybe I make some progress, maybe I get some distance toward my goal, and then I look down to see these feet of clay.

It's enough to stop anyone in their tracks. What keeps us moving forward can only be the deep recognition of and desire for what lies ahead—rest, healing, home. No matter how long it takes, the struggle is a worthy one.

DAY 289

Let us, then, bring joy to this heavenly tribunal, which rejoices in our acts of righteousness. We need not worry about men's opinions, for men can neither reward those who have lived well nor punish those who have lived otherwise.

St. Neilos the Ascetic, "Ascetic Discourse," p. 250

Rejoicing

IF THERE IS NO JOY in it, I may be doing this wrong. This is the advice I hear from a friend when I find, after several months of reading the *Philokalia*, taking it to heart and head, that I am on the floor in my bathroom, and I am weeping for what seems like no reason at all. I have read today about rejoicing, and in the same sitting, I have read today the following from the Psalter: "I wait for the Lord, my whole being waits."

I am keenly aware in this moment that I am disconnected and floating. I want, with all my heart, to be anchored, for my whole being to wait on the Lord, but there are dishes to wash and people to call and life, real life, to live. I don't know what it looks like to wait on the Lord with my *whole being.* I can only see how far I am from the mark. The saving grace seems to be that at the same time I also see the expanse of my capacity to love, and the gentleness of God, and the truth of His mercy.

So my friend tells me to look for the joy in it, and I can see, right away, that he is right. And I think, if there is no joy in it, I may be doing it wrong. I put aside the "mark" I think I'm meant to reach. I put aside the fear of unworthiness and the weeping, and with trembling hands, reach for rejoicing.

Diadochos of Photiki

DAY 290

Introduction by Caroline Jarboe

HAVE YOU EVER LOOKED AT a part of your life from a distance of years and wondered what would be your legacy? How do you trust God when the whole world seems alien and unfamiliar?

St. Diadochos of Photiki would likely have thought about these same questions, because he lived them out himself. It is believed that, toward the end of his life, he and others in Epirus in northern Greece had been captured by a group of Vandals—even though he was the Bishop of Photiki and had represented his bishopric at the Council of Chalcedon, which rejected monophysitism.

Perhaps accordingly, Diadochos was passionately concerned about the importance of holding on to right belief in the face of seductive heresy—and the essential role of prayer and vigilance in preserving a constant communion with God. His most widely known work, *On Spiritual Knowledge and Discrimination*, is known via shorthand as *The One Hundred Chapters*, which spoke of his passion for this persistence.

After his capture by the Vandals, Diadochos and his colleagues were released in North Africa, near Carthage, it is believed. But beyond that final location, nothing is known of Diadochos's life or death.

If he had only known that his words would influence such spiritual giants as John Climacus and Maximos the Confessor—and indeed, the entire Hesychast movement! But the lesson of Diadochos is that legacy belongs to God. It is we who belong to Him.

DAY 291

All spiritual contemplation should be governed by faith, hope and love, but most of all by love. The first two teach us to be detached from visible delights, but love unites the soul with the excellence of God, searching out the Invisible by means of intellectual perception.

"On Spiritual Knowledge and Discrimination," p. 253

Foundation

I WONDER WHAT SPIRITUAL CONTEMPLATION LOOKS like without love. I'm reminded of the description of love that comes from St. Paul in 1 Corinthians: "If I speak in the tongues of men or of angels, but do not have love, I am only a resounding gong or a clanging cymbal. If I have the gift of prophecy and can fathom all mysteries and all knowledge, and if I have a faith that can move mountains, but do not have love, I am nothing. If I give all I possess to the poor and give over my body to hardship that I may boast, but do not have love, I gain nothing."

I wish love were something I could hold in my hands. I wish love had weight and mass and color. It might make things clearer. I could look down at any moment, see it there, remind myself to begin there. Remind myself that love is foundation, not furniture, not decoration, not afterthought.

How does it change my perception of this life if I use love as a starting point, foundational, concrete? Can every decision made and everything seen and everything written or read begin in this way, with love?

DAY 292

The light of true knowledge is the power to discriminate without error between good and evil.

"On Spiritual Knowledge and Discrimination," p. 254

Set Apart

DISCRIMINATION, AT ITS ROOT, COMES from the Latin *discernere*, meaning "to separate, set apart." I am sorting through a load of boxes that have been in storage a long time. I make two piles, "keep" and "throw away." This first box is full of what I've labeled "memorabilia"—artwork, grades, cards, pictures, and letters from the first year we lived in Tennessee. The kids were little then—one, three, five, and eight years old, respectively.

There are notes written to me in Riley's sweet, young-kid handwriting, and large blue lined pages with the alphabet written over and over by Chet. There are photos from the preschool Miles attended and an "invention" Henry drew in ballpoint pen. There are crayon-scribbled pictures ripped from coloring books with no name or date, art projects we made together, magazines tossed in there with no explanation at all.

The "keep" pile is stacking up, the "throw away" pile not so much. My husband asks how I decide which goes where, and I have no answer for this. I cannot remember what made me decide in the moment to keep what is here now, or what I might have thrown away. I have even less of an idea about how to decide now.

DAY 293

When the soul's incensive power is aroused against the passions, we should know that it is time for silence, as the hour of battle is at hand. But when this turbulence grows calm, whether through prayer or through acts of mercy, we may then be moved by a desire to proclaim God's mysteries, restraining the wings of our intellect with the cords of humility.

"On Spiritual Knowledge and Discrimination," p. 255

The Calm Before

THERE'S A REASON MY RESPONSE to feeling stressed, depressed, or just overwhelmed is to retreat under my covers for a time. I cut ties with the outside world. I turn off the music. I close the blinds and let the dark gather. After some time in the dark, in the quiet, alone with my thoughts and prayers, I'm often given the gift of tears. Hard, deep sobbing that moves me beyond words.

For some, this may seem counterproductive. For me, it's protective, even restorative. I take time to get back in touch with my source of strength. To remember where light originates sometimes means entering into the dark and sitting there, waiting. It is a kind of trust, really, this exercise in seclusion. I make the effort to stop making so much effort and just allow myself to *be*.

I never regret that time spent alone, that coveted quiet, those soul-baring tears. I never underestimate the benefit of quieting, the strength of sitting in the dark, the power of deep, wrenching tears. It always ends in gratitude, in calm, in thanksgiving to God.

DAY 294

Spiritual discourse always keeps the soul free from self-esteem, for it gives every part of the soul a sense of light, so that it no longer needs the praise of men.

"On Spiritual Knowledge and Discrimination," p. 255

Word and Light

THIS LINE FOLLOWED ME AROUND the house after I read it this morning. I sat down at my computer, and it rang in my ears as I typed. True words of affirmation stick to me for a long time. They are a kind of fuel for me, a light in dark places; but the fuel burns out, leaving black streaks on the ceiling and walls. This sort of fuel was never meant to burn forever.

It worries me, though, what words of affirmation historically have done for me. I worry that I rely too much on these words from fellow travelers. What makes a person trustworthy? What makes their words ring as truth while others ring hollow?

Today I'm giving St. Diadochos some form, putting his words in my ears, choosing to trust his advice, his affirmations, his admonitions. Today I am lending more weight to this spiritual discourse than I might have before, just to see what it feels like, to see if some sense of this light can find its way in. I wonder if this fuel burns cleaner, burns brighter.

DAY 295

When a man begins to perceive the love of God in all its richness, he begins also to love his neighbor with spiritual perception. This is the love of which all the scriptures speak.

"On Spiritual Knowledge and Discrimination," p. 256

Loving the Neighbors

I AM TRYING TO LOVE MY neighbor the way our Creator loves him, I think to myself. My neighbor cut me off in traffic. My neighbor stole my son's bike from our backyard. My neighbor bullied my daughter, sold me bad goods, called me names when I was too young to know he was a liar.

I am trying to love him, but I am more inclined to complain, to blame, to run far away, to protect myself, to lash out, to hide. What does it mean to love the neighbor who hurts me, whether I know him well or not at all? What does love look like in this situation?

Sometimes running, hiding, blaming, complaining, lashing, or protecting is merited, sometimes necessary for survival. And then, in better moments, in strong moments that took years and years to build, I can see the glimmers of this richness of God's love. In that light, when I want to run, I hope I might run to God, take shelter in God, find solace in God, seek protection in God. In that light, loving my neighbor, even when it doesn't seem appealing, at least seems possible.

DAY 296

If wounds in the body have been neglected and left unattended, they do not react to medicine when the doctors apply it to them: but if they have first been cleansed, then they respond to the action of the medicine and so are quickly healed.

"On Spiritual Knowledge and Discrimination," p. 257

Taking Care

IT'S EARLY FALL, AND MY son walks around in bare feet still. He is almost feral in his need to be barefoot, inside and outside. He takes the dog out, as I have asked, and neglects to put on shoes. A few minutes later, he's limping back into the house, left foot bleeding, gouged on a rusty pipe that was sticking up from the grass in the front of the house. At one time, it was the post for a sign. Now the remnant has taken a bite out of his foot.

The worst part about the trip to immediate care was when they had to irrigate the wound. The physician's assistant flushed the jagged cut again and again, wiping it with gauze every few moments. They had to get all the rust and dirt out or else risk infection.

The cut will heal without stitches, but it must remain clean and dry. He limps from class to class while at school. He limps from the couch to the table at home. He is barefoot, even now, just a flimsy bit of gauze between the floor and his wound, but he takes care to keep his heel lifted, protected, clean; the sting of the cut is a constant reminder.

DAY 297

The deep waters of faith seem turbulent when we peer into them too curiously: but when contemplated in a spirit of simplicity, they are calm. The depths of faith are like the waters of Lethe, making us forget all evil: they will not reveal themselves to the scrutiny of meddlesome reasoning. Let us therefore sail these waters with simplicity of mind, and so reach the harbor of God's will.

"On Spiritual Knowledge and Discrimination," p. 258

Seas and Storms

MY BEST MEMORY OF THE sound of water comes from a trip I took over two decades ago to Italy. It was probably the first time I stayed in a place so beautiful and so peaceful. Our room was high in the side of a cliff overlooking the Tyrrhenian sea. A storm rolled in as the night fell, filling the air with rumbling rolls of thunder and filling the sky with streaks of lightning that seemed to reach deep into the water even as they lit our darkened room. We felt safe there in our room with the lights off and the sliding door open, watching this spectacle of light and sound.

After a few hours, as I was beginning to fall asleep, the storm receded, and the sound became that of waves kissing the shore. From high in the side of the cliff, we could hear it clearly; it was a comforting sound, regular and rhythmic. The storm, too, was a comfort in its own way, a reminder of the powerful nature of things outside of our control.

It is not difficult to feel safe perched high above the water, whether it's a calm sea or a stormy one. Put me in a boat on that sea, and the stakes change. The water, the waves, the storm mean something different for a person at sea. Instead of building a safer room in the side of a cliff, perhaps I really ought to be learning to be a better sailor.

DAY 298

Everything longs for what is akin to itself: the soul, since it is bodiless, desires heavenly goods, while the body, being dust, seeks earthly nourishment. So, we shall surely come to experience immaterial perception if by our labors we refine our material nature.

"On Spiritual Knowledge and Discrimination," p. 259

Hungry

EVERY MORNING I WAKE UP early, make coffee, light a candle on my home altar, kiss my icons, pray until the smell of the coffee catches me. Every morning I get the kids out of bed, get them rolling towards school, and then sit in the silence for a few minutes before the next wave of movement. I am not hungry. I'm never hungry when I wake up.

At around 10 AM my stomach makes noise, reminds me about food. I'm reluctant to leave whatever it is I'm doing to make food, to sit down, to eat. I wonder when it was that I stopped feeling hungry. I wonder if it's something I should worry about, if it's some kind of sickness, or if it's all in my head. I am busy. I am stressed out. I am overwhelmed, but I am not hungry.

Still, the body needs food. It wants, as St. Diadochos suggests, what is akin to it, and so I eat and I live and I go on to do more things. I wonder sometimes if this is a mirror for my spiritual life. If I pray because I am in the habit of praying. Do I feel the longing for prayer the way healthy people feel hunger for food? Is the absence of that longing something to worry about, some kind of sickness, or is it all in my head? The spirit needs food, and so I pray and I live and I go on.

DAY 299

Very few men can accurately recognize all their own faults; indeed, only those can do this whose intellect is never torn away from the remembrance of God.

"On Spiritual Knowledge and Discrimination," p. 260

Mirroring

MY SON COMPLAINS ABOUT AN annoying classmate. I tell him something I heard a long time ago, probably from a magazine article or that psychology class I took in college. "You cannot love or hate anything about another person that you don't already love or hate about yourself." He's skeptical, but I tell him it's science, though I can't remember where I heard it. "I think it's Jung," I say. His thirteen-year-old psyche rejects this, and I let it go.

Other people act like mirrors for us. This I know. It's a gift to remind myself of this when I am apt to complain about someone else—their behavior, their housekeeping, their parenting. And it's a gift, too, to see good in other people and hope, pray, that this is a quality I possess. I want that to be true. It's strange to say that I also want it to be true when I spot flaws in other people—that the same flaws are in me, that I can put my hands on the same kinds of wounds, the same kinds of weapons. My fifty-year-old psyche welcomes this idea, prays for insight and wisdom, for myself and for the mirrors of myself.

DAY 300

In every way, therefore, and especially through peace of soul, we must make ourselves a dwelling-place for the Holy Spirit. Then we shall have the lamp of spiritual knowledge burning always within us; and when it is shining constantly in the inner shrine of the soul, not only will the intellect perceive all the dark and bitter attacks of the demons, but these attacks will be greatly weakened when exposed for what they are by that glorious and holy light.

"On Spiritual Knowledge and Discrimination," p. 260

Homecoming

"ESPECIALLY THROUGH PEACE OF SOUL," he says. This is the part that jumps out. In every way, yes, but *especially* in this way, through peace of soul. Anxiety in my heart feels like a fast pulsing, almost painful. Anxiety in my head is a heavy throbbing, clouding my ability to see or hear anything well. Anxiety in my stomach feels like a giant hand squeezing me around my middle.

Yet I can recognize peace when I feel it in my body, not merely as an absence of anxiety. Peace isn't an empty space waiting to be filled with pain and doubt. Peace has its own rhythm, its own presence.

My soul's anxiety feels less defined, less physical, difficult to articulate with any real precision. If anything, I can only call it a kind of restlessness, a feeling of deep sadness, homelessness. So, then, the peace my soul needs most is to be at home, to be safe and rooted, anchored, embraced. This peace, I imagine, feels like a homecoming.

DAY 301

Our physical sense of taste, when we are healthy, leads us to distinguish unfailingly between good food and bad, so that we want what is good; similarly, our intellect, when it begins to act vigorously and with complete detachment, is capable of perceiving the wealth of God's grace and is never led astray by any illusion of grace which comes from the devil.

"On Spiritual Knowledge and Discrimination," p. 261

What We Crave

SOMETIMES I TRICK MYSELF INTO choosing well. I am craving something that is not good for me—a food, a thought, a purchase, an action. I know it isn't healthy. I know I will regret it later, beat myself up for it, wish with all my heart I'd chosen another option. Still, I will want it. Often, I will go ahead and make the poorer choice.

And, let's not kid ourselves, I will enjoy every single moment of it. I will savor it, tasting it on my tongue and chewing slowly for texture, for sweetness. I will feel greedy for it, not wanting that moment to end, because then the regret will set in and take away any lasting pleasure.

So sometimes I trick myself, or at least delay the thing I think I want until I've had a chance to try whatever my hunger really does require. I'll expect it to be dry or tasteless, but it will surprise me with its savory richness. Subtle flavors mixing with a hint of heat and light. It will fill me completely. I had only to try it once to know the goodness of it.

DAY 302

The experience of true grace comes to us when the body is awake or else on the point of falling asleep, while in fervent remembrance of God we are welded to His love.

"On Spiritual Knowledge and Discrimination," p. 262

Speak

I AM WAKING UP THESE DAYS at 4 AM. I am not *trying* to wake up at 4 AM; my body just shakes me awake for reasons I cannot yet discern. This pattern recurs every now and then, every few years maybe. I wake up, not remembering any dream or reason for waking. My eyes are open, and I'm alert and listening to the soundless night. I feel calm, not sleepy. I'm not worried, not really. I'm barely even thinking.

One of the first nights this began happening again, I thought about God calling Samuel. I said softly to God, "Are You waking me up?" and I waited but heard nothing. I turned over and went back to sleep after a few minutes. The next night, I opened my eyes and said again, "Are You waking me up?" but still, I heard nothing. I turned over and went back to sleep.

I like to think that the answer comes, but maybe I'm not yet ready to hear it when I'm awake. Maybe when I'm sleeping, untroubled by the day's events, God speaks to me so sweetly that my waking self can hardly breathe, and I wake, hopeful and expectant, and waiting for more.

DAY 303

Just as a rough sea naturally subsides when oil is poured upon it, so the soul readily grows calm when anointed with the grace of the Holy Spirit.

"On Spiritual Knowledge and Discrimination," p. 263

Oil

MY FAVORITE PART OF MY chrismation was when I was anointed with the oil—the feel of the priest marking my skin with the cross, and the sound of the words he spoke, "The seal of the gift of the Holy Spirit," followed by the congregation's response, strong and steady in unison, "The seal!" I hadn't expected that part. It made my heart skip a beat each time.

After my chrismation, my godmother told me not to wash off the oil right away. She said that if I could help it, I should not shower until the next day, after I'd received Communion. That night when I got home I still felt the oil on my forehead, my throat, my hands, and my feet. I did as she suggested, left the oil that remained after the service. I let it sink into my skin, and whatever remained before bed, I carefully smoothed into my pores until it disappeared. Years of anxiety about this day, this milestone in my conversion, simply disappeared. I like to imagine it was the oil that calmed the seas of me. When the seas are rough even now, I trace that spot on my forehead, my hands, my feet. I remember that moment and let the seas be calmed once more.

DAY 304

The dreams which appear to the soul through God's love are unerring criteria of its health. Such dreams do not change from one shape to another; they do not shock our inward sense, resound with laughter or suddenly become threatening. But with great gentleness they approach the soul and fill it with spiritual gladness. As a result, even after the body has woken up, the soul longs to recapture the joy given to it by the dream.

"On Spiritual Knowledge and Discrimination," p. 264

In the Dream

I HAVE FAINTED MORE TIMES IN my life than I can count. It started in grade school, usually in church. My overactive imagination led me to consider the nails being pounded into Christ's hands and feet, the sword piercing His side. I'd get lightheaded, a little sick to my stomach, and then find myself suddenly waking up on the cold stone floor of the church, sweaty and shaky.

I dream when I faint. I remember only a small piece of the dream. Usually, it involves a calm place, a field of flowers, the bright sun. I am happy in that place. Then a buzzing starts in my ears, everything turns black, and a pinpoint of light appears, vibrates with the buzzing, and gradually becomes the sounds of people around me, the faces of people around me. It is as if the world comes back into focus and I am awake again. I wake up longing to return to that place, that calm place, that field of flowers. The feeling of it lingers a long, long time.

DAY 305

It is well known that obedience is the chief among the initiatory virtues, for first it displaces presumption and then it engenders humility within us. Thus, it becomes, for those who willingly embrace it, a door leading to the love of God.

"On Spiritual Knowledge and Discrimination," p. 265

Do It Anyway

THE WORD *OBEDIENCE* IS A trigger. I always think it means coercion, giving up my own will. I want to resist when I'm told to obey. I want to choose to ignore whatever is being asked of me.

As a parent, I find myself giving orders to my children, insisting that they obey my instructions. When they say they don't want to do it, I say, "Do it anyway." Sometimes that works; mostly it doesn't.

But the word itself, *obey*, means, at its roots, "to listen" or "to hear." The action required in obedience is listening, hearing, paying attention. "Listen to Me," God instructs. So today I'm working on listening, hearing, paying attention. Instead of plotting an exit or a rebellion in answer to God's call, I want simply to hear Him. I may still say, "No, I don't want to do this thing," and He may further instruct me to do it anyway, but I want, at least, to listen.

DAY 306

Self-control is common to all the virtues, and therefore whoever practices self-control must do so in all things. If any part, however small, of a man's body is removed, the whole man is disfigured; likewise, he who disregards one single virtue destroys unwittingly the whole harmonious order of self-control.

"On Spiritual Knowledge and Discrimination," p. 266

Self-Control

HE HAS TO TOUCH EVERYTHING. He has to put his hands on every single thing before him. This little boy at church traces the lines in the wood of the floors of the church. I stand behind him and his parents at liturgy. I watch them rein him in when he moves too far or too fast. I watch as they instruct him to talk quietly when all he wants to do is shout.

I smile, because I have been there with my own children when they were young. I would get one in line and the other three would spin off. "Herding cats," I say to the woman next to me, and she laughs.

But I smile, too, because I sometimes want to shout when I am meant to whisper. I want to let my attention wander when I am meant to listen. I want to jump or run instead of standing still. I understand the push and the pull of what we want to say or do and the steady hand of self-control. It's a steep climb. There's a learning curve.

DAY 307

We should therefore regulate our food according to the condition of the body, so that it is appropriately disciplined when in good health and adequately nourished when weak. The body of one pursuing the spiritual way must not be enfeebled; he must have enough strength for his labors.

"On Spiritual Knowledge and Discrimination," p. 266

Lifting Heavy

WE BUILD MUSCLE MASS BY lifting heavy. Each time we ask the muscle to do more than it is used to doing, by lifting weights or using body weight against the pull of gravity, we make micro tears in the muscle fibers. When the fibers heal, they heal stronger; the muscle increases in size. And each time we lift after that, the muscle fibers remember, and they recruit help from within themselves. So, when we increase the weight, when we work harder, we're always making progress, building up on this foundation.

Fuel is important, though. Protein and amino acids, carbohydrates, fats, water. All these things help the body to repair the strain on the muscles, help the bones to strengthen to support their weight, help the brain to remember how fortunate we are to breathe air and pump blood. We move to keep moving; we lift heavy to build strength; we eat to fuel the whole system. We cannot do anything well without good fuel.

DAY 308

The soul will not desire to be separated from the body unless it becomes indifferent to the very air it breathes. All the bodily senses are opposed to faith, for they are concerned with the objects of this present world, while faith is concerned only with the blessings of the life to come.

"On Spiritual Knowledge and Discrimination," p. 269

Wants and Needs

I NEED TO EAT GOOD FOOD, need to sleep well, need to breathe clean air, need to move. These are all needs my body has for me. My body reminds me when I don't get enough of these things with rumbling stomach, eye twitching, tight chest, creaking bones. My body tells me what it needs, and it always needs something.

I think of taking my children places they don't necessarily want to be—the store, a long trip in the car, the doctor's office. They tell me what they want, what they need. They tell me what they like or don't like. Like my body, they too are concerned only with this present world. They, too, remind me when they are in need.

It's the quiet moments, at home, comfortable, resting, when we're most cohesive. It's when we're talking or laughing about something that happened that day. We may still be in need. We may still have wants and desires and complaints about the absences of those things, yes, but that drains away. We fold into one another, hands holding, voices mixing, one united purpose of being together, just now, always.

DAY 309

Then the Lord awakens in the soul a great love for His glory: for when the intellect with fervor of heart maintains persistently its remembrance of the precious name, then that name implants in us a constant love for its goodness, since there is nothing now that stands in the way.

"On Spiritual Knowledge and Discrimination," p. 270

Distance

I RAN ALL THE WAY. I could have gone further, in fact, but I ran the required 3.1 miles in my training for my first 5K race for the first time. I was focused on the breathing, the footfalls, the running track. I tried not to worry too much about where I was in the distance, only that I was running and not stopping.

I chose the pace, slow but steady. I don't care how fast I get there, I just want to get there. Each time I felt winded, I slowed down but didn't stop. Each time I thought about quitting, walking home, giving up, I took more air into my lungs but didn't stop. I let my mind wander, took in the scenery of the trees, the litter on the ground, the water beside me. I listened to music I trained to inside. Sometimes I sang along out loud, and I didn't care what anyone I passed thought about it. I pumped my fist in the air when I saw I had gone halfway. I giggled a little when I saw that I was almost at the end of the route.

Six months of running brought me here. Six months of making small efforts, being persistent, and setting clear goals: 3.1 miles, slow and steady; slow down if you must, but do not stop.

DAY 310

Since we are but children as regards perfection in the virtue of prayer, we have need of the Spirit's aid so that all our thoughts may be concentrated and gladdened by His inexpressible sweetness, and so that with all our being we may aspire to the remembrance and love of our God and Father. For, as St. Paul says, it is in the Spirit that we pray when we are taught by Him to cry without ceasing to God the Father, "Abba, Father" (Rom. 8:15).

"On Spiritual Knowledge and Discrimination," p. 271

Instead

THERE ARE A FEW THINGS, still, that derail me in my thinking. I project far into the future sometimes and worry. I reach back into the past and feel depressed. Staying present is where I am lacking. Still, this part of my reading today sticks out: "and so that with *all our being* we may aspire to the remembrance and love of our God and Father."

This is what I want instead. Instead of feeling torn into pieces by the past or future thinking, I want to remember God with all my being. This reading today tells me I *can* be whole; my being *can* be pulled together for its true purpose.

I imagine my heart knitted together again in prayer, stitched with care, my body wrapped in gauze, my soul held tight inside. Every day, I will look at the bandages, not thinking of my injury but hopeful for the restoration, grateful for the care.

I will emerge from recovery, and at last I will be healed, whole. I don't want to ruminate on the hurts of the past or the fear of the future. I want to remember that the One who made me, who cares for me, who holds me so beautifully, is here now. I want to remember God's love with my whole being instead.

DAY 311

Divine justice requires that we receive back not the objects of theft, but the thief himself, freed through repentance from sin.

"On Spiritual Knowledge and Discrimination," p. 273

Love One Another

WE ARE NOT OUR MISTAKES, our errors, our hurts, our sins, our poverty, our judgments, our harsh words, our missed appointments, our dropped vases, cracked plates, burned dinners. We are made by the hands of the Creator of all things.

This is what I'm thinking today as I sit awash in one more in a long line of regrettable things I've just said to someone I love. It won't do to be angry all the time, or sad, or regretful, or shaming, though it often feels as though I spend a lot of time there.

The equation seems simple enough:

He did something. I got mad and said something painful. He was hurt. I was hurt. This space is where forgiveness goes, on this line in the report in my head.

He was sorry. I was sorry. We forgive. The anger is justified; the sadness is valid. The regret is merited; the forgiveness is welcome. Now love one another.

Still, I want to hold on to the hurt. I want to store it up, keep it for later, rekindle the injury if it is needed. But it isn't needed.

God does not store up our mistakes, errors, hurts, or sins. He lifts them from us, sends them out into the wind to be blown away, removes them as far as east from west, welcomes us home, loves us without fail.

DAY 312

Therefore, when we have been made ready, we begin to long sincerely for this gift of contemplative vision, for it is full of beauty, frees us from every worldly care, and nourishes the intellect with divine truth in the radiance of inexpressible light.

"On Spiritual Knowledge and Discrimination," p. 275

Tethering

IT'S A PULLING SENSATION AT the chest, as if a rope has been tied there inside and now someone is on the other end, tugging. Sometimes the tugging is strong and powerful, sometimes a slight, quick pulse, as a kind of reminder that while we're here in the world, there is always some tension, no matter how well things are going.

It seems strange for my brain to go to tethering today when hearing about being freed from worldly care, but there it is. Worldly cares spin me out, leave me floating and grasping at whatever I can grab. Today I recognize that I may yet be "made ready," and the sound of that is a comfort. It ignites, at least in some small part, a sense of longing, a desire to be tethered to the One who made me.

I may never be able to move far enough from the dark to reach the inexpressible light, at least when I am in this world, but I can know that I am connected to that light. I am made by those hands, chosen, beloved of God. That, too, is a comfort.

DAY 313

Ideas of value always shun verbosity, being foreign to confusion and fantasy. Timely silence, then, is precious, for it is nothing less than the mother of the wisest thoughts.

"On Spiritual Knowledge and Discrimination," p. 276

Timely Silence

I'VE DISCOVERED THAT LISTENING IS a gift. I used to be distracted in conversations with people I didn't know very well, thinking as they spoke about what I might say in response. It was one of my introvert tricks. If I could get a response down, I might hide the fact that I was sorely uncomfortable in that conversation. And I wanted to contribute. I wanted to seem as though I was smarter or more interesting than I felt at that moment.

Then, a few years ago, I began to listen instead. To people I knew, people I didn't know at all, people who were somewhere in between. Listening to my children talk on and on about a game I didn't know or care about, for example, used to make my head hurt, but when I chose to listen and let them speak, I was struck by moments of real joy in their faces. This chosen silence, the rapt attention to their words, their ideas, their dreams—it was a gift to me and to them.

There are times in which I will speak, tell my stories, float ideas across the waters of conversation. And there are times, too, during which the best way for me to love the person before me is to listen and listen well.

DAY 314

So long as the soul is worldly-minded, it remains unmoved and untroubled however much it sees people trampling justice under foot. Preoccupied with its own desires, it pays no attention to the justice of God.

"On Spiritual Knowledge and Discrimination," p. 277

Small Things

THE WORLD IS BIG. I know this even as I feel the space between places is shrinking, too. I can hear about what is happening anywhere through the little black box I hold in my hand. I get alerts all night and day. Even when my phone is on vibrate, I hear them. I sit up in bed, fumble for my glasses, read the headline. That's always a mistake.

The trouble with following all the news, all the time, is that rather than feeling more informed, I end up feeling as though I cannot make a difference, as though whatever I have to offer is never nearly enough to help the world be less selfish or cruel. I cannot solve the world's troubles. Like many people, I want to disconnect, to leave it behind, to let everyone else sort it out and get back to my own life.

Here's where a quote from Mother Teresa, one I've held a long time, comes to mind: "Not all of us can do great things. But we can do small things with great love." This is the call I hear today, to put aside the headlines and sensational stories, the overwhelm, the apathy, the disconnect. I wonder what it would look like to work toward doing the small things with great love.

DAY 315

When the soul has reached self-understanding, it produces from within a certain feeling of warmth for God. When this warmth is not disturbed by worldly cares, it gives birth to a desire for peace which, so far as its strength allows, searches out the God of peace.

"On Spiritual Knowledge and Discrimination," p. 278

Building a Fire

SO MUCH DEPENDS ON HOW the wood is stacked. Teepee, lean-to, log cabin—whatever your preferred method, the core elements of fire-building are the same. There must be kindling, good, dry wood, and room for oxygen. If the wood is stacked too tightly, air won't circulate; the fire suffocates before the kindling can catch the wood. Even if the wood does catch, it won't last long. But there's a protection to the structure as well; stacked too loosely, the whole thing can collapse in, scattering the coals, cutting off the flow of air to wood, to kindling, to core.

This is the way of faith, too. So much depends on how we place the elements, how much care we take in the structure of our prayer lives, our parenting, our partnering, our love for other people, our love for ourselves, for our Creator. We may have to practice quite a lot, stacking and kindling and lighting, over and over, in all kinds of weather and seasons, until we get it right.

DAY 316

When someone rids himself of all worldly riches, he discovers the place where the grace of God is hidden. For as the soul advances, divine grace more and more reveals itself to the intellect.

"On Spiritual Knowledge and Discrimination," p. 279

Stuff

THE RULE IN OUR HOUSE used to be that before one of us made a list for Christmas gifts, we had to go through all our stuff and give away or throw away some things to make space. It's not just physical space, but emotional space, too. Do I need this much stuff? Really?

But I ran out of energy to enforce the rule over the years. There were too many people in the house, too much stuff, too little time. Our closets are filled, our drawers too. Once a year I might enter the kids' rooms to clear out a small area, tote away a few bags of "give away" or "throw away." They hardly notice what's missing. But I notice. I like the space that is left there, clean-swept and empty, but not so empty that it must be filled right away. Time and lack of attention to that old, neglected rule will fill up that space after a while, and I'll have no trouble finding yet another place to clear out, to tote away bags of "give away" or "throw away." We don't need this much stuff; we need more clear spaces.

DAY 317

We share in the image of God by virtue of the intellectual activity of our soul: for the body is, as it were, the soul's dwelling-place.

"On Spiritual Knowledge and Discrimination," p. 280

Windows

THE VIEW FROM THE WINDOWS in this house in Chicago is terrible. From where I sit writing today, I can see the alley, the neighbors' yard filled with construction materials for their new garage, phone and electric wires, a tree that is dying. I don't expect it will survive the winter.

It's a funny thing about windows: two-way glass means I'm looking out, judging what I see, but if anyone were to look in, what an invasion it would be. I don't often consider the looking in. I draw the blinds, I turn off the lights. There is no invitation in these windows.

This whole journey into the wilderness of the soul—the reading, the study, the prayer, the daily reflection—cannot merely be an exercise in looking out. This journey must allow for some looking in, as well.

DAY 318

Captivity is one thing, battle is another. Captivity signifies a violent abduction, while battle indicates a contest between equally matched adversaries.

"On Spiritual Knowledge and Discrimination," p. 283

Powerful

WE HAVE ONLY ONE REAL adversary, and he is not more powerful than we are. This is the thought I have as I navigate a particularly hard week. Nothing goes right—the weather, the traffic, the parenting, the workflow. Anxiety comes to visit, tells me lies about the reality of our situation. "There's nothing you can do," it says.

In a quiet moment on a day when nothing goes right, I want to lie down on the bed before the kids come home from school and just give up. Why bother? I wonder.

There's another voice, though, a voice I trust because it is clear and strong and uses words like *hope* and *peace*. It brings me images of clear, running mountain streams and calm falling rain. The voice uses phrases like "you're not alone" and "it's going to be all right." This voice reminds me that I have some power, too. The enemy is not more powerful than I am. I can stand up, face the needs of the day, muddle through until a break comes in the battle. I have some power here.

DAY 319

For what is considered perfection in a pupil is far from perfect when compared with the richness of God, who instructs us in a love which would still seek to surpass itself, even if we were able to climb to the top of Jacob's ladder by our own efforts.

"On Spiritual Knowledge and Discrimination," p. 285

Climbing

My arms are tired from climbing. I am nowhere near perfection today, nowhere near reaching the top of the ladder. I can't even see where the ladder ends. It goes like this a lot.

There are rare days, however, during which I feel I've done so much work. I feel so accomplished, so ready for the next step in my faith. Those days I am putting hands and feet on rungs, strong and steady. No wind blowing, nothing to stop me. Except myself, perhaps.

What is at the top of this ladder? A concrete platform, a diving board, another ladder? Fear is what freezes me here. Fear and nothing else. My arms are strong. My legs are strong. My goal is clear. Up. I panic. I am on this ladder. I am climbing; there is no going down apart from falling. I cannot do it on my own.

DAY 320

When God recedes in order to educate us, this brings great sadness, humility and even some measure of despair to the soul. The purpose of this is to humble the soul's tendency to vanity and self-glory, for the heart at once is filled with fear of God, tears of thankfulness, and great longing for the beauty of silence.

"On Spiritual Knowledge and Discrimination," p. 286

Making Room

My college student daughter wants to stay in New York next year when the school year ends. It's not unexpected. She'll be a junior. She's feeling her life begin. She's using her own hands to construct the framework of her adult life. It's exciting and it's terrifying, too, for us both.

I tell my children that I got a dog because he won't leave me. We train our children to leave us, but we train pets to stay. It would be selfish for me to try to persuade my daughter not to begin this adult life. Still, when she clings to me before she leaves from visiting each break, I hold too, almost afraid to let go. What will become of that space she has held for so long?

When I read this passage today, my first thought is panic. Does God recede from us? No, I don't want to think that's true. And yet, in the light of my experience with my own children, I revisit the idea again, seeing it not as a kind of abandonment but rather as a way of making room. I don't want to let go of my daughter when she clings to me, and yet I must. I have to make room for the new joys that can come, make room for growing, make room for the next stage of her life.

This is what God does with us, and it doesn't feel like letting us go or leaving us. It feels like trust in the process of our becoming. When we're ready, when it's time, He makes room.

DAY 321

When a man stands out of doors in winter at the break of day, facing the east, the front of his body is warmed by the sun, while his back is still cold because the sun is not on it. Similarly, the heart of those who are beginning to experience the energy of the Spirit is only partially warmed by God's grace.

"On Spiritual Knowledge and Discrimination," p. 287

Lake Effect

WINDS COME OFF LAKE MICHIGAN all year round, but in the winter, the wind can produce snow in places along the lake. The rest of the area may not see any precipitation at all. It's Jekyll and Hyde. Turn to the east and see the brilliant snow; turn to the west and see the grey dullness of a winter sidewalk.

Both are real. Both are happening at once. It's science, not magic.

The same is true of the spiritual life. We feel our heart expand even as we realize how much further we have yet to go. We turn to the east and bathe in the white-light snow that glitters like diamonds. We turn to the west, the bare and grey, and remember that winter in Chicago shows us two faces of winter. Both are real. Both are happening at once.

DAY 322

When the intellect begins to perceive the Holy Spirit with full consciousness, we should realize that grace is beginning to paint the divine likeness over the divine image in us.

"On Spiritual Knowledge and Discrimination," p. 288

Effortless

I HAVE WATCHED AN ARTIST AT work on a painting. First the sketch, the form, then the color, the texture, the edges, the fill. It builds layer upon layer upon layer. And, to my eye, it seems finished, but then comes another color, another texture, until I cannot even remember the sketch. It's become more than I could have imagined.

Is the work done in us like something we watch this way, or something we may catch out of the corner of our eye? Can we feel the layers added? Or do we only glimpse this work of the Holy Spirit as we move on with daily life, not stopping to notice that we are, somehow, changed? My face growing slowly brighter, my breathing easier, my moods smoothing, my prayer life constant and vibrant, filling in all those empty spaces.

DAY 323

If we fervently desire holiness, the Holy Spirit at the outset gives the soul a full and conscious taste of God's sweetness, so that the intellect will know exactly of what the final reward of the spiritual life consists.

"On Spiritual Knowledge and Discrimination," p. 289

Taste and See

SOMEONE TOLD ME ONCE THAT I should try a food my child rejects at least twelve times. The idea, I suppose, was that after that many times trying a food, their tastebuds would finally give in, and they'd begin to eat it. I don't know if that ever held true. I lost count after the first few times on certain foods. After the fourth child, I couldn't even keep track of which foods they liked and which they did not like. One kid liked hamburgers, the other hated them. One person liked broccoli, another would avoid it at all costs.

There were a few things that once tasted, all loved. Most were easy to guess—cakes, cookies, soda pop—but there were other non-sweet foods too: stir-fry, chicken curry, homemade whole wheat bread.

These things only needed one taste. The taste transcended our individual needs and desires and found us all on the same level, at least for a while. In time, even those agreed-upon foods and drinks began to cause some dissension. All worldly things fade, shift, change.

There really is no equal to the sweetness of God, the desire to know Him, to seek Him out. The taste we receive does not waver, does not fade, does not fail in any amount of time.

DAY 324

As wax cannot take the imprint of a seal unless it is warmed or softened thoroughly, so a man cannot receive the seal of God's holiness unless he is tested by labors and weaknesses.

"On Spiritual Knowledge and Discrimination," p. 291

Resist

I AM RESISTING THIS HEAT TODAY. "I do not want to be changed," I tell myself, "I am fine as I am." But the heat pours down like a strong light overhead. I can feel the wax of me melting. I wrap my arms around my body, holding it together. My heart is a puddle on the floor. I am resisting this heat, this softening of myself. What if, when all is said and done, I am not made better by all this work? This is the fear that lingers in the heat of temptation and doubt.

I want to throw it all away, move to a cool place and regroup, reform myself the way I think would be best, form my features in a way that is pleasant and beautiful by the world's standards. But I am not a confident sculptor; the materials won't do what I hope they will do. The risk of my becoming cold and brittle and shapeless is real.

So, though I am resisting this heat, I will, nevertheless, give myself over to it in the end because I do trust this Creator. He knows the work, the vision, the materials, better than I ever can.

DAY 325

Humility is hard to acquire, and the deeper it is, the greater the struggle needed to gain it.

"On Spiritual Knowledge and Discrimination," p. 292

Deficient

"ON THE GROUND, FROM THE EARTH." Word origins might be my favorite thing. The definition of this one, *humility*, begins with words like *modest, sweet, lowly.* None of those helps me. I reach further back into the root and see the relationship to *humus*, the Latin word for *soil* or *earth.* This is not lowly or even modest. To be from the earth feels comforting instead of demeaning.

How long have I been thinking that to seek humility means to tear myself down? Make myself less than whoever stands before me? It's not about some deficiency in me; it's about knowing where I began, in the soil, from the earth. It's about remembering my mortality even as I feel assurance in the eternity that lies ahead. We anchor to the earth in body, we anchor to God in spirit; and that's a tension that either holds us upright or tears us apart.

Humility, perhaps, is what is needed to keep us together in that tension.

DAY 326

But when the intellect fully and consciously senses the illumination of God's grace, the soul possesses a humility which is, as it were, natural.

"On Spiritual Knowledge and Discrimination," p. 292

Dark Mornings

THE DAYS HAVE BEEN GRADUALLY getting shorter, the light no longer streaming into my room to wake me before my alarm. The skylights above my head wake me early on summer days, which is unfortunate because just once, on days when the kids don't have to go to school, I'd like to sleep late.

In the summer, sometimes I throw the cover over my head in a halfhearted attempt to block out the light. It never works. My body wants to wake. Truth be told, I'm already well into the habit of rising early by this time. The dark overhead doesn't do much to insulate me from waking.

This natural waking, the body sensing the time even without my eyes sensing the light through closed eyes, is what I imagine it must be like for the intellect to sense God no matter what the season. It keeps a line to Him, a natural grasp of His goodness and mercy, His leading, His light.

DAY 327

The first type of humility is usually marked by remorse and despondency, the second by joy and an enlightened reverence.

"On Spiritual Knowledge and Discrimination," p. 292

Softening

MISTAKES ARE NORMAL, HUMAN, EXPECTED. That will never change. My reaction to my errors can and should change. I want to be a better version of myself. I don't need to be perfect.

I could do without the process, though. I could do without the hot-face moment when I realize my mistake and the creeping flush when others notice too. I could live without the stammering as I try to explain, the awkward moment when we work through it, if we work through it.

The adrenaline rush in those moments tells us there's action needed. When I was younger, it felt like fight or flight. Stand my mistaken ground or run away and avoid repercussions. Not much was solved by either of these choices.

Now, it feels like a softening, recognizing some deeper truth, something that needs my attention. If I'm going to be a better version of myself, I must begin with the admission that I am not already there. There is still work to do. There may always be work to do.

DAY 328

So those who wish to live virtuously should not hanker after praise, be involved with too many people, keep going out, or abuse others (however much they deserve it), or talk excessively, even if they can speak well on every subject.

"On Spiritual Knowledge and Discrimination," p. 293

Alone and Lonely

WHEN THE INVITATION TO A classmate's party arrives in the mail, I ask my youngest son if he wants to go, but he declines. Then a few days later he changes his mind. He wants to go. I cannot figure out yet if he's more an introvert or an extrovert. He doesn't seem to fit the profile of either very well. When I ask him, he tells me he likes to be alone, but he doesn't like to feel lonely, and that strikes a chord in me. I feel it too. I don't always want to go to the party, but I want to be invited, and I want to be missed if I'm not there.

Left to my own devices, I'd stay home alone and maybe not feel at all lonely. I don't have to be with people all the time. Still, I know that I need people. I'm better in community. I'm better with company now and then. This direction from St. Diadochos doesn't feel like a call to avoid people, but rather to embrace some foundational truth about myself. When people speak about finding our "identity in Christ," this is what comes to mind on the heels of the reading today. To live virtuously, we need to look to that which is eternal, foundational, and ever-true. Only God fills this need.

DAY 329

The intellect should therefore devote itself continually to keeping the holy commandments and to deep mindfulness of the Lord of glory.

"On Spiritual Knowledge and Discrimination," p. 293

Guide

ON A HIKE IN THE wilderness, this city girl followed the trail and the guide. I'm not experienced in the outdoors. The trail was easy to follow, the guide knowledgeable. He'd stop every few minutes at first, telling us about the area that surrounded the trail, the trees, the air, the elevation, the history, the landslides.

He moved much faster up the steep incline, and I plodded along at a pace I could handle without becoming too winded. We stopped to rest when I asked, but otherwise we kept moving up, up, up. When I could not navigate some rocks in the road, he offered a hand. The destination was never in question for me. I put my trust in the trail and the guide. I felt challenged, but safe, always safe. When my focus was foggy, when I was unsure of the next steps, the guide knew the way. He was paying attention.

The well-tuned intellect is a guide for us. The trail marks the path, but it is the guide who keeps us moving, knows where we're going, reminds us to rest as needed, and shows us how to appreciate the journey.

DAY 330

Those who desire to free themselves from their corruption ought to pray not merely from time to time but at all times; they should give themselves always to prayer, keeping watch over their intellect even when outside places of prayer.

"On Spiritual Knowledge and Discrimination," p. 293

Keeping Watch

THE ALARM ON MY PHONE marks the liturgy of the hours. It's set for 6 AM, 9 AM, 12 PM, 3 PM, 6 PM, and 9 PM. At first, when I started this practice years ago, each time the alarm went off I would open my prayer book and pray. Now I'm apt to be in the car, the grocery store, the movie theater, or one of my kids' schools. The best I can offer at those hours is the Jesus Prayer. I find my lips moving as I shut off the alarm, already in motion, already in prayer, a habit I cultivated over the course of ten years.

Sometimes I shut off the alarms for a trip or a meeting. My body remembers them, though. My lips will move with the Jesus Prayer without my even realizing it. I wonder in those times whether the prayer is heartfelt, whether the habit is effective at all or just an autonomic response.

It feels different to consider the habit of prayer as "keeping watch." It feels deeper somehow when I consider that I should "give myself" to prayer. Habit is a way in, a starting point, but consciously giving myself over to the moments of prayer is a kind of surrender. This is asking more of us. This is the next step in a life of prayer.

DAY 331

It is the mark of one who truly loves holiness that he continually burns up what is worldly in his heart through practicing the remembrance of God, so that little by little evil is consumed in the fire of this remembrance and his soul completely recovers its natural brilliance with still greater glory.

"On Spiritual Knowledge and Discrimination," p. 294

Burning

THE ROAD TO EMMAUS COMES to my mind from this reading. "Were not our hearts burning within us?" I always remember that part. I put my hand on my chest and try to feel that burning, as the apostles might have felt it when their hearts recognized Christ before their brains told them it was He.

When I am most prone to give into the troubles, the struggle, the weight of the world, I place my hand there again, fingers spread a little. I take a deep breath, feel the fire that reminds me that what I see all around me is not the end of things, but a beginning.

I say yes to this world, with its ticking clocks and honking horns and mortgage to pay and kids to feed, but also yes to the next world. The deeper reality that we are more than a collection of atoms dancing in time with all the other atoms on this planet. This is what that burning in our hearts tells us.

DAY 332

We should pay close attention to maintaining inward awareness during confession, so that our conscience will not deceive itself into believing that the confession it has made to God is adequate; for though we may not be aware that we have done anything wrong, the judgement of God is far more severe than our conscience.

"On Spiritual Knowledge and Discrimination," p. 295

Left Unsaid

I SPILL WORDS OUT ON THE table. I dump them there, sort through with care and thought. "This, I'll take," I say aloud. "This, I'll leave here." I parse the phrases, tell the truth but tell it slant, as Emily Dickinson might say. I don't imagine she thought of confession when she wrote that poem, but sometimes it fits.

I throw around a few vulnerable words, slide them into the phrases gently, hoping they don't open any gaping wounds, hoping they don't tear me up so much that I cannot get out all that I have rehearsed. I place those vulnerable words in there, even so, knowing that they are powerful: greedy, envious, fearful, hurting, lonely, cruel, indifferent.

I place those words believing that I am being truthful, letting God determine what is what, but they turn out to be little landmines every time. I speak them. My heart explodes. The tears come. It takes me a long time to get the rest out, and by then, it's no longer the rehearsed confession, no longer the small offering I carefully crafted. There is now nothing left unsaid.

DAY 333

If we do not confess our involuntary sins as we should, we shall discover an ill-defined fear in ourselves at the hour of our death. We who love the Lord should pray that we may be without fear at that time; for if we are afraid then, we will not be able freely to pass by the rulers of this world.

"On Spiritual Knowledge and Discrimination," p. 295

Emergency Shelter

I CALL IT FREE-FLOATING ANXIETY, AND it happens to me a lot. I'll be sitting at my computer or at the sink, in my car during rush hour, or taking a walk, and a feeling of dread rushes over me. There's no one thing that comes to mind, just a sense of cold weight, like being outside too long in the middle of winter in clothing that is not quite warm enough. I left the house thinking I was all right but then find I was wrong.

I wonder if there is some better preparation for that free-floating anxiety, that cold snap I didn't expect. I wonder if there is some warm place I can go, some shelter from it? Instead of lamenting the cold, I want to open my eyes in those moments and look around, see where I might find a place of refuge, of safety, of warmth.

DAY 334

But the soul which rejoices in the love of God, at the hour of its departure, is lifted with the angels of peace above all the hosts of darkness. For it is given wings by spiritual love, since it ceaselessly carries within itself the love which "is the fulfilling of the law" (Romans 13:10).

"On Spiritual Knowledge and Discrimination," p. 295

Doorways

WHEN WE WERE LITTLE, MY sister and I would stand in doorways and press our arms out from our bodies against the doorjamb as hard as we could for as long as we could. When we couldn't hold it any longer, we'd step out of the doorway, relax our arms at our sides, and let them float out from our bodies as though lifted by unseen hands.

Sometimes, I do it still.

It reminds me of the constant pressure I place on myself, my family, my faith life. I press and press and press against that which is unmoving. I cannot budge it. I don't even think I mean to budge it, only to push for as long as I can, as hard as I can. I'm living for that moment of release, letting myself be lifted, free from the pressure, free from the doorway and self-inflicted pain, lifted as though by unseen hands.

John of Karpathos

DAY 335

Introduction by Summer Kinard

TRANSFORMATION COMES ONLY THROUGH HUMILITY, and humility comes from knowing that one is a creature.

Lurking behind St. John's advice for the monks in India is the specter of the Manichean view of salvation. For the Manicheans, a para-Christian sect popular in India for over sixteen centuries, souls are not creatures but uncreated bits of light separated by matter from the God they fell from. That makes for a life of longing and discipline that shares some of the outward asceticism of Christian monks, but it lacks the transformation that is the hallmark of repentance and closeness and rest in God.

St. John doesn't talk about the Manichean views directly. Rather, he lays out corrective meanings for popular Manichean metaphors and dilemmas. For instance, the Manicheans saw the moon as a repository for transcendent light on its way out of the fallen world. St. John, however, uses the moon as a metaphor for repentance. Tiny particles of God might flee the world literally in the Manichean view, but the Christian monks advised by St. John must work toward true repentance as created human beings.

Suffering led the Manichean sect to see the material world as evil, so that the chosen Manichean ascetics ordered their life with the goal of participating in as little suffering as possible. St. John presents a corrective view of suffering and overcoming. Suffering must be harnessed as a means to humility, which will bring us closer to the God whose grace helps us overcome pitfalls in order to draw near to Him. Dispassion, the end of suffering, is achieved not through fleeing the created world but by training oneself in continuous prayer, so that the suffering of the world motivates fuller trust in the gracious God.

DAY 336

When making a request of an earthly king, sometimes men bring with them as an offering nothing more than a bunch of spring flowers; yet often, so far from rejecting their request the king has even presented them with gifts in return. In the same way I, at your command have gathered from various sources a century of spiritual texts: this is my offering to you who are "citizens of heaven."

St. John of Karpathos, "Texts for the Monks in India," p. 298

Citizens of Heaven

IT WASN'T DOCTRINE, BUT THE picture I had growing up Catholic was that we were building something here on earth, and yet we were also building a house in heaven. I pictured it as a literal house. Every good deed, every kind word, every sacrifice was a brick sent up through the air to build this house in heaven.

It may not be a house, but we are building something here. Every good thing does echo somewhere eternal, moving dirt around in some way we cannot even know. I am already given a home to which to return when my time here is done. I am already accepted into this citizenry for a place I do not yet know.

And there is, it turns out, a whole library of encouragements and opportunities to prepare me for a place I cannot see with these eyes or feel with these fingertips. I have nothing to offer apart from good intentions, best-laid plans, hope I hold in my fist like a collection of dandelions and wildflowers picked from the side of the road, as a gift gathered almost like an afterthought.

DAY 337

The honours of this present life, however splendid, come to an end when we die; but the honours bestowed by God on those whom He regards as worthy are incorruptible and so endure forever.

St. John of Karpathos, "Texts for the Monks in India," p. 298

Enduring

THE FIRST THOUGHT I HAVE is "What is splendid?" and then the answer, "Nothing I can own." Mountain ranges in the morning, covered with snow, quiet. Stunning sunsets. Brilliant sunrises. Rippling water at the edge of a lake. Sleeping babies. The touch of someone who knows me better than anyone else in the world. Kind words. Strong prayers. Lasting friendships.

And what a blessing, each of them. As I reread that partial list of things that are splendid, I find I am struck with gratitude. These are honors that have already been bestowed upon me throughout this short life so far. If this taste of God's blessing is for this life, how can I even bear to think of what may lie ahead in the next?

So this is what endures—though we all will pass away, the good we do here and now, the kindnesses, forgiveness, care, joy, love, and beauty we offer live on in our wake.

DAY 338

The moon as it waxes and wanes illustrates the condition of man: sometimes he does what is right, sometimes he sins and then through repentance returns to the holy life.

St. John of Karpathos, "Texts for the Monks in India," p. 299

Even Keel

TWO STEPS FORWARD, ONE STEP back, I mutter to myself on days like today. I was doing well keeping my temper. I was praying every morning and every evening. I was keeping the fast. I was doing everything right.

At one time in my life, someone described me as "even keel." The face I showed was calm; I seemed in control. I don't think that person knew the waxing and waning that took place under my skin. I took that compliment, though, and I played that part well for a long time, until finally, I didn't.

The tides change with the moon. The seas rise and fall, the waves are sometimes rough, sometimes calm. This boat can only do so much in response to the water it sails. No matter how steady my hand might appear on the wheel, I'm just as prone to panic, to give up, to make mistakes even after long stretches of doing everything right.

DAY 339

If you manage to avoid falling, if you succeed in leaping over the barrier formed by impassioned thoughts, and if you overcome the unclean provocations that the enemy in his ingenuity continually suggests to you, do not ignore the gift conferred to you.

St. John of Karpathos, "Texts for the Monks in India," p. 299

Shame for Falling

IN THE SUMMERS WHEN I was in high school, I worked at an amusement park. A few times daily, I had to go out and sweep the area around the pizza shop where I worked. I'd walk up and down the strip of shops, sweeping as I went. I sometimes traveled the length of the "street," circumnavigating patrons, emptying the litter into the cans that lined the street, and then refilling the little dustpan as I went.

I remember one day it was hot, and I was tired. The crowds were thick and sweaty. While walking and sweeping, I tripped and began to fall forward. A man grabbed my shoulders from behind and steadied me. Once I regained my balance, he asked if I was all right, and I said I was fine.

In that moment, I felt embarrassed. I can still feel the humiliation rattle in my bones. I was sixteen, skinny and awkward. Rather than feeling grateful for not having fallen on my face, I hid for the rest of the day, ashamed that I had almost fallen, ashamed that someone had to keep me from falling.

It is this strange reading of that moment that persists when I avoid falling—shame for even being close to falling. I wish now I could default to gratitude rather than shame.

DAY 340

A monk should practice the virtue of fasting, avoid ensnarement by the passions, and at all times cultivate intense stillness.

St. John of Karpathos, "Texts for the Monks in India," p. 300

Guilt and Noise

I AM AWASH IN GUILT AND noise. The guilt comes because I give myself over to the distractions instead of remaining in prayer. I can't even last a minute before my brain wants to jump onto the next thought train out of town. I thought, after all this time, that I would be better at it.

Intense stillness escapes me. Perhaps it will always escape me. Perhaps, too, I was never meant to capture it. I chase and I chase, and it runs and runs. It's an odd thing to say that I am running after stillness. Even as I type those words, I recognize the complexity of them.

It's not merely a silly notion; that would be easy to correct. It's a complex notion, to want something so badly, something that has no real form or shape. I cannot hold it in my hands. I cannot taste it on my tongue. The ache of what's missing, though, that intense stillness, is real. It is so very real. The best I can do today is to sit in this and wait.

Stop running. Stop chasing. Trust that around the next corner, I may catch a glimpse.

DAY 341

The enemy knows that prayer is our invincible weapon against him and so he tries to keep us from praying. He fills us with a desire for secular learning, and encourages us to spend our time on studies we have already renounced.

St. John of Karpathos, "Texts for the Monks in India," p. 301

Margin

SOMETHING HAS TO GIVE BECAUSE I have no margin right now, no extra time or energy to spare. I need some margin, some breathing space in my life. Prayer gives up its time without any complaining, so that is the first thing to go. I try to reintegrate that morning time into whatever has displaced it, squeezing in a quick few words as I walk out the door, drive around the city, shop for food, pick up the dry cleaning, work on a project for a client.

I tell myself that this is praying without ceasing, and I don't think I'm entirely wrong about that, but the foundation is poor if I let prayer time give way to errands or exhaustion so easily. Breathing space comes from an influx of oxygen that only a habit of prayer can provide.

DAY 342

When we fiercely oppose the passions, the demons trouble us all the more severely with shameful thoughts. At such a time, we should reaffirm our faith in the Lord and set our hope steadfastly in the eternal blessings that He has promised us.

St. John of Karpathos, "Texts for the Monks in India," p. 301

Fighting Back

ETERNAL BLESSINGS SEEM SO FAR away and perhaps even out of reach. When I lift my hands out in front of me, I don't know what I'm hoping to grasp. It's always been my thought-life that suffers temptation. Thoughts are vivid and strong; ideas race through my head, trigger that longing for something other than God.

That longing is temporary and temporal. That longing becomes distorted and disruptive. I try to move it back to its proper place, arms reaching out to God, but the eternal has no form, no substance around which I can wrap my fingers, and so it slips away.

Fight back, I tell myself, when I find myself sliding back into old habits, damaging patterns, shameful thoughts. Fight back.

There's no promise it will get easier, but failing to fight for something better is sure to lead away from God, the source of everything that is good. The only life-giving choice, the hopeful choice, we can make is to continue to fight for what is good.

DAY 343

Some hold that the practice of the virtues constitutes the truest form of spiritual knowledge. In that case, we should make every effort to manifest our faith and knowledge through our actions.

St. John of Karpathos, "Texts for the Monks in India," p. 302

Hope for Heaven

WE HOPE FOR HEAVEN. WE long for it, for connection with God, for reunion with the One who made us. In the meantime, we're here with our houses and cars and families and friends. We're building careers. We're building relationships. None of this is wasted or merely waiting for something better after we die.

What we build, how we love and how we live, this life, the now, matters. What will I leave behind when I exit this life? Will I have nurtured a strong and loving family and network of friends? Will I have contributed to the world in a way that lives long after I'm gone? Even small works—a kind word to a stranger, a little money toward a cause that needs it, consolation to a friend who is wandering—it all matters. We can hope for heaven, but hope now, in this world, translates into acts of kindness and care.

DAY 344

When a man grows inwardly and increases in holiness, he is something great and marvelous. But just as the elephant fears the mouse, so the holy man is still afraid of sin, lest after preaching to others he himself should be cast away.

St. John of Karpathos, "Texts for the Monks in India," p. 303

High Places

WHEN I'M NINETY YEARS OLD, I'm going to be amazing. This is what I think. By that time, I hope I'll have been practicing pursuing God long enough to have made at least a bit of progress. I have awfully far to go, so I'm giving myself this long to evaluate whether I'm getting better at it.

It just cements an inkling I have had for a while now that there is no place high enough for me to feel I've arrived. Until I am done in this world, I will have to struggle and continue to climb. I'll rest and hydrate, take time to appreciate the movement of the sun on the landscape around me, take time to love my fellow travelers, take time to pray and give thanks—but then, the climb again. I don't suppose I'll arrive by age ninety, but I hope I'll be able to look around and see I'm getting closer to the peak.

DAY 345

There is a tiny fish called the remora, which is supposed to have the power to stop a large ship simply by attaching itself to the keel. In a similar manner, by God's permission a person advancing on the spiritual way is sometimes hindered by a small temptation.

St. John of Karpathos, "Texts for the Monks in India," p. 304

Grains of Sand

HALFWAY THROUGH MY RUN, I feel the pebble in my shoe. It rubs on my left foot at the insole. It feels like a grain of sand. I don't think much about it. If I stop, I think, I won't start again. I'm more afraid of my lack of willpower than of a grain of sand in my shoe, so I don't stop and take the pebble out.

I run three miles like that. By the end, I'm limping a bit, but I make it home, proud of the distance I've made, proud of the speed of the run. The next day, a painful red sore has developed. Every step reminds me of the decision to forge ahead despite what felt like a momentary discomfort. The sore takes time to heal, given where it is on my foot. I don't run for a week or more in order to give it time to heal, lest I tear open the wound again.

DAY 346

When you are being tested by trials and temptations, you cannot avoid feeling dejected. But those who till the earth of hardship and tribulation in their hearts are afterwards filled with great joy, tears of consolation and holy thoughts.

St. John of Karpathos, "Texts for the Monks in India," p. 305

Just Wait

IN THE WINTER LIKE THIS, it's hard to recall what might be waiting under the snow and soil. It's still a few months before the snow melts, the soil loosens, and the first green begins to emerge from the ground. Hostas, creeping myrtle, lily of the valley all sleep soundly for now, tucked in and prepared because of the groundwork we did in September and October.

The skies have been gray for weeks; the days are so short it feels as though it's always night; the stress is already ramping up for the holidays with shopping and preparation. I use this time of fasting and prayer to combat the darkness, combat the stress that seems to come as part and parcel of this holiday season. It's preparation, tilling the soil, placing mulch around tender seeds in the ground. While the snow and dark and gray press in, I recall the spring. Redemption returns. Hope is born if I can just wait.

DAY 347

God in His compassion has healed my intellect, and regaining my natural simplicity I can now see the things of this world clearly.

St. John of Karpathos, "Texts for the Monks in India," p. 306

Complicated

As I explain to a coworker how to do a task, I realize that though it's simple, it's difficult to convey. This makes things complicated. I try to distill it down, give only the highlights, hit the finer points in another conversation, but he's lost. We start again, me trying to find the best method to communicate a task over the phone, but I can't use words for it. I'm a tactile learner. I have to be there, put my hands into the software and root around until I find the right buttons to click, the right form fields to fill in, the right address to send it to.

Within a few minutes we find a system. He reads out the page. I picture the page in my head, ask more questions, move us back to another page, another field, another client email address. What takes me ten minutes when I'm doing it on my own on my laptop takes thirty minutes. When we finish, he sees that it's not really all that difficult; we just find ways to make it complicated.

DAY 348

Anyone who devotes himself with special intensity to prayer is assailed by fearsome and savage temptations.

St. John of Karpathos, "Texts for the Monks in India," p. 307

The Other Shoe

THINGS CAN ONLY GO SMOOTHLY for so long before something is bound to break. I don't want to be a pessimist, but life has taught me to expect opposition, discomfort, trouble. What can insulate us from this sort of thing? Enough money? Brilliant children? Perfect parenting?

No, life pushes in. Bad things happen. Good things happen. Neutral things happen. It's a mashup of experiences. It feels unfair to hear that because I'm building up some resistance, I'll be subject to more attack.

It seems the way we handle everything that comes either builds up or tears down. Still, all that vigilance, all that waiting for another shoe to drop can be exhausting. So sometimes after days of wrestling I will lie down and let my muscles recover, let my spirit rest, let my heart even out again.

DAY 349

We should on no account wear ourselves out with anxiety over our bodily needs. With our whole soul let us trust in God: as one of the Fathers said, "Entrust yourself to the Lord, and all will be entrusted to you."

St. John of Karpathos, "Texts for the Monks in India," p. 308

All the White

IT SNOWED THE WHOLE NIGHT. In the morning, I could tell there had been some decent amount of accumulation. The morning was quiet but bright, with snow piled on my windowsill and the small deck outside my bedroom door. The kids slept late, but I was up early enjoying the sound of a city wrapped in this blanket of snow. We had no place to go today. No school. No errands. No work.

I spent an hour just sitting and reading, drinking coffee, and listening to the sounds of neighbors shoveling their walk, winter birds chirping, muffled car tires on the street outside my window. I closed my eyes, ignored my phone and computer, and let the winter day envelop me the way the snowfall enveloped the window boxes, the deck furniture, the backyard, the garage roof.

Before too long, the snow will show signs of car exhaust, footprints, shoveling, melting, but for a short time, it feels good to be wrapped in all that white.

DAY 350

It is God who provides food both for those who eat much and for those who eat little. Bearing this in mind, anyone among you who has a capacious appetite should in future set his faith entirely in God, freeing his intellect from all worldly distractions and anxieties.

St. John of Karpathos, "Texts for the Monks in India," p. 309

Glutton

SELF-CONTROL IS NOT MY SUPERPOWER. It isn't food that reveals this; it's thinking. I'm a glutton for bad thinking. I'm greedy for fears, planning too far ahead, worrying about the future, expecting the worst, wishing for another outcome without doing anything to bring it to fruition.

I spend too much time on bad thinking. It's wasted and useless, and when I'm finished, I have nothing to show for it. How did this advance me in any way? Am I less grouchy for it? No. Less impatient, more loving? Am I filled with gratitude? No. I am filled with nothing good and nothing good for me. My hunger is still there. My stomach is still empty, my body unfueled. How can that be?

So what then? I get caught up on the admonition each week in liturgy to set aside worldly cares. How can I effectively do that, I think, when my whole waking life is worldly? It occurs to me then that here, in my head and my heart, is a place I can begin to change. I can set aside the bad thinking if I want to do it. I can nudge those thoughts as they come in, send them away, move back to the food that restores, that heals, that ministers.

DAY 351

How can we overcome the sinfulness that is already firmly established within us? We must use force. A man labors and struggles, and so by the use of force he escapes from destruction, always striving to raise his thoughts to holiness.

St. John of Karpathos, "Texts for the Monks in India," p. 310

Heeding

THE ONE FACTOR THAT DETERMINES whether my rescue Chihuahua will freak out when he sees another dog on a walk is whether he's willing to look at me. He has to break his laser focus on the other dog and look at me. That's all it takes for me to calm him.

The timing is crucial, though. If he doesn't break the laser focus, he'll move to barking, then more barking, then lunging on the leash. I turn and pull him from the scene. He shakes and whines all the way home. He's not aggressive, he's reactive. He thinks he's supposed to handle some unknown danger. He really doesn't want to do it. And he doesn't have to do it.

So I train him to look at me when he doesn't know what else to do. I reward him for just looking in my direction. I reassure him. I have him sit or even lie down. Within a few minutes, each time he chooses to trust that I have this handled, he relaxes just a little bit more.

It will take a long time to get him to the point of trusting without going through the stress and fear. It may never happen. But we work at it every day, and almost every day we make just a little bit of progress.

DAY 352

Sin drives us towards God, once we repent and have become aware of its burden, foul stink, and lunacy. But if we refuse to repent, sin does not drive us toward God. In itself it holds us fast with bonds that we cannot break, making the desires which drive us to our own destruction all the more vehement and fierce.

St. John of Karpathos, "Texts for the Monks in India," p. 311

Defiant

DIGGING IN, I REASON THAT what I want is perfectly fine. I can think of scores of ways in which the sin I continue to entertain is legitimate, justified even. Digging in, I make a fortress around myself, daring God to prove me wrong.

He won't. He cannot be provoked in this way. And so I am alone in that fortified position, with only my chosen sin to comfort me, and it is no comfort at all, really.

To be clear, when I'm in this place, it's because I made it. It's because I chose it instead of running toward the One who can free me from the burden of my own bad ideas. I can only think it's defiance that leads me here. What do I think I'm gaining by choosing poorly and then sticking with that choice until I'm trapped by it?

DAY 353

Pray then to be sheltered by the cool and refreshing cloud of God's grace, so that you may escape the scorching heat of the enemy.

St. John of Karpathos, "Texts for the Monks in India," p. 312

Shelter

IT'S A FALSE PRESSURE, THIS season. Rather than being immersed in the preparation for the coming Nativity, I am making lists and planning meals and trying to time the ordering of gifts for children and relatives, the travel we'll need to undertake to make sure everyone feels as though they've had the celebration they want.

The journey toward the Nativity started well enough. I had everything well in hand, actually, and then commitments piled up, the calendar sped up, "Five more shopping days until Christmas!" signs popped up wherever I happened to look.

I start saying things like "I just need to get past Christmas and then I can do such and such." And even as I say those words, I recognize the loss in them. How do I resist the temptation to put my head down and barrel through instead of sitting in the sweet comfort of the truth that Christ is coming soon? Maybe this—take shelter here. Sit down in a calm place with a hot beverage, watch the snow fall, read something life-giving, pray in earnest. Everything else will keep.

DAY 354

Glorify our Lord, for He alone is wise: through setbacks of this kind He restrains the presumption that we tend to feel because of our advance in the knowledge of God. Trials and temptations are the reins whereby God in His providence restrains our human arrogance.

St. John of Karpathos, "Texts for the Monks in India," p. 312

Know-It-All

THE OLDER I GET, THE less I feel I truly know. I used to be able to hold forth on a topic, injecting facts and bits of trivia here and there. Now that I'm further down the road in my life, I want to sit back a bit, listen better, hear more, take it in, and compare it with what's been stored up in my brain and heart and soul. What resonates? What does not?

It shows up usually in intellectual conversations. When asked about a book, I used to want to bluff my way through and pretend I'd at least heard of a certain text. I thought it reflected badly on me if I admitted I hadn't read it. How could I call myself an educated person, a well-read author, a smart person, if I haven't read whatever book is being discussed at the moment? But there are millions of books published. The reality of it is that I cannot have read them all, so I give myself permission to say so. It's freeing, and it's honest, finally.

When asked by someone recently about a spiritual matter, I was glad to say, "I don't know." How long did it take me to figure out that it's all right not to know something and also to be able to admit it?

DAY 355

So let us confidently believe that the cold, dark coals of our minds will sooner or later blaze with heat and light under the influence of the divine fire.

St. John of Karpathos, "Texts for the Monks in India," p. 314

Discovery

THE FIRST DISCOVERY IS THAT it is not too late. A fire is built, already assembled, waiting to be lit. There's no deadline to meet, no milestone I have blown past, no expectation unfulfilled. God is waiting for me, and that waiting is eternal.

Unlike anything in this present life, this fire is waiting, built and ready, for whenever I stumble upon it again. And when I do find it there, I pat my pockets for matches or look around for kindling, a piece of flint, anything I can find to ignite it.

Sometimes I look for hours. Sometimes I wander away, too cold to continue, or too distracted by the lights of the city, the light of the moon, the sounds around me. Sometimes I'm just too busy to stop long enough to make the fire, though all it takes is a brief flame held to the pile of dry wood. It's there, already prepared, waiting to be discovered again and again, waiting for my part.

DAY 356

So if you have not yet received the gift of self-control, know that the Lord is ready to hear you if you entreat Him with prayer and hope.

St. John of Karpathos, "Texts for the Monks in India," p. 314

Idling

I'VE BEEN STUCK HERE FOR at least ten minutes. This long line of cars is going east toward the expressway. There may be an accident ahead or construction, but the traffic is stopped, and we are wedged into this line halfway between side streets on which we could escape. We are all idling in this one spot, breathing air polluted by the car before us, polluting the air of the car behind us. Some people turn off the road, decide to try another route, honk or complain, but I'm waiting. I want to go this way. I'm not in a rush. I can wait.

Standing still with engine running. It's a familiar feeling. Idling isn't parked. There is a potential for movement. We're awaiting the return to movement. We're ready for it, revving gently, rocking with the wind, music filtering in my closed window from the westbound cars as they skim past us. Oh, to be westbound today. But my destination is ahead; I do not want to take the side roads, lean on my horn, let my anger rise to my face. This much I can do.

Later today this idling will be over, but I'll remember it, those moments of waiting with engine running, heart beating in anticipation, eyes heavy from the weight of it all.

DAY 357

Fire makes iron impossible to touch, and likewise frequent prayer renders the intellect more forceful in its warfare against the enemy.

St. John of Karpathos, "Texts for the Monks in India," p. 316

Ascending

THE ANXIETY CAN PILE UP so strong and high, as though I've dug myself a well, taking stones down with me, only a bit of daylight high above. At the bottom of that well, I dart from thought to thought in a small circle, put my hands on cold stone, and consider trying to climb. I decide it is no good. I cannot get a grip on anything. I cannot get any height. How did I get here, I wonder?

The trouble with being at the bottom of the well is that I forget it was my hands that cobbled it around me. I dug it, I fortified it, my thoughts, my sins, my fears. Every stone was a fear; every handful of earth was a retreat from the world.

Today I decide to climb. I feel the dirt in between the stones, jam my toes into the cracks and lift. It is slippery, yes, but it is possible. Today I decide to rename the stones as prayer, to focus not on the depth of the well but on the ascent, the daylight above. The climb begins in prayer, is bolstered by prayer, is strengthened by prayer. There is no other way up.

DAY 358

The Holy Spirit whom we worship is all-powerful, and in an astonishing way He brings into existence what does not yet exist within us.

St. John of Karpathos, "Texts for the Monks in India," p. 317

Words

HE SPOKE IT INTO BEING. One word from the lips of God. I wonder what it was about the sound of that word—consonants and vowels, glottal stop, and life bursts into being. What are the words He speaks that bring new life in this heart? What are the words I can use that might echo that creation? I care. I want you to live. Breathe deep. You are mine. I am yours. I love you. I love you. I love you so much I feel I might break into pieces from the grip of it.

Is that the love God spoke? A love so deep, so strong that the world broke into pieces, into being, from the grip of it? All the world, all of life, broke forth from that word, came into being from nothing. In light of this, everything is possible.

DAY 359

When there is no wind blowing at sea, there are no waves; and when no demon dwells within us, our soul and body are not troubled by the passions.

St. John of Karpathos, "Texts for the Monks in India," p. 320

Prince of Peace

WONDERFUL COUNSELOR, MIGHTY GOD, EVERLASTING Father, Prince of Peace. To us a child is born, a child who grew to become the man who calms the waters of the most troubled seas. Today we are given the One who grants us the opportunity to experience the peace that passes understanding, the only peace that is lasting and true.

I'm remembering this today: the occasion of Christ's birth isn't an event of the past but of the present, of the future. Every day can be a remembrance of His coming into our midst. Every day can offer the opportunity to have the stormy waters calmed around me, the opportunity to overcome the passions that seek to derail my progress toward lasting peace.

DAY 360

Let the fire of your prayer, ascending upwards as you meditate on the oracles of the Spirit, burn always on the altar of your soul.

St. John of Karpathos, "Texts for the Monks in India," p. 321

Burns Like Fire

WHEN THE KIDS ARE OUT of school for the holidays like this, I'm reminded how much I rely on the structure of my day to facilitate prayer. Where does prayer fit into a day that departs from its normal course?

They don't get up early for school, so I don't get up early and pray. We all meander into the kitchen; my morning routine is dashed on the rocks of vacation time. My usual practice of praying for the kids after I drop them at school is missing. They're here with me now. I don't remember to pray because I can simply lay my hands on them, kiss the top of their heads, tell them I love them. It makes me wonder if my practice of prayer is based on absence alone, on the fear of letting go, on felt need.

How do I build this practice of prayer so that it burns in me like fire, not filling a need, not filling an absence, but burning to give light and heat and life?

DAY 361

What have we gained, they ask, we who suffer affliction in soul and body, always praying and singing psalms? Do not those who neither pray nor keep vigil enjoy happiness and success throughout their lives?

St. John of Karpathos, "Ascetic Discourse," p. 322

Comparison

"COMPARISON IS THE THIEF OF joy," said Eleanor Roosevelt, and I believe her. I believe her because I know it too well. I am forever looking around to see who might have it better than I do at this moment. Whenever I spot someone who seems to have it together or someone who receives recognition for their work before I have, I move to tear them down brick by brick. If I can tear them down, it means I am okay.

But I'm *not* okay when I do that.

Tearing someone else down to feel better about my own circumstances does not elevate me in the least. It only makes me petty and vindictive. Does it calm my anxiety about money or parenting, marriage, friendships, career goals? No. The kind of reassurance I need to truly find calm in these circumstances doesn't come from this sort of destructive brickwork, but through prayer, putting my trust in the One who made me that my path is my own.

DAY 362

But all the grim things that befall us on the ascetic way—torments, pain, confusion, shame, fear, and despair—lead finally to endless joy, inexpressible delight and unutterable glory.

St. John of Karpathos, "Ascetic Discourse," p. 324

Wordless

I DON'T OFTEN FIND MYSELF WITHOUT words, but when my friend described his experience in the middle of a snow-covered highway, I had nothing to say. He had a terrible month, full of loss and hardship. He had long nights of working late, missed deadlines, disappointment, financial crises, worry, doubt, and fear from all sides.

He described the trip he took when he was finally able to get away and try to regroup. As he drove into the mountains, the snow began in earnest, piling up on the highway. He pulled over, he said, got out of his car and just stood there. No one else was on the road at that time of night. He stood in the quiet, listening to the snow fall on the mountain road, listening as it blanketed everything, and just took it in, becoming a witness to this miraculous, unexplainable moment of good.

And though, as he told me the story, I was hearing my teenagers argue downstairs, car alarms blaring outside my Chicago house, I was transported there, to that place. The calm of it overcame me. I was suddenly on that road just then, and there were no words I could offer, and there were no words that were needed.

DAY 363

What is it that so distresses you? No stain is intrinsic. If a man has tar on his hands, he removes it with a little cleansing oil; how much more, then, can you be made clean with the oil of God's mercy.

St. John of Karpathos, "Ascetic Discourse," p. 324

Forever

MISTAKES I HAVE MADE OVER the years fade with time, but I never seem to let them go. I hold onto them as I hold onto a favorite T-shirt on which I've managed to spill motor oil. The stain that's left behind is the size of my palm. I stop trying to remove it after the first attempt. It's stubborn, and maybe there is a part of me that is resigned to it. This is forever, I think, I did this.

Yet I'm not willing to throw out that article of clothing. I wear it around the house, covering it with a pullover sweater, always remembering it's there under the scratchy wool. I don't want to throw away the shirt. It means something to me, even with the stain there.

This is where I'm stuck—remembering that the stain is not the shirt and the shirt is not me. I am not the sum of my past missteps, sins, transgressions, or shortcomings. I don't have to carry them around with me like this. I am forgiven, given a new garment to wear.

DAY 364

As we look up to Him with cries of distress and continual lamentation, it is He Himself that we breathe.

St. John of Karpathos, "Ascetic Discourse," p. 325

Touch

WHEN MY CHILDREN WERE YOUNG and got hurt, I would hold them first, tell them I know it hurts, then tend to the wound. That embrace was foundational. Triage of the soul first. That embrace said, "I am here, so you are not alone." That embrace said, "I can handle your pain." That embrace allowed the child to face the hurt and then face whatever it would take to heal the hurt.

This is what God does for us when we lift up our hurts to Him, when we reach up toward Him in the face of injury. I run to Him because I need to know He is there, that I am not alone, that He can handle my pain. With practice, I hope I begin to reach up to Him as a first action when I'm hurt, not as a last resort after I've tried to close the gaping wounds myself. With practice, I hope it is His touch I seek out, His healing I receive, His air I breathe.

DAY 365

I have written at length in order to strengthen those in danger of falling away through apathy.

St. John of Karpathos, "Ascetic Discourse," p. 326

Easy

THIS APATHY IS A KIND of internalized exhaustion. It didn't come on all at once; it built, layer upon layer, over days or weeks or months, maybe years. It is these turning points in the calendar that give me hope. Winds are due for changing, so where do we go from here?

Easy is the word that creeps back time after time. Facing the start of the new year, I find I have a choice to make. How do I want to live this next part of my life? What does this new year have for me? Ideally, it would be nice if it whatever it is, it's easy.

Even as I consider it, I recognize the fingerprints of that stored-up exhaustion. Apathy wants the easy route, the easy plan, the easy choice, because this last year has been hard fought, filled with struggle.

I take a moment to look at my arms, now muscled with the work done this last year. The hard work of the struggle shows under my skin. I can lift more. I can go farther. I can breathe deeper. The strength didn't come all at once. It came almost without my noticing. I am stronger than I have been because of the struggle, because of the terrain of the road, because of the hope for a life well lived.

Acknowledgments

We become truly personal by loving God and by loving other humans. . . . In its deepest sense, love is the life, the energy, of the Creator in us."

—Met. Kallistos Ware

A GREAT DEAL OF ORDINARINESS HAPPENED while I was writing this book. I hammered the outline into shape in my head, usually in the shower or while cooking, sometimes stopping whatever I was doing to make a note on my phone or on a random piece of paper I found on the counter. I was greatly distracted for at least a year that way; laundry went undone, kids went without haircut appointments or new shoes to replace the ones with the soles that had come unglued in gym class—things like that.

The actual writing part was not distracting as much as ever-present. Though I got into a rhythm of writing in the mornings to keep on track and stay out of the oncoming traffic of my family life and work commitments, Lord knows that didn't always go to plan. The work was always looming in the background no matter what else I had to do, and it weighed on my entire clan at times, I know. So, while doing the work is beautiful and life-giving to me, it is messy, especially to people who are watching it unfold in real time.

For the time and energy and sacrifice of my long-suffering family while I was immersed in this three-year labor of love, I say, I'm eternally grateful. Thanks for picking up the slack until I surfaced again.

All along the road I had guides for the reading and the writing of this work. Some were well aware of their contribution: Fr. Kaleeg Hainsworth, Fr. John Baker, Dr. Nicole Roccas, Fr. Andrew Stephen Damick, Scott Cairns, and Karen Beattie, to name the front-line workers there. Others were probably not so much aware of their massive contribution to my understanding and digesting of the materials that fueled this *Wilderness Journal*, but every conversation along the way was a signpost, a resting place in the shade, a drink of water, a shared snack of trail mix (the kind with real chocolate chips).

Finally, to my fellow pilgrims along this Orthodox path, in my immediate church family, the greater family of faith, and my lovely publishing family at Ancient Faith, I am deeply and profoundly grateful for you all.

—ADC